INSPIRE / PLAN / DISCOVER / EXPERIENCE

VIENNA

DK EYEWITNESS

VIENNA

CONTENTS

DISCOVER 6

EXPERIENCE VIENNA 60

NEED TO KNOW 218

Left: Stephansdom's Gothic ornamentation and tiles
Previous page: The Baroque Karlskirche at sunrise

DISCOVER

WELCOME TO
VIENNA

Once the capital of a great empire, with Baroque pomp at every turn to prove it, modern Vienna remains a city at the very heart of Europe. A cornucopia of culture, it puts art, architecture, music and theatre at centre stage. Whatever your dream trip to Vienna includes, this DK Eyewitness Travel Guide is the perfect companion.

1 Statue of Athena outside Vienna's Parliament.

2 A cup of coffee at Café Landtmann.

3 Relaxing by the Riesenrad in Prater.

4 MuseumsQuartier's busy courtyard in the evening.

Vienna is a city steeped in history: from Roman ruins at the foot of the Hofburg to the tallest tower of Gothic Stephansdom, the city's landmarks are testament to its imperial power. So, too, are the impressive collections of fine art and antiquity that fill Vienna's peerless museums. The Habsburgs' legacy aside, Vienna's art and architecture scene packs a punch – this is the home of the Secessionist movement and Jugendstil, Gustav Klimt, Egon Schiele and Otto Wagner. From creative innovators to big thinkers: in the capital's iconic *Kaffeehäuser* revolutions have been planned, politics debated and scientific ideas theorized. And did we mention Freud?

But this is a city that also likes to be entertained. As the home of the waltz, lavish operas and the unsurpassable Vienna Philharmonic, no place offers a better opportunity to dress in your finest and indulge in some of the world's most celebrated music. There are simple pleasures to be found in the ubiquitous coffee houses and cosy local *Beisln*, too. Mouthwateringly decadent chocolate cakes, crisp apfelstrudel and schnitzel the size of dinner plates are the stuff of foodie dreams.

Though Vienna's centre is compact, there's a lot to see and do here. We've broken the city down into easily navigable chapters, with detailed itineraries, expert local knowledge and colourful, comprehensive maps to help you plan the perfect visit. Whether you're staying for a weekend, a week or longer, this Eyewitness guide will ensure that you see the very best Vienna has to offer. Enjoy the book, and enjoy Vienna.

REASONS TO LOVE
VIENNA

Small but steeped in imperial splendour, Vienna delights at every turn. Any list of its treasures must include its magnificent museums, famed *Kaffeehäuser* and glorious music scene. Here are a few of our favourites.

1 KAFFEEHÄUSER

A Viennese institution and ubiquitous across the city, every *haus* has a story to tell. Savouring coffee and cake in a centuries-old café is a time-honoured tradition.

2 STEPHANSDOM

The seat of the church in Austria, this cathedral is the city's soul and centre of an empire *(p66)*. Climb the striking Gothic tower for the best views in all Vienna.

3 SACHERTORTE

The ingredients of this darkly decadent chocolate cake have been a secret since its creation in 1832. Taste the "original" recipe, with a dollop of cream, at Hotel Sacher *(p159)*.

CLASSICAL MUSIC 4

Once home to fine classical composers, Vienna's music scene is world famous *(p34)*. Tickets for the Vienna Boys' Choir and the Philharmonic are the hottest in town.

BEISLN 5

Why not join the locals and head to a *beisl*? These cosy Viennese bistros are the perfect place to enjoy hearty homemade classics like temptingly crisp Wiener schnitzel.

JUGENDSTIL 6

Jugendstil emerged in the 20th century in a flourish of avant-garde architecture and art. Kirche am Steinhof *(p196)* and the Wagner Apartments *(p160)* are glorious examples.

BAROQUE PALACES 7

Few royal dynasties match the Habsburgs for pomp, as attested by the delightful palaces dotting Vienna. The Belvedere is among the most stunning *(p170)*.

PRATER 8

Vienna's green lung, this huge park is home to the Wiener Reisenrad, the iconic Ferris wheel *(p186)* that was immortalized in Carol Reed's 1949 film noir *The Third Man*.

9 HUNDERTWASSER-HAUS

Marvel at this iconic building on the city's outskirts *(p184)*. All curving irregularity and eyewateringly bright colour, this is an expression of sheer architectural exuberance in contrast to the stately palaces.

10 MUSEUMS-QUARTIER

This modern art complex hums with activity day and night (p128). Head to the world's largest collection of Schieles at the Leopold Museum, or just chill in the main courtyard.

OPERA 11

Head out in your finest garb to the Staatsoper for an opulent night at the opera (p156). This is the realm of Neo-Classical splendour and musical prestige. Tickets are like gold dust.

MARKETS 12

Exotic food at the Naschmarkt (p158) and antiques at the Flohmarkt – Vienna is a treat for street shoppers. Advent turns the city's market squares into Christmas wonderlands.

EXPLORE
VIENNA

This guide divides Vienna into six colour-coded sightseeing areas, as shown on this map. Find out more about each area on the following pages. For sights beyond the city centre see p182 and for days out from Vienna see p208.

WÄHRING

GÜRTEL

GÜRTEL

WÄHRINGER

WÄHRINGER

WÄHRINGER STRASSE

SPITALGASSE

Narrenturm

HERNALSER GÜRTEL

KINDERSPITALGASSE

SPITALGASSE

ALSER STRASSE

OTTAKRINGER STRASSE

Museum für
Volkskunde

LAUDONGASSE

JOSEFSTADT

LERCHENFELDER GÜRTEL

LERCHENFELDER GÜRTEL

JOSEFSTÄDTER

Maria Treu
Kirche

LANGE GASSE

OTTAKRING

THALIASTRASSE

STRASSE

KOOPSTRASSE

LERCHENFELDERSTRASSE

**MUSEUM AND
TOWN HALL
QUARTER**
p124

GABLENZGASSE

NEULERCHENFELD

NEUBAU

BURGGASSE

SCHMELZ

KAISERSTRASSE

WESTBAHNSTRASSE

SIEBENSTERNGASSE

HÜTTELDORFER STRASSE

NEUBAUGÜRTEL

NEUBAUGÜRTEL

LINDENGASSE

MARIAHILFERSTRASSE

Haus des Meeres–
Aqua Terra Zoo

MARIAHILF

MARIAHILFER GÜRTEL

LINKE WIENZEILE

LINKE WIENZEILE

Wien

SCHÖNBRUNNER STRASSE

MARGARETEN

WESTERN EUROPE

North
Sea

DENMARK

NETHERLANDS

POLAND

BELGIUM

GERMANY

CZECH
REPUBLIC

SLOVAKIA

FRANCE

VIENNA

SWITZERLAND

AUSTRIA

HUNGARY

ITALY

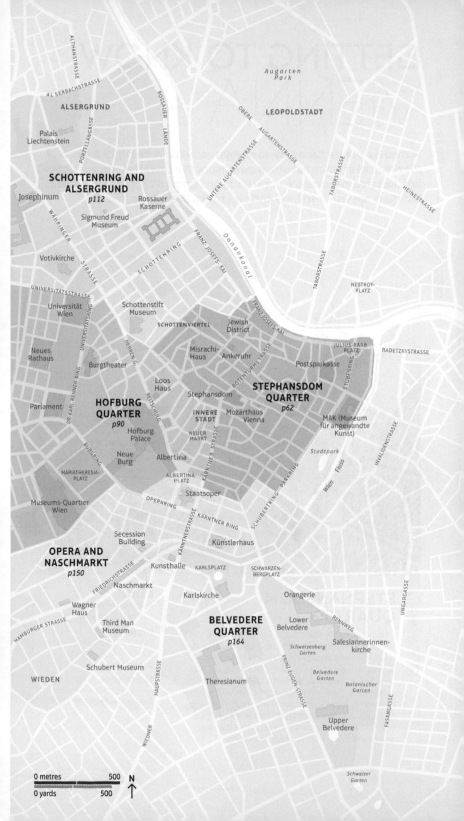

ALTHANSTRASSE

ALSERBACHSTRASSE

ALSERGRUND

ROSSAUER LÄNDE

Augarten Park

OBERE AUGARTENSTRASSE

LEOPOLDSTADT

TABORSTRASSE

HEINESTRASSE

Palais Liechtenstein

PORZELLANGASSE

SCHOTTENRING AND ALSERGRUND
p112

UNTERE AUGARTENSTRASSE

Donaukanal

Josephinum

Rossauer Kaserne

Sigmund Freud Museum

WÄHRINGER STRASSE

FRANZ-JOSEFS-KAI

TABORSTRASSE

NESTROY-PLATZ

Votivkirche

SCHOTTENRING

UNIVERSITÄTSSTRASSE

Schottenstift Museum

Universität Wien

UNIVERSITÄTSRING

SCHOTTENVIERTEL

Jewish District

FRANZ-JOSEFS-KAI

JULIUS-RAAB-PLATZ

RADETZKYSTRASSE

Neues Rathaus

HERREN-G.

Misrachi-Haus

Ankeruhr

Postsparkasse

STUBENRING

Burgtheater

BÄTSCHLG.

DR.-KARL-RENNER-RING

Loos Haus

Stephansdom

ROTENTURMSTRASSE

INVALIDENSTRASSE

Parlament

HOFBURG QUARTER
p90

INNERE STADT

STEPHANSDOM QUARTER
p62

MAK (Museum für angewandte Kunst)

BURGRING

Hofburg Palace

NEUER MARKT

Mozarthaus Vienna

Neue Burg

Albertina

KÄRNTNER STRASSE

Stadtpark

MARIATHERESIA-PLATZ

ALBERTINA PLATZ

Wien Fluss

Museums-Quartier Wien

OPERNRING

Staatsoper

SCHUBERTRING

PARKRING

Secession Building

KÄRNTNER RING

KÄRNTNER RING

Künstlerhaus

OPERA AND NASCHMARKT
p150

FRIEDRICHSTRASSE

Kunsthalle

KARLSPLATZ

SCHWARZEN-BERGPLATZ

KÄRNTNERSTRASSE

UNGARGASSE

Naschmarkt

Karlskirche

Orangerie

Wagner Haus

HAMBURGER STRASSE

Third Man Museum

BELVEDERE QUARTER
p164

Lower Belvedere

RENNWEG

Salesiannerinnen-kirche

Schwarzenberg Garten

Schubert Museum

HAUPTSTRASSE

WIEDEN

Theresianum

PRINZ-EUGEN-STRASSE

Belvedere Garten

Botanischer Garten

FASANGASSE

WIEDNER

Upper Belvedere

Schweizer Garten

0 metres   500

0 yards   500

N

GETTING TO KNOW
VIENNA

Vienna is a compact and easy-to-navigate city composed of 23 districts *(Bezirke)*, all of which have their own distinctive character. Famous sights are clustered in the centre, encircled by the grand Ringstrasse boulevard, but there are visitor-friendly enclaves to discover all over the city.

PAGE 62

STEPHANSDOM QUARTER

Dominated by the magnificent Gothic cathedral, this is Vienna's first port of call for most visitors, its winding cobbled streets and spacious squares buzzing with activity. Along with fine medieval and Baroque churches, the area is home to the city's most historic coffee houses and many stylish shops, as well as a few overpriced, touristy restaurants you would do well to avoid. Music lovers should head for the Mozarthaus: nowhere else did he compose more work than in his apartment in the shadow of Stephansdom.

Best for
Religious landmarks, medieval architecture, coffee houses

Home to
Stephansdom, Jewish Quarter, MAK (Museum für angewandte Kunst)

Experience
The joy of whiling away hours in a classic coffee house

PAGE 90

HOFBURG QUARTER

Home to the magnificent Hofburg Palace, this has been the beating heart of imperial Vienna since the 13th century. Both history and fine art fans, as well as those fascinated by the opulent lifestyles of the Habsburgs, are in for a treat. While there may be large crowds and long queues for most of the palace's attractions at any time of the year, the sublime green Burggarten and Volksgarten make for a welcome respite and a chance to recharge your batteries.

Best for
Imperial grandeur, sumptuous Baroque palaces

Home to
The Hofburg Complex

Experience
The sight of the Lipizzaner horses being put through their paces at the Spanish Riding School

$\rightarrow$

PAGE 112

SCHOTTENRING AND ALSERGRUND

This lively student and business district buzzes with activity. One of Vienna's most multicultural neighbourhoods, it offers a wide selection of bars, and street food from across the globe. In contrast to the student vibe, this is also the place for museums dedicated to Sigmund Freud – who taught at the university – and Johann Strauss, the so called "Waltz King". The Neo-Gothic Votivkirche presides over the skyline, and the Freyung is one of the city's most elegant squares.

Best for
Student life, cheap eats

Home to
Sigmund Freud Museum

Experience
A wander around Freud's old haunts and intellectual hangouts

PAGE 124

MUSEUM AND TOWN HALL QUARTER

This is home to the city's big hitters, the major cultural sights and the Austrian parliament, mostly nestled along the Ringstrasse. Both the Kunsthistorisches and Naturhistorisches museums hold Habsburg treasures beyong compare, and the modern MuseumsQuartier is a lively hub of contemporary art. To the west, Spittelberg's streets are among the most picturesque and atmospheric in all Vienna. At night, head to the Burgtheater for world-class theatre.

Best for
Museums and galleries

Home to
MuseumsQuartier Wien, Kunsthistorisches Museum, Naturhistorisches Museum, the Burgtheater

Experience
Diving into the best of Viennese high culture

PAGE 150

OPERA AND NASCHMARKT

Three great cultural institutions dominate the northern part of this area – the Academy of Fine Arts, the Staatsoper and the Secession Building. To the south is the Naschmarkt, Vienna's liveliest daily market, overlooked by Otto Wagner's glorious Jugendstil apartments; the bustling flea market held here on Saturday is not to be missed. Shoppers will find more to enjoy along the city's main retail street, the pedestrianized Mariahilferstrasse, with its many lovely boutiques, department stores and cafés.

Best for
Musical overtures, Jugendstil architecture

Home to
Staatsoper, Secession Building

Experience
Bartering for one-of-a-kind souvenirs at the Naschmarkt

→

PAGE 164

BELVEDERE QUARTER

An effortlessly elegant quarter, the Belvedere was developed after the final retreat of the Turks in 1683 allowed the city to expand. Stretching from the majestic Karlsplatz, with its *Jugendstil* pavilions and the monumental Musikverein – home of the peerless Vienna Philharmonic Orchestra – to the sublime gardens of the Belvedere Palace, this is Vienna at its most grandiose and confident, an entire district built on the cusp of imperial greatness. If all this splendour gets too much, seek respite in the Botanical Gardens, a verdant oasis of calm in the city centre.

Best for
Grandiose Baroque buildings, classical music

Home to
The Belvedere, Karlskirche, Botanical Gardens

Experience
The very best of fin-de-siècle Vienna

PAGE 182

BEYOND THE CENTRE

So compact is Vienna (and so well served by public transport) that few places require much effort to get to, even those beyond the city centre. Top of the list is Schönbrunn, summer residence of the Habsburgs and one of the finest royal palaces in the world. On the east bank of the Danube, and as emblematic of Vienna as any grand palace, a visit to the Prater and its Ferris wheel remains a quintessential Viennese experience.

Best for
Rococo palaces, green spaces, military history

Home to
Prater, Schönbrunn, Hundertwasserhaus, Heeresgeschichtliches Museum, Zentralfriedhof

Experience
A bird's-eye view of Vienna from the top of the Prater's Wiener Riesenrad

DAYS OUT FROM VIENNA

Vienna is surrounded by beautiful, varied countryside, the perfect place for long walks, gentle hikes and enjoying a slower pace of Austrian life. There are Hungarian-style plains, Alpine mountains and idyllic lakes all within an hour or two's journey from the city centre. From the Vienna Woods to small town spa retreats, the mysteries of Mayerling – where late-19th-century history took a decisive turn – to the holy significance of Heiligenkreuz, there are plenty of day trips all within easy reach of the city.

Best for
Getting outdoors, off-the-beaten-track sights, Austrian life

Home to
Mayerling and the Vienna Woods

Experience
Hiking through spectacular Austrian scenery

←

1 Performing at the Vienna State Opera.

2 Tempting Wiener schnitzel.

3 Stephansdom's interior.

4 Bustling shopping street leading to the Hofburg Palace.

With its sumptuous coffee houses, imperial architecture and tree-lined boulevards, along with an astonishing array of museums, Vienna is a treasure trove for travellers. These itineraries will help you to make the most of your visit.

24 HOURS

Morning

Begin your day in the heart of the city with a tour of the Stephansdom (p66). Vienna's iconic cathedral has withstood the ravages of both time and history to become the city's defining landmark. When you've finished admiring the cathedral's stunning towers, crypts and altars, head up to the top of the 137-m (450-ft) Gothic spire to take in the view. For a long, leisurely lunch, Figlmüller is nearby (p77). A Viennese institution, this cosy *biesl* has been serving generous portions of wonderful local food since 1905. Order the exceptionally succulent Wiener schnitzel – it is widely regarded as the city's best.

Afternoon

When you're suitably refreshed, the magnificent Hofburg Palace (p94), the centre of Habsburg power for centuries, is just a short walk away. Once you've had your fill of imperial splendour, take a peek at the elegant interior of the Looshaus which sits adjacent to the palace on Michaelerplatz (p106). Wander in the palace gardens, and pay your respects to Mozart at Viktor Tilgner's memorial,

before ending your afternoon with a trip to the Spanish Riding School (p100). The 80-minute shows of outstanding horsemanship have remained unchanged for decades but still thrill the crowds. Book tickets online in advance to skip the long queues.

Evening

Music was for centuries Vienna's gift to the world, so dress up – Austria is a stickler for tradition – and settle in for a night at the opera. The Vienna Staatsoper (p156) was the first of the grand Ringstrasse buildings to be completed, and if you are lucky you may catch a performance of *Don Giovanni*, the first opera performed here back in 1869. Whichever production you see, the cast, orchestra, conductor, sets and costumes are guaranteed to be world class. If you can't grab a ticket for a performance (and they can be hard to come by), a guided tour is a great way to see inside the superb Neo-Renaissance building. The Hotel Sacher's restaurant (p158) opposite the opera house is a suitably swish venue at which to close the evening with dinner and a nightcap.

←

1 Admiring mumok's collection of modern art.

2 A family at the Prater.

3 A lively performance at the Burgtheater.

4 Relaxing in the Burggarten.

2 DAYS

Day 1

Morning MuseumsQuartier Wien (p128) is one of the largest urban complexes of contemporary art and culture in the world. Devote your morning to the Leopold Museum (p131), particularly the Secession and Art Nouveau exhibition on the ground floor. If you are with the kids, the ZOOM Kindermuseum next door is an exciting place for them to explore. Alternatively, marvel at mumok's collection of modern art, with masterpieces by Warhol, Picasso and Yoko Ono. After, relax in the grand courtyard; known as "Vienna's living room", it is open around the clock.

Afternoon For lunch, have a picnic and recharge your batteries in the nearby Burggarten, and make a quick visit to the Schmetterlinghaus (Butterfly House) to view the collection of butterflies (p99). Then head to the Ringstrasse's palatial Kunsthistorisches Museum to enjoy the astonishing array of fine art and antiquities. Much of the collection is derived from those of Habsburg monarchs, accumulated over centuries (p132).

Evening A bar hop through the city centre is a great way to discover Vienna's fabulous nightlife, and there is no better place to get things under way than with a perfectly mixed cocktail or two at the American Bar (p109). Sky Bar (p75) on Kärtner Strasse has some of the best views of the Stephansdom. Meanwhile, renowned jazz bar Porgy & Bess is well suited for late-night drinks with music into the small hours (p75).

Day 2

Morning A gentle tram trip around the Ringstrasse is a pleasant way to start the day, and from the city centre line D will drop you off right outside the Belvedere Palace (p170). So stunning is the symmetry of the palace and its gardens that many visitors simply admire the building and move on, but make time to see the plentiful treasures housed inside. The Klimt Collection features an extensive array of Jugendstil art, including Klimt's famous The Kiss.

Afternoon For lunch, make for the top deli Lingenhel Käserei, on Landstrasser Hauptstrasse, a great place to stock up on fabulous salami and cheese (www. lingenhel.com). Suitably refuelled, make for the great green Prater (p186). The park was once an imperial hunting ground and its tree-lined avenues and verdant meadows are perfect for leisurely strolls. Kids will love the miniature railway and funfair. No visit to Vienna would be complete without a spin on the Prater's Wiener Reisenrad Ferris wheel, with its fabulous views across the city.

Evening Take the tram back to the city centre, to the Museum and Town Hall Quarter, and savour an early supper at upmarket Vestibül restaurant, which serves classic fare with a contemporary twist, like decadent lobster currywurst (p145). Catch a modern show (many are subtitled in English) at the magnificent Neo-Classical Burgtheater to round off the day (p138).

←

1 Lively MuseumsQuartier.

2 A show at the grand Raimund Theatre.

3 A tram on the Ringstrasse.

4 Schönbrunn Palace's Neptune fountain.

4 DAYS

Day 1

Morning Start the day with breakfast at Café Landtmann (p145), where Freud used to have coffee, and duck into the Sigmund Freud Museum (p116). Clear your head after with a walk in the Liechtenstein Garden Palace (p120). For lunch, have a Viennese classic at Gasthaus Wickerl (p121).

Afternoon Walk off lunch in nearby Domgasse, taking in the many fascinating buildings, incuding the Mozarthaus (p78). Jump on a Ringstrasse tram for a tour of the city's most grandiose architecture.

Evening Listening to the dulcet tones of the Vienna Boys' Choir (p198) at the Musikverein (p177) is the perfect way to unwind at the end of the day.

Day 2

Morning Escape the bustle of the city centre at the Rococo Schönbrunn Palace (p188), the Habsburg's summer residence. Take the Imperial Tour before exploring the beautiful palace gardens.

Afternoon Go bargain-hunting at the Naschmarkt (p158) and don't miss the Otto Wagner-designed Jugendstil apartment buildings which overlook the market (p160).

Evening The MuseumsQuartier's courtyard is something of a meeting point for young Viennese before they head to the area's pubs and clubs (p128). Club Donautechno will have you dancing the night away, while hip bookshop-bar Phil offers a more laid-back atmosphere (p161).

Day 3

Morning Head out to the Vienna Woods (p210). Start in Nussdorf and take a gentle walk up to the look-out point at Stefaniewarte atop the Kahlenberg, a 484-m- (1,585- ft-) high mountain, for views of the Danube valley. In great weather, the terrace of the Kahlenberg restaurant is ideal for a hearty lunch.

Afternoon Explore the vineyards around the villages of Grinzing (p197), Nussdorf and Kahlenbergerdorf on the banks of the Danube, all well known for producing excellent white wines such as crisp Grüner Veltliner. Some of the wineries offer tastings and tours.

Evening Dine in a traditional *Heurige* (Austrian tavern) before heading back to the city centre. Grinzing and Nussdorf have plenty to choose from (p197).

Day 4

Morning Begin an eclectic day at the bizarre Hundertwasserhaus (p184) and make time for a coffee in the Art Café on the ground floor. Then head to the Museum of Applied Arts (MAK), which showcases a rich array of Austrian decorative arts (p72). At lunchtime, TIAN will convince you that Vienna can do veggie food as well as anywhere (p77).

Afternoon Wander the Spittelberg (p143), one of the most colourful neighbourhoods in the city. Biedermeier and Baroque architecture abounds here, and in summer the area hosts a craft market. Nearby, Amerlingbeisl is a good choice for afternoon tea (p145).

Evening Pick up tickets for a show at the Raimund Theatre (p51), one of Vienna's oldest, which today stages musicals from Broadway classics to original productions. Then pop to Bauernbräu just around the corner (www.bauernbraeu.com), a quintessential Viennese pub serving hearty food and good beer.

Kaffeehaus Institutions

There's nothing like sipping a frothy coffee and enjoying the cosy hum of a Viennese coffee house. A place of everyday elegance, this is where history is made and debates settled, where locals linger over the papers or chat with friends. Menus feature complicated brews, newspapers are fastened in wooden holders, and smartly dressed waiters bring a glass of tap water to accompany every coffee – it's a highly ritualized affair. Head to Café Landtman (p145) for outdoor seating and an extensive cake list. Café Central serves Austrian classics (p111), while Café Prückel's 1950s-style interior, designed by Oswald Haerdtl, is particularly Instagram-friendly (www.prueckel.at). This is traditional Vienna at its best.

Did You Know?

Coffee beans were introduced to Vienna by its Turkish invaders in the 17th century.

→

Perusing the lengthy menu at Café Central

VIENNA FOR
COFFEE CULTURE

Like the Parisian bistro or London pub, the *Kaffeehaus* is a Viennese institution. Whether it's indulging in a leisurely Wiener Melange at a sumptuous traditional coffee house or sipping a flat white in a hip "Third Wave" café, there are plenty of ways to get your caffeine fix in this city.

THE ORIGINAL SACHER

Forget schnitzel, Vienna's culinary gift to the world is the Sachertorte, a chocolate cake created by pastry chef Franz Sacher in 1832 for Prince Metternich. Franz's son Eduard opened Hotel Sacher (p159) in 1876, where the "original", secret-recipe Sachertorte can be tasted. The cakes at rival bakery Demel are just as delicious (p105).

A Slice of History

Coffee with cake is a classic combination to be enjoyed throughout Central Europe, and Vienna is no exception, with sweet treats at every café. Enjoy the famous chocolate cake at lavishly decorated Café Sacher (p158). Kaffee Alt Wien is renowned for tempting crisp apfelstrudel, a Viennese staple served with sweet vanilla custard (www.kaffeealtwien.at).

Slices of Sachertorte ↑
with fresh cream

TOP 5 TRADITIONAL COFFEES

Schwarzer (or Mocca)
Espresso, served as a *kleiner* (single) or *grosser* (double).

Wiener Melange
A milky coffee topped with foam.

Einspänner
Espresso topped with whipped cream.

Maria Theresa
Black coffee served with orange liqueur and whipped cream.

Turkische
Thick, dark and very sweet, this drink is served in a copper pot.

The "Third Wave"

In recent years, small stylish "Third Wave" coffee shops have sprung up across the city, with a new generation of baristas revitalizing classic coffee. Leading the pack are tiny Kaffeemodul *(www.kaffeemodul.at)* and trendy Kaffemik *(www.kaffemik.at),* where you can sip beverages brewed from freshly roasted beans in sleek surrounds, plus cool Café Espresso, which has a distinct American diner feel *(www.espresso-wien.at).*

← The sleek, modern interior of laid-back coffee shop Kaffemik

Intellectual Hangouts

Once the meeting place of writers and freethinkers, the grand Viennese coffee house can still draw a clever crowd. Café Prückel offers live classical music and is popular with locals playing lively games of bridge. Quaint Kleines Café attracts a loyal clientele of thespians and artists, along with university students sipping *Schwarzers* and idling on their laptops *(p75)*.

→ Locals relaxing in Franziskanerplatz outside Kleines Café

Baroque Splendour

After the defeat of the Turks in 1683, the 17th and 18th centuries saw a flurry of construction, and Baroque palaces sprang up across Vienna. In the centre, the Belvedere *(p170)* and Hofburg *(p94)* are the most stunning. On the outskirts you'll find majestic Schönbrunn, once the imperial family's summer residence *(p188)*. Mid-19th-century architects combined Baroque and Neo-Gothic elements, creating a unique style visible along the grand Ringstrasse *(p142)*.

→

The grand, curving façade of the magnificent Hofburg palace

VIENNA FOR
ARCHITECTURE

From sumptuous Secessionist icons, through the monumental housing estates of "Red Vienna" to the innovative Hundertwasserhaus, there's more to Vienna's architecture than imperial palaces. Stroll the streets for a glimpse of the intriguing buildings that shape this iconic city.

Late 20th Century

Vienna's eclectic mix of modern buildings will entice architecture enthusiasts. On the outskirts, maverick eco-designer Friedensreich Hundertwasser's fairy-tale apartment block is the most visited *(p184)*. In the centre, Hans Hollein's Hass-Haus *(p81)*, an icon of Postmodern architecture, faces the Stephansdom, reflecting the tiled Baroque roof in its curving mirrored façade.

> 💬 INSIDER TIP
> ### Take a Tour
> Join a walking tour led by Architekturzentrum Wien for fascinating insights into Vienna's architecture. Walks set off from spots across the city. Register your attendance online in advance *(www.azw.at)*.

Hundertwasserhaus, a fabulous undulating kaleidoscope of colour ↑

Red Vienna

"Red Vienna" was the city's nickname during the 1920s and 1930s, when the Social Democratic Party governed Vienna following more than 600 years of imperial rule. The period saw a boom in the construction of utilitarian social housing, of which Karl Ehn's Karl-Marx-Hof in Heiligenstadt is the most famous. Head out of the city centre by tram to see this splendid, streamlined example, the world's longest residential building (p199).

TOP 5 GEMS OF ARCHITECTURE

Stephansdom
A soaring Baroque and Gothic cathedral (p66).

Palmenhaus
Schönbrunn's stunning glass palm house (p188).

mumok
An imposing breeze-block art gallery (p129).

Postsparkasse
Modernist masterpiece by Otto Wagner (p74).

Haas-Haus
A mirrored icon of Postmodernism (p81).

← The imposing exterior of the Karl-Marx-Hof

Otto Wagner's Pavillon Karlsplatz, detailed in delicate gold filigree ↑

Flourishing Jugendstil

In 1896, a new generation of avant-garde artists, architects and designers launched an architectural revolution: Vienna Secession was born. The movement's roots in Jugendstil (Art Nouveau) are evident in the richly decorative motifs that pattern the buildings of this era. Look out for Secession accents throughout the city: the Wagner Apartments feature floral ceramic and gold detailing (p160); the Hofpavillon (p202) and Pavillon Karslplatz (p177) are monuments in gold and green; and the Secession Building (p154) is renowned for its golden filigree dome, sometimes referred to as the "Golden Cabbage".

HABSBURG LEGACY

Avid collectors and patrons of the arts, the Habsburg emperors amassed thousands of rare treasures over their 650-year-long rule *(p55)*. Precious masterpieces of the imperial collection are housed in the great Kunsthistorisches Museum *(p132)*, which was opened to the public by Emperor Franz Joseph I in 1891. The museum's Picture Gallery holds treasures that were accumulated by Archduke Ferdinand II, Emperor Rudolf II and Leopold Wilhelm, including rare works by Dürer and Bruegel.

The spacious interior of the Kunsthistorisches Museum's Picture Gallery ↑

VIENNA FOR
ART LOVERS

Vienna is a true wonderland of creative arts. World-class museums and galleries exhibit an astonishing array of visual art, from works of ancient antiquities and medieval religious pieces, to dazzling 19th- and 20th-century masterpieces, including works by history's finest artists.

The Cult of Klimt

In the late 19th century Vienna was the centre of the Secession movement *(p155)*, of which artist Gustav Klimt was a leading figure. There are plenty of places to see stunning examples of his work: the Belvedere houses *The Kiss (p170)*, the Secession Building *(p154)* holds his astonishing *Beethoven Frieze*, and Klimt's sumptuous gilded frescos adorn the Kunsthistorisches Museum's walls and ceilings *(p132)*.

←

Visitors admiring Klimt's gilded *The Kiss (1907-8)* at the Belvedere

32

The Great Masters

Lovers of classical paintings are well-served at the Kunsthistorisches Museum *(p132)*. Wander sumptuous galleries and enjoy a superb hoard of Old Masters – here you'll find the world's largest collection of Bruegel's alongside Giuseppe Arcimboldo's curious portraits composed from fruit and vegetables, and works by Rembrandt, Caravaggio, Titian and Holbein. Meanwhile the Albertina *(p98)* houses over 140 masterpieces by German renaissance master Albrecht Dürer, alongside drawings by Hieronymus Bosch, Raphael and Rubens.

1 million

Prints of Old Masters are housed in the Albertina, including drawings by Dürer and Klimt.

Take to the Streets

Vienna's street art scene has blossomed in the 21st century, so keep your eyes peeled as you stroll the city's boulevards. The best can be found in Mariahilf and around Naschmarkt *(p158)*. In the vibrant MuseumsQuartier *(p128)*, look for outdoor installations, and while wandering the pedestrianized Graben spot outsized displays of modern art in the Kunstplatz *(p104)*.

→

A street art installation by Julien Berthier sitting in the Graben's Kunstplatz

20th Century

Along with Baroque opulence and grand Old Masters, Vienna's modern galleries hold plenty of contemporary art. Stunning Expressionist works of Schiele and Kokoschka abound at the Belvedere *(p170)* and Leopold Museum *(p128)*. Also at the MuseumsQuartier, mumok's extensive modern art collection combines Post-Pop, Nouveau Realist and avant-garde art in futuristic gallery spaces *(p131)*.

←

Wally Neuzil by Schiele at the Leopold Museum

TOP 4 VIENNESE MUSIC MAKERS

Wolfgang Amadeus Mozart (1756-91)
Wrote his most famous works in Vienna.

Joseph Haydn (1732-1809)
Composed pieces such as *The Creation* here.

Johannes Brahms (1833-1897)
Musical director of the Vienna Singakademie.

Johann Strauss (1825-99)
Composed the *Blue Danube,* the unofficial national anthem.

The incomparable Vienna Philharmonic Orchestra during a performance ↑

VIENNA FOR
CLASSICAL
MUSIC LOVERS

Once the music capital of Europe and home to scores of illustrious classical composers, Vienna still draws musicians and music-lovers from across the globe. With its magnificent venues and thriving concert and festival scene, the city is one of the greatest classical music destinations in the world.

Tracing the Tradition

With the Habsburgs as the city's musical paymasters, 18th-century Vienna was a breeding ground for luminaries of classical composition. Today, there are historic musical sights at every turn. Visit the Deutschordenhaus where Brahms once resided or the Pasqualatihaus *(p146),* the most famous of 30 abodes occupied by Beethoven.

←

Exterior of the Pasqualatihaus, inhabited by Beethoven in the early 19th century

Viennese Venues

The Vienna Philharmonic Orchestra moved to the Musikverein (p177) in 1870 – Strauss conducted a premiere of his waltz *Freuet Euch des Lebens*, or "Enjoy Life", at the opening. Renowned worldwide for its impeccable acoustics, the venue is still home to the orchestra. The opulent Staatsoper (p154) puts on nearly 300 performances each year, with a varied programme of ballet and opera.

INSIDER TIP
Schönbrunn's Summer Eve

Each summer the Vienna Philharmonic Orchestra hosts the Sommernachtskonzert, a free open-air concert at the Schönbrunn Palace (www.sommer nachtskonzert.at).

Musical Museums

Music-lovers and kids alike will adore the Haus der Musik (p80), a high-tech interactive sound museum. Climb the piano steps or try your hand at conducting a virtual version of the Vienna Philharmonic. At the Kunsthistorisches Museum (p132), the Sammlung Alter Musikinstrumente boasts a huge collection of ornate and ancient musical instruments.

$\longrightarrow$

An interactive muscial exhibit at the Haus der Musik

Choral Sounds

Vienna has a distinguished choral heritage. The world-famous Vienna Boys' Choir (p198) was founded in 1498 by the great patron of the arts, Maximilian II. Today the boys perform at the Burgkapelle (p96): tickets are snapped up quickly, so make sure to book in advance. The Wiener Singakademie, founded in 1858, was conducted variously by Brahms, Strauss and Gustav Mahler and still performs regularly at the Wiener Konzerthaus.

$\longleftarrow$

The renowned Vienna Boys' Choir mid-performance

Sweet Treats

You can't visit Vienna without trying the cake, and with cafés and *konditoreien* (bakeries) on every corner, travellers are spoiled for choice. Indulge your sweet tooth at Hotel Sacher *(p158)* for a slice of the eponymous chocolate cake, or at chic Café Landtman *(p145)*, where you'll find perfect apfelstrudel rich with butter and raisins. At legendary Demel *(p105)*, the elaborate displays of cakes and chocolates are a feast for the eyes as well as the taste buds.

→

A tempting display of delicious cakes for sale at Demel

VIENNA FOR
FOODIES

Austria's capital brings together fresh produce and great ingredients from across the country in its thriving foodscape. From hearty traditional fare at a cosy *beisl* to mouthwatering patisserie in a chic classic café, these are some of the city's must-eats.

BEYOND THE SCHNITZEL

Despite some rather meat-heavy menus, those that shy from the schnitzel needn't go hungry. Topping a decent showing of veggie eateries is Wrenkh, where meat dishes come second to innovative vegetable creations *(p77)*. In the busy Stephansdom quarter, TIAN Wien's green courtyard is a veggie oasis *(p77)*, and outside the city centre, branches of the burger joint Swing Kitchen do a roaring trade in vegan fast-food *(www. swingkitchen.com)*.

Sizzling Street Food

Dominating the market scene for five centuries, the bustling Naschmarkt *(p158)* is home to hundreds of stalls offering fresh produce and international street food, while the up-and-coming Karmelitermarkt district holds a wide array of Middle Eastern eateries and artisanal bakeries. For on-the-go sustenance, look out for the many excellent *würstelstände* (sausage stands) serving freshly grilled sausages with lashings of *senf* (mustard).

One of the many vibrant *würstelständes* found throughout Vienna ↑

A Bite in a Beisl

The traditional place for neighbours to eat, drink and gossip, the *beisl* – a kind of homely bistro-pub hybrid – is a Viennese staple. This is the place to go for generous portions of hearty Austrian fare: unctuous goulash with pillowy bread dumplings, buttery cheese-laden *kaiser spitzel* (a kind of Austrian gnocchi) and, of course, the ubiquitous Wiener schnitzel.

Head to Alsergrund where Greichenbeisl and Beim Czaak *(p77)* keep it classic, or to Spittelberg's Amerlingbeisl *(p145)*, serving traditional dishes with a modern twist.

←

A traditional dessert of *marillenknödel* (apricot dumplings), served at a *beisl*

(p77) (p145)

TOP 5 VIENNESE SPECIALITY DISHES

Wienerschnitzel
Wafer-thin veal cutlet fried in breadcrumbs.

Knödel
Dumplings served savoury with stews, or as dessert with fruit and cream.

Tafelspitz
Boiled beef with apple and horseradish sauces, the favourite dish of Emperor Franz Joseph I.

Kartoffelpuffer
Vienna's original street food: potato pancakes served with sour cream.

Apfelstrudel
Layers of flaky buttery pastry encasing apple, cinnamon and raisins.

Contemporary Cuisine

Traditional eateries dominate, but there's more to Viennese cooking than schnitzels and strudel. For clean modern flavours make for trendy Heuer am Karlsplatz *(p158)*, or try a contemporary take on French and European cuisine at Leopoldstadt's hip Skopik and John *(www.skopikundlohn.at)*.

↑ Diners enjoying the innovative cuisine at Skopik and John

The Coffee House Set

UNESCO describes the Viennese coffee house as "a place where coffee, time and space are consumed, but only the coffee is found on the bill". Open to anyone for the price of a hot drink, the democratic nature of this Viennese institution made it the ideal place to share new, often radical ideas. Freud's Vienna Psychoanalytic Society first met at Café Korb (www.cafekorb.at), while Vienna's Secession movement was founded at Café Sperl (www.cafesperl.at).

→

Sigmund Freud *(left, seated)* and the Vienna Psychoanalytic Society

VIENNA'S
INTELLECTUALS

Vienna's coffeehouses and universities have been a hotbed of cerebral discussion for centuries, encouraging a cross-fertilization across disciplines that has inspired countless great thinkers. Walk in the footsteps of the city's intellectual icons to stimulate your own imagination.

The Vienna Circle

The "Vienna Circle of Logical Empiricism" was a formidable group of philosophers, scientists, logicians and mathematicians, which included Philipp Frank and Hans Hahn. Chaired by Moritz Schlick, the philosophical association met regularly at the University of Vienna *(p145)* during the 1920s and 1930s. In 1936, Schlick's murder on the steps of the university brought the circle's decade of enlightened discussions to an abrupt end.

→

Students at work in the University of Vienna's elegant library

Did You Know?

Freud's daughter Anna was also a famous and respected psychologist.

Vienna's Revolutionaries

Vienna's status as the capital of an empire that included Slavic lands made it the perfect refuge for eastern Europeans looking to plot revolutions. Lenin, Trotsky and Stalin all lived as fugitives in Vienna around 1912–13, and could often be found debating ideas and playing chess in Café Central (p109). Stalin wrote *Marxism: The National Question* with Nikolai Bukharin during his time in the city, while Trotsky launched the influential *Pravda* newspaper.

← A statue of writer Peter Altenberg sits in Café Central

THE WITTGENSTEIN FAMILY

Second only to the Rothschilds in wealth, the Wittgensteins were one of the richest and most eccentric families in early 20th-century Europe. Father Karl accrued vast fortunes as a steel tycoon, and was a generous patron to the Secession movement. His son Ludwig was the protegé of Bertrand Russell and became one of the great philosophers of the 20th century, while Ludwig's elder brother Paul was a renowned pianist, for whom Ravel composed the *Piano Concerto for the Left Hand* (Paul lost his right arm during World War I).

On the Couch

Vienna and Freud go hand in hand – locals joke that Vienna's nickname the "City of Dreams" owes its genesis to Freud's writings on the subconscious. A city resident from 1860 to 1938, Freud studied at the university and wrote many of his greatest works here. Young intellectuals, including Carl Jung and Otto Rank, were drawn to Freud's rooms on Berggasse 19 for lively discussions – visitors can explore these lodgings today as the fascinating Freud Museum (p116).

↑ Learning about Freud's work at the Sigmund Freud Museum

The Prater at Sunset

Immortalized in *The Third Man*, the Prater *(p186)* is home to the impressive Wiener Reisenrad ferris wheel – the view of the Danube and the city centre from the top is a must for any photographer. Feet firmly on the ground, snap a shot of the wheel at sunset, as the lights of the fairground start to sparkle in the twilight. The park's lovely tree-lined paths are similarly photogenic, particularly during autumn.

←

A night shot of the Wiener Reisenrad ferris wheel in the Prater

VIENNA FOR
PHOTOGRAPHY

From its generous imperial boulevards to serene green spaces, Vienna is a photographer's dream. There are iconic shots around every corner, so keep your camera at the ready to snap the perfect picture of this beautiful city. Here's an insider's guide to Vienna's most photogenic spots.

Baroque Elegance

Stunning Schönbrunn *(p188)* is the finest of Vienna's palaces and its elegant gardens, complete with follies and reflective pools, will tempt any lens. Crowds can often spoil photos of the Hofburg Palace *(p94)*, so get there early for the perfect shot, or wait until evening to capture its illuminated façade. At the Belvedere *(p170)*, splendid gardens slope down from the palace towards the city, so a grand panorama of Vienna will grace the background of every shot.

Across the Water

Since 1875, it has been the Danube Canal, and not the Danube itself, which has flown through the centre of Vienna. The best views of the river, and ample opportunity for great photos, can be found from the top of the Donauturm in Donaupark (p199), while on summer evenings shots across the water from east to west are hard to get wrong. A river boat trip is a great way of getting your lens as close to the water as possible.

→

Looking across the Danube to the city from Donaupark

Hundertwasserhaus

With its multicoloured exterior and irregular design, the spectacular Hundertwasserhaus is one of the most Instagrammed sights of the city (p184) – and it's not hard to see why. The psychedelic patterns, dazzling coloured tiles and wavy façades are sure to liven any photo library. Have some fun experimenting with different angles to get a shot that stands out from the crowds.

←

Shooting a low-angle view of the colourful Hundertwasserhaus

Up Above the Stephansdom

With it's intricately patterned tiled roof, the gothic St Stephen's Cathedral is an iconic image of Vienna (p66). The best shots can be captured from above: climb the 343 steps of the south tower for a breathtaking 360-degree vista of the city's skyline, and a fabulous close-up of the astonishing roof.

↑

The sumptuously lit exterior of the Schönbrunn Palace

→

A panorama of the city from the top of the Stephansdom

By the River Danube

In summer, make for the sandy beaches on the banks of the Donaukanal, or take a dip at Badeschiff, a floating river swimming pool *(p74)*. Rowing and pedal boats are available for hire from the Hofbauer Marina close to Alte Donau metro station, while the tranquil Danube Island offers lovely canal views.

💬 **INSIDER TIP**
Rundumadum

The mammoth 120 km (74 miles) Rundumadum hiking trail encircles the city in 24 easy stages. Collect pins at the five "stamping points" to prove you completed it.

Relaxing along the bank of the Danube canal in summer ↑

VIENNA FOR
THE GREAT OUTDOORS

More than half of Vienna is made up of green spaces. With gorgeous landscaped gardens and pleasant parks in its centre, and wild romantic woods and miles of gentle hiking trails just beyond its periphery, the city offers a plethora of ways to enjoy the great outdoors.

On Two Wheels

When it comes to cycling, Vienna's pedal-power is a match for Amsterdam. With 1,300 km (800 miles) of pleasant cycle paths, flat wide roads and more than 100 city bike stands across central Vienna, it is easy to hire a bike and cycle the city. Take to the cycling track along the Danube embankment or head to the mountain bike terrain of the popular Vienna Woods *(p210)*.

←

Enjoying a leisurely cycle along one of the city's numerous bike paths

Wander the Vienna Woods

On the city outskirts, there are over 240 km (150 miles) of marked hiking trails through tranquil woods to enjoy *(p210)*. Impeccably well signposted and easily reached by public transport, a walk through the woods is a wonderful way to while away an afternoon. The city's longest trail begins at the end of tramline D in the winemaking town of Nussdorf and leads to the Stefaniewarte on the Kahlenberg *(p197)*.

→

Beams of sunlight streaming through the Vienna Woods

Grandee Gardens

The sumptuous gardens of Vienna's palaces are delightful places for a picnic or a gentle stroll. The Schönbrunn *(p188)* and Belvedere *(p170)* palaces are the best known, but the Augarten *(p198)* is the city's oldest Baroque garden and offers an extensive network of shady avenues.

→

The beautifully landscaped gardens at Schönbrunn Palace

THE REPUBLIC OF KUGELMUGEL

Since 1976, this unusual micronation has claimed its territory in a bizarre ball-shaped house, located in the Prater since 1982. The republic declared its independence after a dispute between the Vienna council and the house's owner, Edwin Lipburger, who was jailed for his refusal to pay taxes and for printing his own stamps. The republic currently has 650 non-resident citizens.

Tracing the footsteps ↑
of Harry Lime on the
Third Man tour

VIENNA
OFF THE
BEATEN TRACK

Vienna packs a serious punch when it comes to quirky offbeat sights. Catacombs and crypts, bizarre museums and a self-declared microstate will pique the interest of even the most jaded traveller. This is the best of the out-of-the-ordinary attractions the city has to offer.

Underground Vienna

Escape the crowds at the Stephansdom *(p66)* by descending the steps to its crypt and catacombs. A centuries' old burial site, this creepy chamber holds Maria Theresa's stomach among its more unusual exhibits. Meanwhile, beneath the Kapuzinerkirche, emperors and empresses rest in elaborately decorated sarcophagi within the atmospheric vaults of the Kaisergruft *(p108)*.

→

The decorated tomb
of Franz Joseph in
the Kaisergruft

Take a Tour

Guided walking tours by "Space and Place" offer an alternative perspective of the city: if you've had your fill of imperial splendour, join their Vienna Ugly Tour to discover 19 of the city's least attractive buildings, including the Federal Ministry on Vordere Zollamtstrasse and the Hungarian Cultural Centre on Hollandstrasse *(www.spaceand place.at/vienna-ugly)*. Alternatively, follow in the footsteps of Orson Welles's Harry Lime and descend into the underworld of Vienna's impressive 19th-century sewer system on the intriguing *Third Man* tour *(www.drittemanntour.at)*. For something a little more salubrious, go on a shopping adventure with Lucie, an American expat and fashionista who leads travellers around the best of Vienna's chic fashion spots, introducing them to the city's lesser-known boutiques and hidden gems of couture *(www.shoppingwithlucie.com)*.

Admiring the ↑
exhibits at the
Globe Museum

Learning about the ↑
history of art forgery at
the Museum of Fakes

Unusual Museums

Forget the crowds of the MuseumsQuartier – make instead for the quaint Globe Museum *(p108)* or discover the art of forgery at the Museum of Fakes *(www.faelschermuseum.com)*. The Bestattungsmuseum houses morbid but fascinating exhibits exploring burial rituals through the ages *(p195)*.

The Third Man

Post-World War II Vienna, a city caught between old and new, and split between the occupying American, British, French and Soviet forces, was the setting for the classic film noir *The Third Man*, written by Graham Greene. Directed by Carol Reed, the black-and-white 1949 murder mystery stars Orson Welles at his most malevolent. Devotees can revel in the hoard of treasures at the Third Man Collection *(p161)* or reenact the film's final scene in the grimy sewers of the city on the Third Man Tour *(wwwdrittemann tour.at/en)*. Pay your respects to the film's most iconic scene by riding the Prater's landmark ferris wheel *(p186)*.

→

The moody streets of Vienna, in Carol Reed's *The Third Man*

Did You Know?

The Burg Kino cinema screens *The Third Man* every Tuesday, Friday and Sunday *(www.burgkino.at)*.

VIENNA FOR
FILM BUFFS

Vienna's imperial past and history of Cold War intrigue have sparked the imagination of writers and directors from around the world. Film lovers can track down iconic scene locations, enjoy the city on screen at thriving cinemas or revel in movie magic at fantastic festivals.

Vibrant Venues

The Austrian Film Museum, housed in the Albertina building *(p98)*, has a lively programme of classic and contemporary cinema *(www.filmmuseum.at)*. Meanwhile METRO Kinokulturhaus, part of the Filmarchiv Austria, is dedicated to preserving the country's rich cinematic history and offers a calendar of thought-provoking films *(www.filmarchiv.at)*.

←

Keen cinemagoers visiting the METRO Kinokulturhaus

TOP 5 FILM SETS IN VIENNA

The Piano Teacher
A thriller starring Isabelle Huppert, set at Vienna Conservatory.

Funny Games
Director Michael Haneke made two versions of this thriller.

The Night Porter
Postwar Vienna is at its most sinister in Liliana Cavani's erotic thriller.

Before Sunrise
Richard Linklater's 1995 romantic film.

The Third Man
The Prater's ferris wheel was immortalized in this drama.

EMPRESS SISSI ON SCREEN

Married at 16 to Franz Joseph I, the Empress Elisabeth, known as Sisi (1837–1898), was adored by the Austrian people for her beauty, dignity and elegance. She has been idolized in many films, none more lavish than the 1955 Austrian-made *Sissi*. In Hollywood's depiction of Sisi's life, the 1968 film *Mayerling*, Ava Gardner plays the empress in the time before her son's death.

A screening at the Viennale festival with an arriving film star *(inset)* ↑

Film Festivals

With a splendid calendar of festivals, Vienna has plenty to keep film fanatics entertained. The Viennale *(www.viennale.at)*, running since 1960, is the largest and takes place each October at classic cinemas in the city, including Gartenbaukino and Urania. For those seeking more niche events, try the Vienna Independent Film Festival *(www.vienna-film-festival.com)* or the Kino am Dach *(kinoamdach.at/)*, a summer film festival hosted on the roof of the city library.

EAT

Kolariks Praterfee

This place on Prater's main avenue has kid-sized portions of all your Vienna favourites, including schnitzel.

🏠 Prater 128 Waldsteingartenstraße
🔲 kolarik.at

€€€

Eis Greissler

Tuck into a dizzying array of ice cream and flavours at this popular local spot.

🏠 Rotenturmstraße 1
🔲 eis-greissler.at

€€€

VIENNA FOR
FAMILIES

From hands-on museums to quirky sights, funfairs to picnics in parks, Vienna is a wonderful place to explore with kids in tow. Aside from city-centric sights, there is also plenty of scope for fun on the water including boat trips and the Danube beaches – when the weather is warm.

Cycle the City

With miles of cycling paths both through the city centre and the Vienna Woods (p210), hiring a bike is a great way to explore. There are plenty of parks to stop at around the city: in the centre, the lush green spaces at the Burggarten and Volksgarten are perfect for picnics. Hop off your bikes for the rides at the Prater funfair (p186), or at Schonbrünn palace, with its tricky maze (p188).

→

Enjoying a family day out at the Prater funfair

Rainy-Day Activities

Vienna has a number of indoor activities that will light up grey and miserable days. The Haus des Meeres *(p160)*, a colourful aquarium in the Mariahilf district, has shoals of tropical fish to observe, and kids can dive into the water themselves at Diana-Bad indoor water park *(www.dianabad.at)*. To get around town in the rain, hop on the yellow No 1 tram, which trundles around Vienna's Ringstrasse. Grab a window seat to spot the city's impressive imperial buildings.

←

The magical world of the sea on show at Haus des Meeres aquarium

Puppet Performance

The Marionette Theater at Schonbrünn Palace *(p188)* has been entertaining audiences with its puppets for over 200 years. They now have a kid-friendly program including shows like *Aladdin* and *Hansel and Gretel*. For a more modern performance, head to the kid-centric space Dschungel Wien *(www. dschungelwien)* which stages dance and dramas.

→

Having fun onstage at Dschungel Wien

Get Interactive

Vienna's museums will spark young minds with a range of activities and exhibits. At the Museumsquartier's ZOOM *(p128)*, there are hands-on craft workshops where kids can get creative. Children will love climbing the musical piano staircase at the Haus der Musik *(p80)*, while the Technisches Museum has excellent technology-focused activities *(p202)*.

←

Kids using drills and other tools in fun workshops at ZOOM

VIENNA
AFTER DARK

Vienna doesn't go to sleep when the sun goes down: this 24-hour city serves everything from classic cocktails to happening hops, crowded clubs to jiving jazz venues, magic musicals to brilliant burlesque. Whatever entertainment keeps you awake at night, you're sure to find it here.

TOP 5 VIENNESE DANCE CLUBS

Pratersauna
A massive club playing techno and electro.

Sass
An opulent space with mellow vibes.

Cabaret Fledermaus
An eclectic mix of music in stylish surrounds.

Flex
An established venue in a disused metro tunnel.

DonauTechno
Expect pumping techno and crazy light shows.

Feel the Beat

In Vienna, clubs offer both tectonic techno beats and quirky and eye-catching designs. The massive Pratersauna nightclub *(www.pratersauna.tv)*, housed in an old spa, draws crowds all year; its pool is open in warmer months. In summer, outdoor clubs pop-up on the Danube embankment and floating bar Badeschiff's *(p74)* DJs spin tunes by its pool long into the night.

↑ Dancing to the light-up beats at the iconic Pratersauna club

All of Wien's a Stage

From Broadway musicals to underground comedy, Vienna's stages entertain year-round. There are big productions at the Raimund Theatre and Ronacher *(www. musicalvienna.at)*, dramas at the venerable Burgtheater *(p138)* and Theater an der Wien *(p158)*, stand-up comedy at Casa Nova *(www.casanova-vienna.at)* or burlesque and drag shows at Volkstheater's Rote Bar *(www.volkstheater.at)*.

←

The cast of *Mary Poppins* performing at glitzy Ronacher theatre

WIEN WINE

For those seeking a taste of rural Austria, the villages surrounding Vienna are known for their wine-making and are home to large numbers of *Heurigen* – vineyard taverns serving classics and plates of cheese and charcuterie alongside fine wine from local vineyards. The best *Heurigen* are found at the charming nearby towns of Nussdorf, Kahlenberg and Grinzing *(p197)*.

Jumping Jazz Clubs

Jazz is big news in Vienna, and the eclectic Porgy & Bess *(p75)* attracts famous international acts and a crowd of music lovers. Jazzland is the oldest jazz club in the city, dating back to 1972, and is the place to see Austrian greats *(www.jazzland.at)*. It's also one of the venues for the JazzFloor festival, which brings together leading acts from around the world each November.

←

Acts playing in a former church crypt at Jazzland

By the Glass

Here, sophisticated bars sit cheek by jowl with casual taprooms and microbreweries. For high-end drinks seek out minimalist Ebert's Cocktail Bar *(p161)*, or for cocktails with a rooftop panorama of the city try Sofitel Hotel's Das LOFT *(www.dasloftwien.at)*. The beer scene is booming: try a brew at 7 Stern Bräu brewery *(p143)* or at Beaver Brewing Tour *(p119)*.

→

The colourful ceiling by Pipilotti Rist at Das LOFT

A YEAR IN
VIENNA

JANUARY

New Year Celebration Concerts *(1 Jan)*. Musical celebrations at the illustrious Musikverein and Konzerthaus are a national institution.

△ **Wiener Eistraum** *(Jan–Mar)*. The Rathausplatz is transformed into a huge ice rink that attracts ice skaters of all ages.

FEBRUARY

Carnival *(Fasching)* *(Feb)*. The start of Lent is marked by a carnival with food, drink and general merriment.

△ **Opera Ball** *(late Feb)*. For one night only, the Staatsoper stage becomes a dancefloor, host to the capital's most glamorous ball.

MAY

Genussfestival *(early May)*. Held in the Stadtpark, this food festival shows off the best of Austrian food and its most skilful chefs.

△ **Wiener Festwochen** *(May–Jun)*. A cultural festival showcasing contemporary outsider arts, music and theatre, opening with a free open-air concert in the Rathausplatz.

JUNE

Vienna Pride *(early Jun)*. Each year, the joyous celebrations include a Pride Run, beach parties, discussions and cultural events, and the raucous Rainbow Parade around the Ringstrasse.

△ **Donauinselfest** *(late Jun)*. The Danube Island Festival is the largest open-air rock and pop music event in the world. Admission is free.

SEPTEMBER

△ **Vienna Fashion Week** *(mid-Sep)*. Held at the MuseumsQuartier, this is the capital's premier fashion event.

Vienna Contemporary *(late Sep)*. Austria's largest international contemporary art fair takes place at the Marx Hall.

Vienna Design Week *(late Sep)*. Ten-day annual design bash with shows, pop-up exhibitions, tours, workshops and parties across the city.

OCTOBER

△ **Long Night of the Museums** *(early Oct)*. Some 130 of the city's museums stay open until 1am, with one ticket covering them all.

Viennale *(Oct)*. This fine film festival attracts international stars of cinema.

Wien Modern *(Oct–Nov)*. A leading festival of contemporary classical music, with peformances at over 30 venues across the city.

MARCH

Osterklang *(before Easter)*. In the run-up to Easter, this is a spring celebration of music and dance at Theater an der Wien, with opera, ballet and classical music.

△ **Easter Markets** *(Mar or Apr)*. The main market takes place outside Schönbrunn Palace.

APRIL

△ **Vienna City Marathon** *(early Apr)*. Over 30,000 participants pound the streets of Vienna during Austria's biggest road race.

Vienna Blues Spring Festival *(Apr–May)*. The city gets the blues during this long-standing festival, with rockers and blues legends performing at the Reigen and Theater Akzent.

JULY

△ **ImPulsTanz** *(Jul–Aug)*. Europe's biggest dance festival presents contemporary performances by young artists across the city.

Oper Klosterneuburg *(Jul–Aug)*. One of Austria's most eagerly anticipated social events, with operas held at Klosterneuburg Monastery.

Musikfilmfest *(Jul–early Sep)*. Summer evening concerts and film screenings are held at an open-air cinema in the Rathausplatz, with pop-up food stalls suppling tasty treats.

AUGUST

Feast of the Assumption *(15 Aug)*. One of the biggest festivals in the Catholic calendar sees church services and processions celebrating the Virgin's arrival in heaven

△ **Sturm Season** *(late Aug)*. As the autumn grape harvest begins, *sturm* (fermented grape juice) can be enjoyed in the many *Heurigen* (vineyard taverns) on Vienna's outskirts.

NOVEMBER

△ **All Saints' Day** *(1 Nov)*. Catholics honour the dead by laying flowers and lighting lanterns on graves.

Vienna Boys' Choir Annual Open Day *(mid-Nov)*. For one afternoon, visit the Vienna Boys Choir at their boarding school in the Baroque Augarten Palace.

Klezmore Festival *(mid-Nov)*. A Klezmer music festival attracting performers from across the world to Vienna's theatres, clubs and churches.

DECEMBER

△ **Christmas Markets** *(throughout)*. For festive cheer head to the Belvedere's Christmas village or the Rathausplatz's Christkindlesmarkt.

Midnight Mass *(24 Dec)*. Across the Catholic world, believers gather for a service just before midnight on Christmas Eve.

Kaiserball at the Hofburg *(31 Dec)*. Tickets for the New Year's Ball at the Hofburg, a prestigious social event, are highly prized.

A BRIEF
HISTORY

With its strategic location on the Danube, Vienna was occupied variously by the Celts, Romans, Babenbergs and Habsburgs, each contributing to making this one of Europe's wealthiest cities. While no longer the heart of an empire, the Austrian capital remains a global centre of finance, politics and culture.

Early Vienna

The region around Vienna was first inhabited in the late Stone Age, and Vienna itself was founded as a Bronze Age settlement in around 800 BC. Settled by Celts from about 400 BC, it was incorporated by the Romans into the province of Pannonia in 15 BC. The garrison of Vindobona, allied to the nearby town of Carnuntum, was established by the beginning of the 1st century AD, its population reaching 20,000 by AD 250. Vindobona was later overrun by Barbarian tribes, and the garrison was reduced to ruins by the Huns in 433. Rome's influence on the region diminished and in the 8th century,

1 The walled city, a magnet for traders over the centuries.

2 Artist's impression of the Roman garrison of Vindobona.

3 Otto I expelling the Hungarians in 955.

4 Tomb of Friedrich II, the last Babenberg ruler.

Timeline of events

800 BC
Bronze Age settlers on what is now Hoher Markt.

250
Vindobona develops as a garrison town, and its population reaches 20,000.

433
Vindobona destroyed by the Huns; centuries of invasions by Barbarian tribes ensue.

2000 BC
Indo-Germanic settlements on the slopes of northwest Vienna.

15 BC
The Celts, present since 400 BC, are defeated by the Romans, who found Vindabona.

the Frankish Emperor Charlemagne made Vienna part of his Eastern March (borderland territory), and so by extension it became part of the Holy Roman Empire.

Medieval Vienna

In 955 the Holy Roman Emperor Otto I expelled Hungarian tribes from the Eastern March. Just over two decades later, he made a gift of Vienna to the German Babenberg dynasty, who, despite further incursions by the Hungarians, restored the city's status as a centre of trade and culture.

Friedrich II, the last of the Babenburg dynasty, died in battle against invading Hungarian forces in 1246. In the period that followed, rival factions vied for power until the Bohemian ruler Ottakar II subdued the warring nobles and took control. He then made an unsuccessful bid for the Imperial throne, after which he was ousted by the Habsburg count Rudolph I, King of Germany. Over the centuries the power of the Habsburg rulers grew, and when Rudolph's descendant Friedrich V was elected Emperor in 1452, the Habsburg dynasty and the Holy Roman Empire fused into a single entity, with Vienna as its hub.

WHERE TO SEE MEDIEVAL VIENNA

Gothic churches in the city include the Stephansdom (p66), the Burgkapelle (p96), Augustinerkirche (p98), Ruprechtskirche (p75) and Maria am Gestade (p83). Medieval houses that have survived include the Basiliskenhaus in Schönlaterngasse (p77).

883
First mention of Wenia (Vienna), derived from the Celtic word for the Wien river.

1030
The Hungarians besiege Vienna.

1156
Heinrich II Jasomirgott moves his court to Vienna; builds Am Hof.

1278–82
Rudolf I becomes ruler of Austria.

1452
Friedrich V elected Holy Roman Emperor; Vienna made seat of Empire.

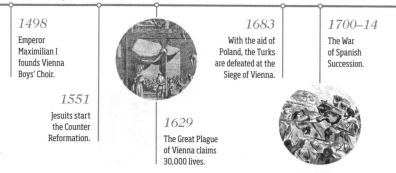

Renaissance Vienna

Because of the balance of power existing in the electoral college, from 1452 onwards Habsburgs were invariably elected Holy Roman Emperor, and by the 16th century their empire had expanded into Spain, Holland, Burgundy, Bohemia and Hungary. Under the relatively enlightened rule of Maximilian I (1508–1519), Vienna was transformed into a centre for the arts. But the city was under constant threat: from Turkish attacks, the plague, and disputes between Protestants and Catholics, finally resolved when the Jesuits spearheaded the Counter-Reformation.

Baroque Vienna and the Napoleonic Wars

The Turkish threat was ended for good in 1683, when Kara Mustapha's forces were repelled at the city's gates. Under Karl VI the city expanded and the Karlskirche and the Belvedere palaces were constructed. Around the Hofburg, mansions for noble families sprang up, and under rulers such as the beloved Maria Theresa Vienna enjoyed a lively era as a resplendent imperial capital. But with the rise of Napoleon Bonaparte (1769–1821), Vienna was once again under threat. Napoleon's

MARIA THERESA'S RULE

The long reign of Maria Theresa was a time of serenity, wealth and sensible administration, despite a background of frequent wars. The vast palace of Schönbrunn was completed by the Empress, who also presided over Vienna's rise as the musical capital of Europe.

Timeline of events

1498
Emperor Maximilian I founds Vienna Boys' Choir.

1551
Jesuits start the Counter Reformation.

1629
The Great Plague of Vienna claims 30,000 lives.

1683
With the aid of Poland, the Turks are defeated at the Siege of Vienna.

1700–14
The War of Spanish Succession.

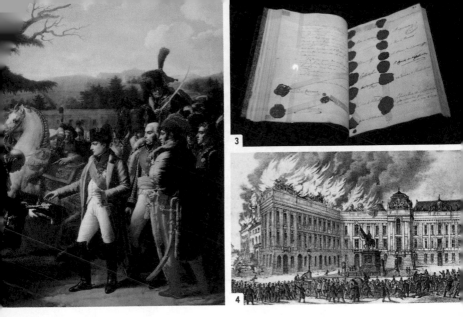

defeat of Austria at Austerlitz in 1805 was a humiliation for Emperor Franz I. His foreign minister, Prince Metternich, took the reins and, in a gesture of appeasement, arranged for Napoleon to marry the emperor's daughter. In a matter of years, Napoleon himself was defeated and in the subsequent Congress of Vienna, which sought to restore a peaceful balance of power in Europe, Austria regained some of its lost territories. On the domestic front, however, Metternich seized the opportunity to impose a reactionary and autocratic rule, and Austria's middle classes, excluded from political life, became increasingly disaffected.

The 1848 Revolution

An anti-establishment revolution in which the middle classes sided with the workers and nationalist movements elsewhere in the Habsburg empire drove Metternich from power in 1848. However, having appointed a series of liberal governments to appease the revolutionaries, newly appointed Ferdinand I lost military support and was forced by the counter-revolution to abdicate in favour of his nephew Franz Joseph. As emperor, Franz Joseph ushered in a new age of grandeur, despite the dwindling power of the Habsburgs.

1 Massed Turkish forces besieging the city walls.

2 Napoleon accepting the surrender of the city.

3 Signed and sealed pages of the Congress of Vienna.

4 The Hofburg burns in the 1848 revolution.

Did You Know?

The Congress of Vienna was not a formal congress but a year-long series of private, often secret, discussions.

1740
Maria Theresa ascends to the throne.

1809
Napoleon moves into Schönbrunn Palace and marries Franz I's daughter Maria Louisa.

1812–14
Napoleon defeated by the combined forces of Russia, Prussia, England and Austria.

1814–15
Congress of Vienna held; Austria loses Belgium but gains parts of Italy.

1848
Revolution in Vienna; Metternich forced from office, and Emperor Ferdinand I abdicates.

Austro-Hungarian Empire

Austria's reign in the German-speaking world ended with its defeat in the Austro-Prussian War of 1866. Reconciliation with Hungary and the creation of the Austro-Hungarian Empire in 1867 did something to restore prestige. A time of intellectual ferment in Vienna, this was the age of Freud and the writers Karl Kraus and Arthur Schnitzler, and of the Jugendstil arts movement. But Austro–Hungary's annexation of Bosnia-Herzegovina in 1908 increased tensions with Russia and in 1914, Franz Ferdinand, heir to the Austrian throne, was murdered in Sarajevo, precipitating World War I.

First Republic and World War II

The loss of Austria's territories after defeat in World War I forced Karl I to abdicate, and the country was declared a Republic, shrinking from an empire of 50 million people to a state of 6.5 million. Frequent armed clashes between nationalists – some supporting unification with Germany – and Communists followed, culminating in a short but bloody civil war in 1934. Despite government efforts to preserve independent

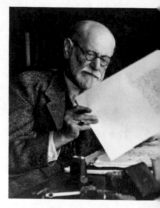

↑ Sigmund Freud, a key figure in Vienna's avant-garde intelligentsia

Timeline of events

1867
Hungary granted autonomy, leading to Dual Monarchy with separate governments.

1897
Secession movement ...rmed by 19 painters and ...chitects breaking with ...he art establishment.

1914
Death of Franz Joseph.

1918
Declaration of Austrian Republic after abdication of Emperor Karl I.

1934
Socialists banned after street fights in Vienna with government troops.

statehood, an economic boycott by Nazi Germany left people with little choice but to vote for unification (*Anschluss*) in 1938. Austria ceased to exist and became part of Germany for the duration of World War II.

From Postwar Restoration to the Modern Era

At the Moscow Conference in 1943, the Allied forces decided to restore an independent Austrian state. In 1945, Austria was divided into four occupation zones by the Allied powers, and a new president and government were elected. De-Nazification continued until 1948; in 1955 the Austrian State Treaty restored Austria to full sovereignty, and foreign troops were withdrawn.

For 50 years political life in Austria was controlled, relatively uneventfully, by either the Christian-Democratic Party (ÖVP) or the Socialist Party (SPÖ). The 1990s, however, saw the rise of the right. In 2000, Austria was sanctioned by the EU after the right-wing Freedom Party became part of a coalition government that has since adopted contentious measures regarding ethnic minorities and refugees. But regardless of the country's politics, its capital remains hugely popular with visitors and locals alike.

1 Gavrilio Princip shooting Franz Ferdinand. ↑

2 Memorial to the fallen of the civil war of 1934.

3 The signing of the Austrian State Treaty.

4 The MuseumsQuartier in present-day Vienna.

Did You Know?

In 2018, Vienna topped the Economist Intelligence Unit's ranking of "the world's most liveable cities".

1955
On 15 May the Austrian State Treaty brings to an end the Allied occupation.

1995
Austria joins the European Union.

2011
World dignitaries attend the funeral of the "last emperor", Otto von Habsburg.

1938
Hitler enters Vienna and pronounces *Anschluss* with Nazi Germany.

1978
First section of the U-Bahn system opened.

EXPERIENCE

The ornate interior of the Prunksaal

STEPHANSDOM QUARTER

The cobbled streets and spacious squares of this ancient quarter form the heart of the Austrian capital. The site was first occupied over 2,000 years ago by the Romans, who were drawn to the surrounding area by its valuable resources, among them gold. Established around AD 100, this military settlement was known across the Roman Empire as Vindobona. Later overrun by invading Barbarian tribes, and destroyed by the Huns in 403, little trace of the Roman garrison survives.

The most profound influence on Stephansdom was made by its subsequent inhabitants and early Habsburg rulers, with its winding lanes following the compact arrangement of medieval settlements. The historic soul of Vienna still dominates the skyline – the magnificent Gothic Stephansdom. A parish church had stood on this site since the 12th century, but the foundation stone of the cathedral seen today was laid by Duke Rudolf IV, "the Founder", in 1359.

Today, buildings in this area house government offices and businesses, and the largely pedestrianized streets brim with traditional taverns and stylish shops and boutiques.

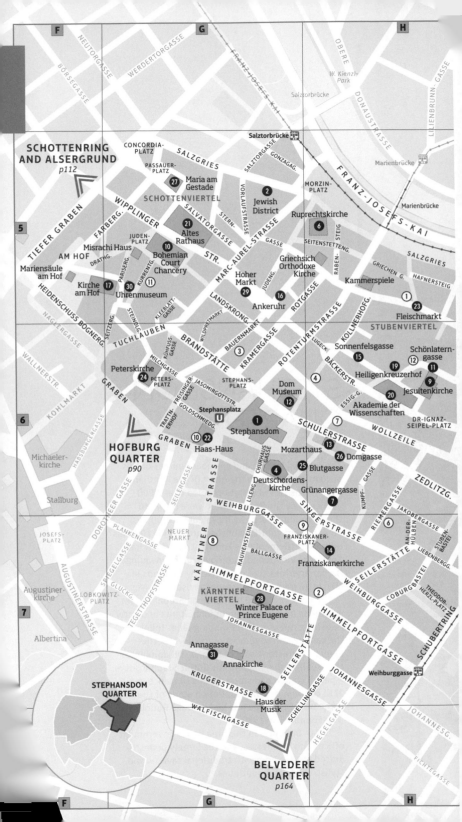

F G H

NEUTORGASSE
BÖRSEGASSE
WERDERTORGASSE
OBERE DONAUSTRASSE
LILIENBRUNN-GASSE
W. Kienzl-Park
Salzbrücke
Marienbrücke
Salztorbrücke
FRANZ-JOSEFS-KAI
Marienbrücke

SCHOTTENRING AND ALSERGRUND
p112

CONCORDIA-PLATZ
PASSAUER-PLATZ
SALZGRIES
SALZTORGASSE
GONZAGAG.
MORZIN-PLATZ
27 Maria am Gestade
SCHOTTENVIERTEL
WIPPLINGER
SALVATORGASSE
STERN-
VORLAUFSTRASSE
2 Jewish District
Ruprechtskirche **6**
SEITENSTETTEN.
RABEN-STEIG
SALZGRIES
GRIECHEN G.
HAFNERSTEIG

5

TIEFER GRABEN
AM HOF
FARBERG.
JUDEN-PLATZ
21 Altes Rathaus
10 Bohemian Court Chancery
MARC-AURELI-STRASSE
GASSE
Griechisch Orthodoxe Kirche
JUDENG.
Kammerspiele **1**
Fleischmarkt **23**

Mariensäule am Hof
Misrachi Haus
DRATHG.
PARISERG.
KURRENTG.
Hoher Markt
ROTGASSE
Schönlatern-gasse **12**

Kirche am Hof **17**
30 Uhrenmuseum
11
STEINDLG.
KLEEBLATT-GASSE
29 Ankeruhr
16
ROTENTURMSTRASSE
KÖLLNERHOFG.
LUGECK
BÄCKERSTR.
STUBENVIERTEL
Sonnenfelsgasse
15
Heiligenkreuzhof
19
11
Jesuitenkirche **9**

NAGLERGASSE
WALLNERSTR.
HEIDENSCHUSS BOGNERG.
TUCHLAUBEN
BRANDSTÄTTE
KÜHFUSS-GASSE
WILDPRETMARKT
KRAMERGASSE
LANDSKRONG.
BAUERNMARKT
SEITZERG.
MILCHGASSE
3
Dom Museum **12**
ESSIG-G.
Akademie der Wissenschaften **20**

6

KOHLMARKT
HABSBURGERGASSE
Peterskirche **24**
PETERS-PLATZ
GRABEN
FREISINGER-GASSE
JASOMIRGOTTSTR.
STEPHANS-PLATZ
SCHULERSTRASSE
4
7
WOLLZEILE
DR-IGNAZ-SEIPEL-PLATZ

Michaeler-kirche
Stallburg
GRABEN
STRASSE
TRATTN-ERHOF
GOLDSCHMIEDG.
Stephansplatz
10 **22**
Haas-Haus
1 Stephansdom
CHURHAUS-GASSE
Mozarthaus **13**
26 Domgasse
Blutgasse **25**
Grünangergasse **7**

JOSEFS-PLATZ
AUGUSTINERSTRASSE
HOFBURG QUARTER
p90
SEILERGASSE
DOROTHEER GASSE
4 Deutschordens-kirche
RIEMERGASSE
JAKOBERGASSE
ZEDLITZG.

Augustiner-kirche
Albertina
LOBKOWITZ-PLATZ
PLANKENGASSE
SPIEGELGASSE
TEGETTHOFFSTRASSE
NEUER MARKT
KÄRNTNER
RAUHENSTEIG
BALLGASSE
WEIHBURGGASSE
SINGERSTRASSE
9 FRANZISKANER-PLATZ
Franziskanerkirche **14**
SEILERSTÄTTE
AN-DER-HÜLBEN
LIEBENBERGG.
STUBEN-BASTEI
COBURG BASTEI
THEODOR HERZL-PLATZ

7

GLUCKG.
8
HIMMELPFORTGASSE
KÄRNTNER VIERTEL
Winter Palace of Prince Eugene **28**
JOHANNESGASSE
2
HIMMELPFORTGASSE
WEIHBURGGASSE
SCHUBERTRING

Annagasse
31
Annakirche
KRUGERSTRASSE
18
Haus der Musik
WALFISCHGASSE
SCHELLINGGASSE
HEGELGASSE
JOHANNESGASSE
Weihburggasse
FICHTEGASSE
JOHANNESG.

STEPHANSDOM QUARTER

BELVEDERE QUARTER
p164

F G H

STEPHANSDOM QUARTER

Must Sees

1 Stephansdom
2 Jewish District
3 MAK (Museum für angewandte Kunst)

Experience More

4 Deutschordenskirche
5 Postparkasse
6 Ruprechtskirche
7 Grünangergasse
8 Dominikanerkirche
9 Jesuitenkirche
10 Bohemian Court Chancery
11 Schönlaterngasse
12 Dom Museum
13 Mozarthaus
14 Franziskanerkirche
15 Sonnenfelgasse
16 Ankeruhr
17 Kirche am Hof
18 Haus der Musik
19 Heiligenkreuzerhof
20 Akademie der Wissenschaften
21 Altes Rathaus
22 Haas-Haus
23 Fleischmarkt
24 Peterskirche
25 Blutgasse
26 Domgasse
27 Maria am Gestade
28 Winter Palace of Prince Eugene
29 Hoher Markt
30 Uhrenmuseum
31 Annagasse

Eat

1 Griechenbeisl
2 TIAN Wien
3 Wrenkh
4 Figlmüller
5 Beim Czaak

Drink

6 Porgy and Bess
7 Diglas
8 Sky Bar
9 Kleines Café

Stay

10 DO & CO

Shop

11 Grimm Bakery
12 Wiener Rosenmanufaktur

① ⓂⒶ

STEPHANSDOM

📍G6 🏠Stephansplatz 1 ⓊStephansplatz 🚌1A, 2A, 3A 🕐9–11:30am & 1–4:30pm Mon–Sat, 1pm–4:30pm Sun & hols 🌐stephanskirche.at

Situated in the very centre of Vienna, Stephansdom is the historic soul of the city, and its chief place of worship. Its soaring towers, impressive crypt and ornately carved altars make this Gothic cathedral the capital's most iconic sight.

A church has stood on this site for over 800 years. It is thought that its first iteration was constructed on the ruins of an ancient Roman cemetery. The first Romanesque building on this plot was consecrated by the Bishop of Passau in 1147, and following its destruction, a second was erected in 1230. All that remains of the original 13th-century Romanesque church are the Giants' Doorway and Heathen Towers. The Gothic nave, choir and side chapels are the result of a rebuilding programme in the 14th and 15th centuries, initiated by Duke Rudolf IV (1358–65), while some of the outbuildings, such as the Lower Vestry, are 18th-century Baroque additions. In a vault beneath the altar are urns containing the internal organs of some of the Habsburgs. According to legend, the North Tower, begun in 1450, was never completed because its master builder, Hans Puchsbaum, broke a pact he had made with the devil by speaking a holy name. The devil then caused him to fall to his death.

↑ The maginificent tiled roof and one of the twin Heathen Towers overlooking Vienna

JOHANNES CAPISTRANUS

On the exterior northeastern wall of the choir is an elaborate pulpit built after the Hungarian victory over the Ottomans at Belgrade in 1456. It was from here that the Italian Franciscan monk Giovanni da Capestrano (1386–1456) is said to have preached against the Turkish invasion of Vienna in 1451. The 18th-century Baroque statue above it depicts the triumphant saint - known in Austria as Johannes Capistranus - trampling on a defeated Ottoman invader.

→ Franciscan monk Capistranus, depicted in marble on the pulpit

↑ The cathedral's imposing Gothic and Romanesque exterior, brightly uplit in the evening

230,000
—
Glazed tiles cover Stephansdom's roof, depicting the coats of arms of Vienna and Austria.

Stephansdom's fine Gothic façade facing busy Stephansplatz ↑

Timeline

1359
▲ Duke Rudolf IV lays the foundation stone of the Gothic reconstruction of the church.

1359–1440
Main aisle, southern arches and southern tower built.

1711
Pummerin bell cast from remains of retreating Turks' guns.

1916
▼ Emperor Franz Joseph I's funeral is held here.

1948
▲ Reconstruction carried out after World War II.

↑ Grand nave leading to the High Altar depicting the martyrdom of St Stephen

Exploring Stephansdom

The lofty vaulted interior of Stephansdom holds a collection of art spanning centuries. Masterpieces of Gothic sculpture include the intricate Pilgram's Pulpit, figures of saints adorning the piers, and the canopies or baldachins over many of the side altars. Left of the High Altar is the 15th-century winged Wiener Neustädter Altar, bearing painted images of 72 saints. The most spectacular Renaissance work is Friedrich III's tomb, while the 17th-century High Altar adds a flamboyant Baroque note.

The North Tower's construction ended in 1511. In 1578 it was topped with a Renaissance cap.

A flight of steps leads to the 18th-century catacombs.

The 12th-century Giants' Doorway and Heathen Towers allegedly stand on the site of an earlier heathen shrine.

The 15th-century Pilgram's Pulpit

HIDDEN GEM
The Catacombs

Under the cathedral, vast catacombs hold the bones of Vienna's plague dead in a mass grave and bone house, along with urns containing the internal organs of members of the Habsburg dynasty.

Main entrance

Singer Gate was once the entrance for male visitors. A relief above the door depicts scenes from the life of St Paul.

← The magnificent Gothic Stephansdom, first consecrated in 1147

The 137-m- (450-ft-) high Gothic spire, or steffl, houses stairs that visitors can climb to reach a viewing platform.

THE PUMMERIN BELL

The North Tower's Pummerin or "Boomer" bell is a potent symbol of Vienna's turbulent past. The original was cast from melted-down cannons abandoned when the Turks fled Vienna in 1683. In a fire of 1945, the bell crashed down through the cathedral roof. In 1952, a new, even larger bell was cast using the remains of the old one.

The cathedral roof's fine glazed tiles were carefully restored after bomb damage during World War II.

↑ Worshippers lighting votive candles at a chapel in the cathedral

↑ The ornate Pilgram's Pulpit, the work of the talented sculptor Anton Pilgram

Southeastern entrance

Lower Vestry

② Ⓜ ▢ ⓐ

JEWISH DISTRICT

📍 G5 🏛 Misrachi-Haus: Judenplatz 8; Stadttempel: Seitenstettengasse 4
Ⓤ Schwedenplatz 🕐 Times vary, check websites for details Ⓦ Misrachi-Haus:
www.misrachi.at; Stadttempel: www.ikg-wien.at

Vienna has been home to a Jewish community for almost 900 years, and, in spite of the decimation of the Jewish population during the Holocaust, much of the city's rich Jewish heritage endures, ready to be explored.

For centuries the heart of the Jewish district, today the Judenplatz is surrounded by shops and restaurants. There are some solid early 19th-century apartment blocks and on Ruprechtsplatz, and in the former town hall, a kosher restaurant, Alef Alef. Behind the restaurant a tower, the Kornhäuselturm, is named after Josef Kornhäusel, an architect from the Biedermeier period. At No 4 Seitenstettengasse is the great Stadttempel, designed by Kornhäusel in the 1820s, Vienna's only synagogue to survive the Holocaust. In 1895, the first Jewish Museum was founded here but it has since moved to two separate locations at Dorotheergasse and the late-17th century Misrachi-Haus on the Judenplatz, the site of the Jewish ghetto in medieval times. Besides the archeological remains of a 500-year-old synagogue and a monument to the Austrian victims of the Holocaust by Rachel Whiteread, the Misrachi-Haus is home to an exhibition detailing the pogrom of 1421.

VIENNA'S JEWISH COMMUNITY

A Jewish community has existed in Vienna since the 12th century, with Judenplatz and the Stadttempel at its core. In 1421 almost the entire Jewish population was burned to death, forcibly baptized or expelled on the orders of Albert V. Thereafter Jewish fortunes fluctuated, with periods of prosperity alternating with expulsions. By the late 19th century the city's cultural and intellectual life was dominated by Jewish people, only for the population to be decimated during the Holocaust. Today, the number of Jewish people in the city is around 15,000, just 10 per cent of pre-World War II numbers.

Did You Know?

Vienna's Jewish district is affectionately known as "Matzo Island".

→
Rachel Whiteread's concrete cuboid Holocaust Memorial in the Judenplatz

← The interior of the elegant Biedermeier-style Stadttempel Synagogue

→ Hebrew inscription above the discreet façade of Stadttempel synagogue on quiet Seitenstettengasse

Did You Know?

Designed by Heinrich
von Ferstel, the MAK
was inspired by
London's Victoria and
Albert Museum.

↑ Grand façade of
the MAK overlooking
the Ringstrasse

③ (icons)

MAK (MUSEUM FÜR ANGEWANDTE KUNST)

📍J6 🏠Stubenring 5 ⑤Landstrasse ⓤStubentor 🚋2 🚌3A, 74A 🕙10am–6pm Tue–Sun (to 10pm Tue) 🚫1 Jan, 25 Dec 🌐mak.at

Both a showcase for Austrian decorative arts and a repository for beautiful objects from around the world, this fine museum was originally founded in 1864 as a collection of art and architecture. It has expanded and diversified over the years to include objects representing new movements and contemporary design.

The Museum of Applied Arts, or MAK, houses an extensive collection of modern and antique furniture, textiles, glass, carpets, East Asian art and fine Renaissance jewellery. In 2012, it was completely renovated and new multimedia exhibitions were added. The basement houses the MAK Design Lab, MAK Forum and MAK Gallery. Most of the permanent collection is displayed in the ground-floor galleries, which include the Asia and Carpet and Textiles collections. The impressive arcaded Main Hall houses temporary exhibitions.

↑ Ornate Chinese Tang dynasty tomb figure in the Asia Collection

The columned Main Hall, decorated in Florentine Renaissance style ↑

THE WIENER WERKSTÄTTE

In 1903, architect and designer Josef Hoffmann (1870–1956) and artist Kolo Moser (1868–1918) founded a cooperative arts and crafts workshop, the Wiener Werkstätte. This promoted all forms of design, including postage stamps, book illustrations, furniture, fabric, jewellery and interiors. The MAK houses the Werkstätte's archives of sketches, fabric patterns and fine pieces of furniture.

↑ Fine tulle and cotton embroidered gowns in the Textiles Collection

EXPERIENCE MORE

4

Deutschordenskirche

📍G6 🏛Singerstrasse 7 ⓊStephansplatz 🚌1A, 2A, 3A ⏱Times vary, check website 🚫Sun, Mon & public hols 🌐deutscher-orden.at

This church belongs to the Order of Teutonic Knights, a chivalric order that was established in the 12th century. It is 14th-century Gothic, and though restored in the 1720s in Baroque style by Anton Erhard Martinelli, it retains Gothic elements such as pointed arched windows. Numerous coats of arms of Teutonic Knights and memorial slabs are displayed on the walls. The Flemish altar-piece is from 1520 and incorporates panel paintings and carvings of scenes from the Passion beneath a number of very delicate traceried canopies.

Situated just off the church courtyard, the Order's Treasury now serves as a museum, displaying various fine collections acquired by its Grand Masters over the centuries. The starting point is a room housing a large collection of coins, medals and a 13th-century enthrone-ment ring. A second room contains chalices and Mass vessels worked with silver filigree, while a third displays maces, daggers and ceremonial garb. The museum also exhibits some striking Gothic paintings and a Carinthian carving of St George and the Dragon (1457).

5

Postsparkasse

📍J6 🏛Georg-Coch-Platz 2 ⓊSchwedenplatz 🚌3A 🚋1, 2 ⏱10am-5:30pm Mon-Fri 🌐otto wagner.com

This building, housing the Imperial Royal Post Office Savings Bank, offers a wonderful example of early Modernist architec-ture, and represents its architect's first

← Madonna and Child statue in the Deutschordenskirche

💬 INSIDER TIP
Take the Waters

In summer, cool off at the Badeschiff, a float-ing pool on the Danube Canal. Take an early morning swim followed by breakfast, and in the evening enjoy craft beers at the beach bar (*www.badeschiff.at*).

move away from *Jugendstil*. Designed between 1904 and 1906 by Otto Wagner, the structure was built in steel and concrete, and still has an unashamedly modern appearance, with square marble plates and iron bolts patterning its façade. Decorative elements – the sculptures of heroic angels adorning the bank's roof, and the curving lines of the interior – owe much to the Secession movement, of which Wagner was an important member.

Wagner was a Modernist pioneer, incorporating func-tional elements into his decorative schemes. Inside, the lofty, atrium-like banking hall, or "Grand Kassenhalle", is encircled by tubular heating ducts and metal columns clad in aluminium.

←
The lofty central
hall of Otto Wagner's
grand Postsparkasse

the 15th century. Visitors
not attending a service in the
church are expected to make
a donation.

_____

6
Ruprechtskirche

**⊙H5 ⚲Ruprechtsplatz
ⓊSchwedenplatz ⊙10am-
noon Mon-Fri, 3-5pm Mon,
Wed, Fri; for Mass 5pm Sat
(6pm Jul & Aug) ⓦruprechts
kirche.at**

St Ruprecht's is cited as the
oldest church in Vienna, with
origins in the 11th century.
Venerating Vienna's medieval
patron saint of salt mer-
chants, Rupert of Salzburg,
the church overlooks salt
wharfs on the Danube Canal.
At the foot of the main tower,
a statue portrays Rupert with
a tub of salt.
    Inside, the church reveals
the results of frequent resto-
rations: the chancel has two
panes of Romanesque
stained glass; the choir dates
from the 13th century;
and the vaulted south
aisle was added in

7
Grünangergasse

**⊙H6 ⓊStephansplatz
🚌1A, 2A, 3A**

This quiet lane takes its
name from Zum Grünen
Anker at No 10, a former
guesthouse that was
frequented by composer
Franz Schubert during the
19th century. There are a
number of notable buildings
that are worth a glance along
the way. The doorway of
No 8, for instance, features
charming carvings of bread
rolls and pretzels. The
building is known as the
Kipferlhaus after a Viennese
crescent-shaped bread roll.
    At No 4, the former
Fürstenberg Palace,
dating from 1720, boasts
a fine Baroque doorway
with carved hounds
racing to the top of
the keystone.

DRINK

Porgy & Bess
This is one of Vienna's
top jazz and live music
nightspots, attracting
a roster of international
stars and an easy-
going crowd

**⊙H7 ⚲Riemergasse 11
ⓦporgy.at**

_____

Diglas
A delightful classic
Viennese café,
complete with velvet
furnishings, this place
heats up in the
evenings, with live
piano music.

**⊙H6 Ⓤ Wollzeile 10
ⓦdiglas.at**

_____

Sky Bar
Head to this
sophisticated spot for
jazz and great vistas
across the city.
Sip cocktails at sun-
down and enjoy a
fantastic view of
the Stephansdom.

**⊙G7 ⚲Kärntner
Strasse 19 ⓦsteffl-
vienna.at**

_____

Kleines Café
This lovely 1970s
creation harks back to
the city's *Jugendstill*
days. The outdoor
seating area is a
pleasant place to enjoy
a glass of wine on a
warm evening.

**⊙G7
⚲Franziskanerplatz 3**

←
The Romanesque
Ruprechtskirche beside
the Danube Canal

8

Dominikanerkirche

📍H6 🏛Postgasse 4
📞512 43 32 🚇Stephans-
platz, Schwedenplatz
🚌2A 🕐7am–6pm daily

Dominican monks came to Vienna in 1226, and by 1237 they had built a church here. In the 1630s Antonio Canevale designed the present church, with its majestic Baroque façade. The central chapel on the right has swirling Rococo grilles and candelabra, and there is a beautiful gilt organ above the west door with casing from the mid-18th century. Frescoes by Tencalla and Rauchmiller are note-worthy, as is the high altar.

9

Jesuitenkirche

📍H6 🏛Dr-Ignaz-Seipel-
Platz 1 📞51252320
🚇Stubentor, Stephansplatz,
Schwedenplatz 🚌2A
🕐7am-7pm (8am Sun & hols)

Andrea Pozzo, an Italian architect, redesigned the Jesuitenkirche between 1703 and 1705 and its broad, high façade dominates the Dr-Ignaz-Seipel-Platz. In the 1620s the Jesuits moved their headquarters here to be near the Old University, which they controlled. The Jesuit order was a dominant force behind the Counter-Reformation and not afraid of making a statement. The grand redesign of the church highlighted their power.

The interior has marble columns screening side chapels, trompe l'oeil effects on the ceiling decoration and richly carved pews.

10

Bohemian Court Chancery

📍G5 🏛Judenplatz 11
📞531110 🚇Stephansplatz
🚌1A, 2A, 3A 🕐8am-
3:30pm Mon-Fri

Vienna's Habsburg rulers were also kings of Bohemia, which was governed from this magnificent palace (1709–14). Its architect, the profoundly influential Johann Bernhard Fischer von Erlach, was con-sidered to be the finest of the day. Later, Matthias Gerl was engaged to enlarge the Chancery, working between 1751 and 1754 to provide the additional accommodation needed for the Ministry of the Interior. The most spectacular parts of the building are the massive Baroque portals. The elegantly curved window frames on the first floor are also particularly noteworthy.

The interior of the building is now used as a courthouse. Its two courtyards are not as impressive as they once were, partly because of the reconstruction undertaken after serious bomb damage during World War II.

The Jesuitenkirche's interior, and its imposing Baroque façade (inset)

↑ Narrow, picturesque Schönlaterngasse in a revitalized historic part of the city

⑪ Schönlaterngasse

📍H6 Ⓤ Stephansplatz, Schwedenplatz 🚌1A, 2A, 3A

This attractive curving lane derives its name (Pretty Lantern Lane) from the handsome wrought-iron lantern that is clamped to No 6. The lantern is a copy of the 1610 original, now in the Wien Museum Karlsplatz (p176). At No 4, a solid early-17th-century house stands in the curve of the street.

On the façade of No 7, the Basiliskenhaus, which dates from medieval times, there is an artist's impression of a basilisk, dating from 1740. Legend has it that a serpent was discovered in 1212 in a well by the house. No 7a was home to the composer Robert Schumann from 1838 to 1839, and No 9 is the **Alte Schmiede**. The old smithy from which it takes its name has been reassembled in the basement. This complex also contains an art gallery and a hall used as a venue for occasional events, including poetry readings and music workshops.

Alte Schmiede

🕘9am–5pm Mon–Fri 🌐 alte-schmiede.at

⑫ 🎨 🎭 🛍️ Dom Museum

📍G6 Ⓐ Stephansplatz 6 Ⓤ Stephansplatz 🚌1A, 2A, 3A 🕘10am–6pm Wed–Sun (to 8pm Thu) 🌐dom museum.at

The Cathedral Museum, or Dom und Diözesan-museum as it is sometimes known, reopened in 2017 after four years of renovation. All of the old treasures are on display, including 16th- and 17th-century carvings and personal gifts from Duke Rudolf IV to the cathedral. His shroud is housed here, along with a well-known portrait of him by a Bohemian master dating from the 1360s.

Added to the museum since the renovation are a number of Modernist and contemporary paintings and sculptures, and galleries now include an extensive collection of modern pieces, including works by Chagall, Klimt and contemporary Austrian artists. The creative displays juxtapose the old with the new, the purpose being to show a continuity in underlying religious themes across the ages, expressed in changing styles and also in materials as varied as paint, glass and metal.

EAT

Griechenbeisl
Located in the old meat market, this traditional *beisl* is the city's oldest guesthouse, once frequented by Beethoven, Brahms and Schubert.

📍H5 Ⓐ Fleischmarkt 11 🌐 griechenbeisl.at

€€€

TIAN Wien
Expect fresh flavours and innovative vegetarian dishes at this modern Michelin-starred eatery.

📍H7 Ⓐ Himmel-pfortgasse 23 🌐 tian-restaurant.com

€€€

Wrenkh
This is one of the city's best restaurants, serving mostly vegetarian dishes in sleek, upmarket surrounds.

📍G6 Ⓐ Bauernmarkt 10 🌐 wrenkh-wien.at

€€€

Figlmüller
Try the fabulously large schnitzel at this cosy traditional dining spot.

📍H6 Ⓐ Wollzelle 5 🌐 figlmueller.at

€€€

Beim Czaak
Opened in 1926, this authentic, rustic *beisl* serves tasty Austrian fare in traditional dining rooms.

📍H6 Ⓐ Postgasse 15 🌐 czaak.com

€€€

← The Renaissance façade of Franziskanerkirche, with the Moses Fountain in front

finely modelled pulpit dating from 1726, and richly carved pews. A dramatic high altar by Andrea Pozzo rises to the full height of the church. Only the front part of the structure is three-dimensional – the rest is trompe l'oeil. Look out for the 1725 *Crucifixion* by Carlo Carlone among the works of art in the side altars.

It is usually necessary to ask a passing monk if you would like permission to view the church organ. It is worth being persistent, as this is the oldest in Vienna (1642), designed by Johann Wöckerl. The organ is beautifully painted, with a focus on various religious themes and subjects.

13 🗺️ Ⓜ️
Mozarthaus

📍 H6 🏛️ Domgasse 5
Ⓤ Stephansplatz 🚌 1A, 2A, 3A 🕐 10am-7pm daily
🌐 mozarthausvienna.at

Mozart and his family lived in a seven-room apartment on the first floor of this building from 1784 to 1787. Of the great composer's total of 11 residences in the city, this is the one where he is reputed to have spent his happiest times. Perhaps that is the reason why a significant number of his masterworks were composed here, including the exquisite Haydn quartets, a handful of piano concertos and *The Marriage of Figaro* opera.

The building was restored in 2006 to commemorate the 250th anniversary of Mozart's birth. It contains exhibitions on two of the upper floors, the original apartment that he and his family occupied, and the Bösendorfer Saal, where concerts and events are held.

Did You Know?

The Franziskanerkirche is dedicated to St Jerome, the patron saint of librarians and translators.

14
Franziskanerkirche

📍 H7 🏛️ Franziskanerplatz 4
Ⓤ Stephansplatz 🚌 1A, 2A, 3A 🕐 6:30am-noon & 2-5:30pm Mon-Sat, 7am-5:30pm Sun 🌐 wien.franzis kaner.at

During the 14th century, the Franciscans took over this church, which was originally built by wealthy citizens as a "house of the soul" for prostitutes wishing to reform. The present church was built in south German Renaissance style in 1601–11.

The façade is topped by an elaborate scrolled gable with obelisks. The Moses Fountain in front of the church was the work of the Neo-Classicist Johann Martin Fischer in 1798.

The interior is in full-blown Baroque style and includes a

15
Sonnenfelsgasse

📍 H6 Ⓤ Stephansplatz, Schwedenplatz

Fine houses line this pleasant street. Though by no means uniform in style, most of the dwellings on the north side of the street are solid merchant and patrician residences dating from the latter part of the 16th century. No 19, built in 1628 and renovated in 1721, was formerly part of the Old University. No 11 has an impressive courtyard, and a number of the overlooking balconies have been glassed in to their full height so as to provide extra living space. No 3 bears the most elaborate façade, and houses a *Stadtheurige* called the Zwölf Apostelkeller. This is an urban equivalent of the traditional *Heurigen*, wine growers' inns found in the villages outside Vienna (p197).

The street was named after a soldier Joseph von Sonnenfels, who became Maria Theresa's legal adviser.

Under his guidance the Empress reformed the penal code and abolished torture.

16
Ankeruhr

📍 G5 🏠 Hoher Markt 10
Ⓤ Stephansplatz, Schwedenplatz 🚌 1 A, 2A, 3A

Commissioned by the Anker Insurance Company, this Art Nouveau masterpiece, which was revealed in 1914 atop a covered bridge (known as the Uhrbrücke or Clock Bridge) between two buildings, is the work of Franz Matsch, a close associate of artist Gustav Klimt. At noon every day, the clock puts on a show, with 12 historical figures parading across the clock face. These include Marcus Aurelius, Empress Maria Theresa and Joseph Haydn, each one accompanied by music from their era. The tunes, including works by Wagner and Mozart, were originally played by a mechanical organ containing an incredible 800 tubes. The organ was damaged during World War II to such an extent that it couldn't be repaired and was replaced by recorded music. Comparisons with the Prague Astronomical Clock are inevitable, though this is a less intricate timepiece.

17
Kirche am Hof

📍 G5 🏠 Schulhof 1 📞 533 8394 Ⓤ Herrengasse
🕐 4:30–6pm Mon–Sat, 7am–7pm Sun

This Catholic church, which is dedicated to the Nine Choirs

↑ The exquisite face of the ornate Ankeruhr on the Uhrbrücke

of Angels, was founded by Carmelite friars in the late 14th century. The façade was redesigned in 1662 by the Italian architect Carlo Carlone to provide space for a large balustraded balcony. Today the church is where Vienna's large Croatian community comes to worship.

Take a walk around the back of the church into Schulhofplatz to look at the tiny restored shops which occupy the space between the buttresses of the Gothic choir.

↑ Looking towards the altar within the grand Kirche am Hof

18 ⊘ ⊙ ⊡ ⊡

Haus der Musik

📍G7 🏠Seilerstätte 30 Ⓤ Stephansplatz, Stubenring 🚌1A, 2A, 3A 🕐10am-10pm daily 🌐hdm.at

The House of Music is a sound museum that delights adults and children alike. Its high-tech interactive displays include "experience zones" such as the Instrumentarium, with its giant instruments, and the Polyphonium, which is a collection of different sounds. The museum's staircase acts as a piano.

19

Heiligenkreuzerhof

📍H6 🏠Schönlaterngasse 5 📞5125896 Ⓤ Schwedenplatz 🚌1A, 2A, 3A 🕐6am-9pm Mon-Sat

In the Middle Ages, rural monasteries expanded and established buildings in the cities. Secularization in the 1780s diminished such holdings, but this one, belonging to the abbey of Heiligenkreuz (p210), survived. The buildings around the courtyard housing the city's Applied Arts College present a serene 18th-century face. On the south side, the

Young visitors engaging with an exhibit at the Haus der Musik →

Bernhardskapelle, dating from 1662 but altered in the 1730s, is a Baroque gem. Across from the chapel a patch of wall from Babenberg times has been exposed: a reminder that, as so often in Vienna, the building is much older in origin than it at first appears.

20

Akademie der Wissenschaften

📍H6 🏠Dr-Ignaz-Seipel-Platz 2 Ⓤ Schwedenplatz, Stubentor 🕐8am-5pm Mon-Fri 🌐oeaw.ac.at

Once the centrepiece of the Old University, the Academy of Sciences was designed in 1753 by Jean Nicolas Jadot de Ville-Issey as the Aula, or great

←
An ornate fountain outside the Akademie der Wissenschaften

hall. It has an impressive Baroque façade and fine rooms. A double staircase leads up to one of the grandest salons in Vienna.

Elaborate frescoes adorn the ceilings of the Ceremonial Hall, and its marble walls have Rococo plasterwork. Haydn's Creation was performed here in 1808 in the presence of the composer: it was the eve of his 76th birthday and his last public appearance.

21

Altes Rathaus

📍G5 🏠Wipplinger Strasse 8 Ⓤ Schwedenplatz 🚌1A, 3A 🚋1 🕐Times vary, check website 🌐doew.at

This building at Wipplinger Strasse was once owned by the German brothers Otto and Haymo of Neuburg, who conspired to overthrow the Habsburgs in 1309. The property was confiscated by Prince Friedrich the Fair and donated to the city. Over the

following centuries the site was expanded to form the complex of buildings that until 1883 served as the city hall, or Rathaus. The entrance of the Altes Rathaus (Old Town Hall) is festooned with ornamental ironwork. Located in the main courtyard is the Andromeda Fountain. Designed in 1741, it was the last work by sculptor Georg Raphael Donner. The fountain depicts Perseus rescuing Andromeda.

A door leads from the courtyard to the Salvatorkapelle (St Saviour's chapel), the only surviving building of the original medieval town house and the former Neuburg family chapel. It has since been enlarged and renovated, but retains its fine Gothic vaults. The walls are lined with old marble tomb slabs, some from the 15th century. Its pretty organ dates from around 1740 and is sometimes used for recitals. The chapel has an exquisite Renaissance portal, facing Salvatorgasse. Dating from 1520 to 1530, it is a rare example of Italianate Renaissance style.

Today the Old Town Hall houses offices and shops, as well as the District Museum, which examines the first municipal district of Vienna (roughly covering the area within the Ring). Of much greater interest is the Museum of the Austrian Resistance Movement, devoted to the memory of those who risked their lives by opposing the Nazis during World War II.

Did You Know?

Haas-Haus's curved façade was inspired by the shape of the Roman fort that once stood on this site.

22

Haas-Haus

G6 Stephansplatz 12 5356083 Stephansplatz 8am-2am daily

Designing a modern building directly opposite the iconic Stephansdom was a difficult task, and the city entrusted it to one of Austria's leading Postmodernist architects, Hans Hollein. The result is the iconic 1990 Haas-Haus, a shining, partly mirrored structure of glass, steel and blue-green marble that curves elegantly into the street. The building has a very pleasingly asymmetrical appearance, with decorative elements such as lopsided cubes of marble attached to its façade, a protruding structure high up resembling a diving board and a Japanese-style bridge inside. Along with space for offices, the atrium within the Haas-Haus has cafés, shops, a restaurant and the upmarket DO & CO hotel *(p79)*.

HIDDEN GEM

Stock im Eisen

This *Nagelbaum* or "Nail Tree" is a medieval trunk into which hundreds of nails have been driven for good luck. It sits behind protective glass on Stephansplatz, on the corner of Graben and Kärntner Strasse.

The curved, partly mirrored façade of Hans Hollein's Haas-Haus

23
Fleischmarkt

📍 H5 🚇 Schwedenplatz
🕐 9am–4pm Mon–Fri

Fleischmarkt, the former meat market, dates from 1220. A small cosy inn called the Griechenbeisl (p77) is its best-known landmark. On its façade is a woodcarving of a bagpiper known as *Der liebe Augustin* (Dear Augustin). Rumour has it that during the 1679 plague, this bagpiper slumped drunk into the gutter one night and, taken for dead, was put in the plague pit. He woke, attracted attention by playing his pipes and was rescued. Miraculously, he did not catch the plague.

Next to the Griechenbeisl is the beautiful Neo-Byzantine Griechische Kirche (Greek Church of the Holy Trinity). The architect Theophil Hansen created its rich, gilt structure in the 1850s. A passage links the Griechenbeisl to Griechengasse. *Griechen* refers to the Greek merchants who settled around Fleischmarkt in the 18th century.

24
Peterskirche

📍 G6 🏠 Petersplatz 6
📞 53364330 🚇 Stephansplatz 🚌 1A 🕐 7am–8pm Mon–Fri, 9am–9pm Sat, Sun & hols

A church has stood here since the 12th century, but the oval structure you see today dates from the early 18th century. A number of architects collaborated on the design, notably Gabriele Montani. The interior is amazingly lavish, culminating in an exuberant, eye-catching pulpit (1716) by the sculptor Matthias Steindl. The richly clothed skeletons on the right and beneath the altar are the remains of early Christian martyrs originally deposited in the catacombs in Rome. Frescoes inside the huge dome by J M Rottmayr depict the Assumption of the Virgin.

In 1729 Lorenzo Mattielli designed the sculpture of St John Nepomuk to the right of the choir. This priest earned his sainthood by being thrown into the Vltava River in Prague

Did You Know?

Peterskirche was inspired by the design of St Peter's Basilica in the Vatican, Rome.

in 1393 after he refused to reveal the secrets of the confessional to King Wenceslas IV; his martyrdom by drowning later became a favourite subject of artists.

25
Blutgasse

📍 G6 🚇 Stephansplatz
🚌 1A, 2A, 3A

This street is said to have acquired its gruesome name – Blood Lane – after a massacre in 1312 of the Knights Templar (a religious military order) in a skirmish so violent that the streets flowed with blood. But there is no evidence to

support this story and the street's charm belies its name. Its tall apartment buildings date mostly from the 18th century. Walk into No 3 and see how the city's restorers have linked up the buildings and their courtyards. At No 9, the Fähnrichshof houses are particularly impressive.

26 Domgasse

H6 **Stephansplatz**
1A, 2A, 3A

Domgasse boasts some interesting buildings, including Mozarthaus Vienna (p78) and the Trienter Hof, with its airy courtyard. No 6 is a house of medieval origin called the Kleiner Bischofshof (Small Bishop's House): it has a 1761 Matthias Gerl façade. Next door is the site of the house where Georg Franz Kolschitzky lived and, in 1694, died. It is said that he claimed some Turkish coffee beans as a reward for his bravery in the 1683 Turkish siege, and later opened Vienna's first coffee house. The truth of this story, however, is doubtful.

27 Maria am Gestade

G5 **Salvatorgasse 12**
53395940 **Stephansplatz** **2A** **7am-7pm daily; tours by appointment only**

One of the city's oldest sights is this lofty Gothic church with its 56-m- (180-ft-) high steeple and immense choir windows. There are recordings of the church from as early as 1158, but the present building dates from the late 14th century, with restoration evident from

←
The beautifully ornate façade of Baroque Peterskirche

↑ Rich decoration and stained glass within Maria am Gestade

the 19th century. The church has had a chequered history and Napoleon's troops used it as an arsenal during their occupation of Vienna in 1809.

Inside, the nave piers are enlivened with Gothic canopies which shelter statues from various periods: medieval, Baroque and modern. The choir contains High Gothic panels (1460) depicting the Annunciation, the Crucifixion and the Coronation of the Virgin. Behind the high altar the windows contain medieval stained glass, which has been carefully restored with surviving fragments.

Tucked away on the north side of the choir is a chapel with a painted stone altar from 1520. The main parts of the interior are visible from the front entrance, but to walk around inside you need to make an appointment.

The decorative interior of the Peterskirche

←

The imposing entrance to the 18th-century Winter Palace of Prince Eugene

(Nuptial Fountain), also known as the Josefsbrunnen. Emperor Leopold I vowed to commemorate the safe return of his son Joseph from the Siege of Landau and commissioned Johann Bernhard Fischer von Erlach to design this monument, which was built by von Erlach's son Joseph Emanuel between 1729 and 1732. The fountain celebrates the betrothal of Joseph and Mary and bears figures of the high priest and the couple, with gilt urns, statues of angels and fluted columns supporting an elaborate canopy.

Linking two office buildings on the square is the bronze and copper Anker Clock (Ankeruhr), set atop the Uhrbrücke or Clock Bridge (p79). Noon is the best time to visit, when all the clock figures are on glorious display.

Römermuseum

◈ ◷9am–6pm Tue–Sun & hols ◷1 Jan, 1 May, 25 Dec
🅦 wienmuseum.at

ROMAN VIENNA

Vindobona was established by the Romans in 15 BC to guard the northern reaches of the Empire from a strategic point on the Danube. For 350 years, soldiers kept marauding tribes at bay, and at its peak the encampment boasted 30,000 inhabitants. Many buildings were left behind, but the vast majority of these lie buried beneath the city today. The Hoher Markt is Vienna's most impressive site of Roman excavations.

㉘

Winter Palace of Prince Eugene

🅠 G7 🅐 Himmelpfortgasse 4–8 🅤 Stephansplatz
🚌 1A, 2A, 3A

The sumptuous and elegant Winter Palace was commissioned in 1694 by Prince Eugene of Savoy, Archduke of Austria and a brilliant military commander. The work was entrusted to Johann Bernhard Fischer von Erlach and later to his rival, Johann Lukas von Hildebrandt in 1702, both of whom were among the foremost Baroque architects of their time.

The result is an imposing town mansion, with one of the most magnificent Baroque edifices in Vienna. Maria Theresa purchased the palace for the state in 1752 and it was home to the Ministry of Finance from 1848 until 2006. In 2018, the palace was closed to the public indefinitely.

㉙

Hoher Markt

🅠 G5 🅤 Stephansplatz, Schwedenplatz 🚌 1A, 2A, 3A

Hoher Markt is the oldest square in Vienna. In medieval times, fish and cloth markets as well as executions were held here.

Today it is possible to view the subterranean ruins of a former Roman garrison, Vindobona, at the fantastic **Römermuseum**, which is located beneath the square. Discovered after World War II, the ancient foundations exhibited here show groups of houses bisected by straight roads leading to the town gates. It seems probable that they were 2nd- and 3rd-century officers' houses. The excavations are well laid out and exhibits of pottery, reliefs and tiles supplement the ruins.

In the centre of the square is the Vermählungsbrunnen

> At every full hour, each of the museum's three floors resound in an incredible cacophony of clocks striking, chiming and playing.

30 ♿

Uhrenmuseum

📍 G5 🏠 Schulhof 2
Ⓤ Stephansplatz 🚌 1A, 2A, 3A 🕐 10am-6pm Tue-Sun 🔒 1 Jan, 1 May & 25 Dec 🌐 wienmuseum.at

You don't have to be a clock fanatic to enjoy a visit to this fascinating clock museum. Located in the beautiful former Obizzi Palace (1690), the museum contains a fine collection of clocks and gives visitors a comprehensive account of the history of chronometry through the ages, and of clock technology from the 15th century through to the present day.

There are more than 3,000 exhibits, some of which were accumulated by an earlier curator, Rudolf Kaftan, while others belonged to the novelist Marie von Ebner-Eschenbach. On the first floor are displayed the mechanisms of tower clocks from the 16th century onwards, alongside painted clocks, grandfather clocks and pocket watches. On the other floors are huge astronomical clocks and a wide range of intriguing novelty timepieces, with many dating from the Beidermeier and belle époque eras.

A major highlight is the Cajetano clock, an elaborate astronomical clock created by David Cajetano, which dates from the 18th century. It has 150

↑ Annagasse, lined with shops and places to eat, leading to the Annakirche

gears and wheels, and over 30 readings and dials that show the dates of solar and lunar eclipses and the movement of the planets.

At every full hour, each of the museum's three floors resound in an incredible cacophony of clocks striking, chiming and playing. All are carefully maintained to keep the correct time.

31

Annagasse

📍 G7 Ⓤ Stephansplatz 🚌 1A, 2A, 3A

Now splendidly Baroque, Annagasse dates from medieval times. It is pedestrianized and a pleasant place for browsing in its various bookshops. Notable buildings include the luxurious Mailberger Hof and the stucco-decorated Römischer Kaiser hotel. No 14's lintel features a Baroque carving of cherubs making merry, while above this is a relief of the blue carp that

← An ornate exhibit in the Uhrenmuseum

gives the house, once a pub, its name: Zum Blauen Karpfen. No 2 is the 17th-century Esterházy Palace, which is now a casino.

Annagasse's most stunning building is surely its church, the lovely **Annakirche**. There has been some form of chapel in Annagasse since 1320, but the present Annakirche was built between 1629 and 1634, and later renovated by the Jesuits during the early 18th century. Devotion to St Anne has deep roots in Vienna and this intimate church is often filled with quiet worshippers.

The finest exterior feature of the church is the moulded copper cupola over the tower. The ceiling frescoes, painted by Daniel Gran, who was a leading painter of the Austrian Baroque period, are now fading but his richly coloured painting glorifying St Anne on the high altar is still striking. The first chapel on the left houses a copy of a carving of St Anne from about 1505 – the original is in the Dom Museum (p77). St Anne is portrayed as a powerfully maternal figure and shown with her daughter, the Virgin Mary, who in turn has the baby Jesus on her knee. The carving is attributed to the sculptor Veit Stoss.

Annakirche

🏠 Annagasse 3b 🕐 7am-7pm daily 🌐 annakirche.at

A SHORT WALK
OLD VIENNA

Distance 2 km (1 mile) **Nearest U-Bahn**
Stephansplatz **Time** 30 minutes

This part of the inner city retains its compact medieval layout of cobbled lanes, winding alleys and spacious courtyards. The influence of the Church is still evident here. As you stroll, you'll notice remains of orders such as the Dominicans, the Teutonic Knights and the Jesuits. Dominating the area is the 137-m-(450-ft-) spire of Stephansdom, the heart of Vienna for centuries. Despite its ancient origins, there's plenty of activity in this quarter. Stephansplatz throngs with visitors all day, and nearby bars and restaurants buzz with people long into the night.

↑ Great Gothic Stephansdom seen from Stephansplatz

*Much of the **Dom Museum** collection was donated by Duke Rudolf IV (p77).*

Stephansdom
took centuries to build and is rich with medieval and Renaissance monuments (p66).

FINISH

STEPHANS-
PLATZ **START**

ESSIG

STOBELGASSE

BLUTGASSE

GRÜNANG

A remarkable Treasury of objects collected by German aristocrats lies alongside the Gothic church of **Deutschordenskirche** *(p74).*

SINGERSTRASSE

Courtyards like this are typical of the tenement houses on **Blutgasse** *(p82).*

Mozarthaus Vienna, *where the composer lived from 1784 to 1787 (p78)*

Did You Know?

Stephansdom's tallest tower is known as *Alter Steffl* - in English this translates as "Old Steve".

Grünangergasse *(p75) and pretty* **Domgasse** *(p83) are full of intriguing houses with unique details.*

The **Akademie der Wissenschaften** *is decorated with Rococo ceiling frescoes (p80).*

The lantern at No 6 gave charming **Schönlaterngasse** *its name (p77).*

One of Vienna's most ornate churches, the **Jesuitenkirche** *was built by the Jesuits in the 1620s (p76).*

Locator Map
For more detail see p64

SCHÖNLATERNGASSE

BÄCKERSTRASSE

DR. IGNAZ-SEIPELPLATZ

POSTGASSE

WOLLZEILE

SCHULERSTRASSE

KUMPFGASSE

Dominikanerkirche
was originally consecrated on this site in 1237, but the present Baroque church dates from the 1630s (p76).

| 0 metres | 50 |
| 0 yards | 50 |

N ↑

→ Dominikanerkirche's richly decorated Baroque interior

HOFBURG QUARTER

What began in the 13th century as a modest city fortress, the Hofburg or "Castle of the Court" grew over the centuries into the extensive palace that marks the heart of this stately quarter. For some 650 years the palace was the nexus of the vast Habsburg empire, which grew to include Spain, Holland, Burgundy, Bohemia and Hungary by the 16th century. The winter residence of the Habsburgs, the Hofburg was still being expanded upon until a few years before the collapse of the empire in 1918.

The presence of the court had a profound effect on quarters surrounding the palace. Majestic streets Herrengasse and Bankgasse are lined with ostentatious dwellings built by the nobility in their eagerness to be as close as possible to the seat of Austro-Hungarian imperial power.

Since 1946 the Hofburg's Leopoldine Wing has been home to Austria's elected president, and the once private Burggarten is open to the public. The Kaiserappartements and Albertina, former state apartments and art collections, today draw crowds with hoards of imperial treasure and world-class collections of fine art.

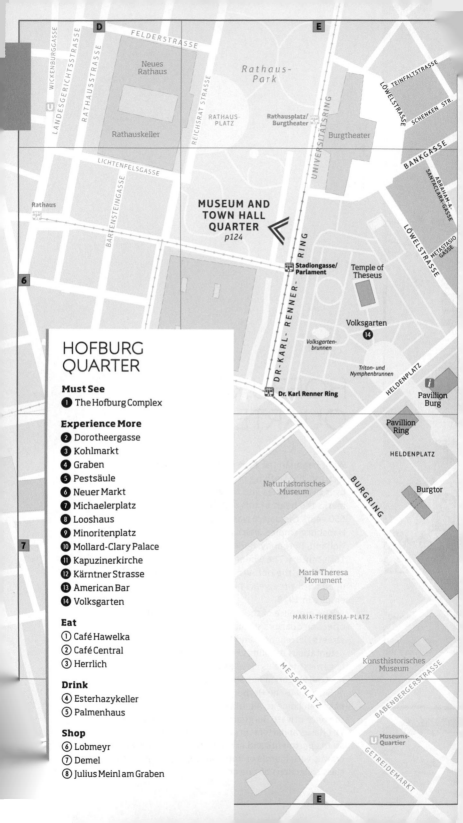

MUSEUM AND
TOWN HALL
QUARTER
p124

HOFBURG QUARTER

Must See
1. The Hofburg Complex

Experience More
2. Dorotheergasse
3. Kohlmarkt
4. Graben
5. Pestsäule
6. Neuer Markt
7. Michaelerplatz
8. Looshaus
9. Minoritenplatz
10. Mollard-Clary Palace
11. Kapuzinerkirche
12. Kärntner Strasse
13. American Bar
14. Volksgarten

Eat
1. Café Hawelka
2. Café Central
3. Herrlich

Drink
4. Esterhazykeller
5. Palmenhaus

Shop
6. Lobmeyr
7. Demel
8. Julius Meinl am Graben

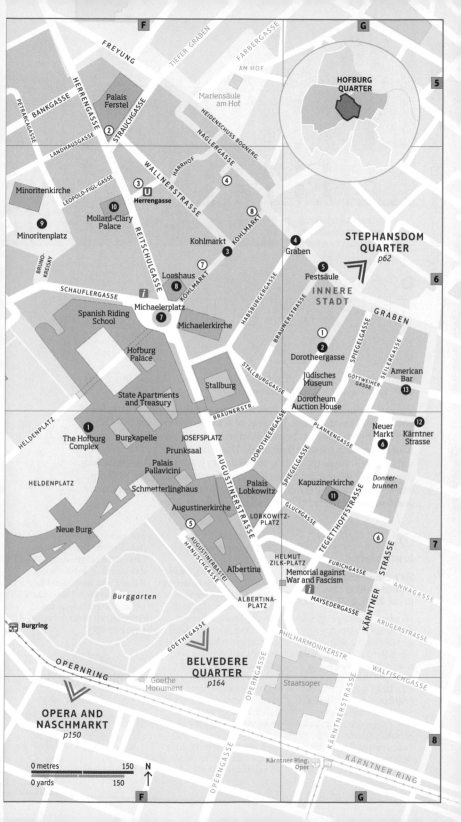

The grand Hofburg entrance, Michaelertor, surmounted by a dome ↑

THE HOFBURG COMPLEX

📍G7 🚪Michaelerplatz 1, A-1010 Ⓤ Stephansplatz, Herrengasse 🚆D, 1, 2, 71
🚌1A, 2A to Michaelerplatz 🌐hofburg-wien.at

The vast Hofburg, Vienna's former imperial palace, is a lavish complex of buildings in the city centre. The seat of Austrian power since the 13th century, the complex has been developed over the years by successive rulers all anxious to leave their mark. The result is a range of architectural styles, from Gothic to late 19th-century historicism. The Neue Burg (New Palace) is the most recent and grand section. Today the Hofburg houses the office of the Austrian president, museums and galleries, the Austrian National Library, and the Spanish Riding School.

① Josefsplatz

📍F7 🚪Augustinerstrasse Ⓤ Stephansplatz, Herrengasse 🚆D, 1, 2, 71 🚌1A, 2A

Surrounded on three sides by the Hofburg Palace, this pleasant square offers fine views of the Baroque architecture of the complex. At the centre of the Josefsplatz is an equestrian statue (1807) of Emperor Joseph II by sculptor Franz Anton von Zauner, which was modelled on that of Marcus Aurelius on Rome's Capitoline Hill. Despite his reforms, Joseph II was a true monarchist, and during the 1848 Revolution (p57) loyalists used the square as a gathering place.

Facing the Hofburg are two palaces. No 5 is the Pallavicini Palace (1783–4), a blend of Baroque and Neo-Classical styles by Ferdinand von Hohenberg. It was a notable location which features in renknowned Viennese film noir *The Third Man*, as the home of Harry Lime's impressive apartment block. No 6 is the 16th century Palffy Palace. On the right of the Prunksaal (p97) is the Redoutensaal. Built in 1750–60, it was the venue for balls in imperial times. To the left is an extension to the Prunksaal which was built a few years later. Both were designed by court architect, the Austrian-Italian craftsman Nikolaus Pacassi, who was a favourite of Empress Maria Theresa and worked extensively on the rennovations of Schönbrunn palace (p188).

Did You Know?

The oldest surviving part of the Hofburg is the Schweizertrakt, which dates back to the 13th century.

② ⟨⟩ ⟨⟩

Burgkapelle

⚲ F6 **🏠 Hofburg, Schweiz-erhof** **Ⓤ Herrengasse** **🕐 10am–2pm Mon & Tue, 11am–1pm Fri** **🚫 Public holidays** **🌐 hofmusik kapelle.gv.at**

From the Schweizerhof, steps lead up to the Burgkapelle (Court Chapel), also known as the Hofmusikkapelle. This is the oldest part of the palace complex, originally built in 1296 but modified 150 years later. The chapel's interior reveals its medieval origins, with Gothic carvings and statuary in canopied niches. There is also a splendid bronze crucifix (1720) by the court jeweller Johann Känischbauer. On Sundays, visitors can hear the Wiener Sängerknaben, the **Vienna Boys' Choir** *(p198)*, performing high mass.

⟨⟩ **Vienna Boys' Choir**

🕐 Jan–Jun & Sep–Dec: 9:15am Sun (book via chapel website)

The Hofburg Complex, in the centre of Vienna ↓

Viktor Tilgner's Mozart Memorial (1896) stands just inside the Ringstrasse entrance.

Anton Dominik von Fernkorn designed this monument to Prince Eugene (1865).

↓ N

Red and black Schweizertor (Swiss Gate) leads to the Schweizerho

The curved façade of the Michaelertrakt

Classical statuary on display at the Neue Burg's Ephesos Museum

③

Neue Burg

📍G7 🏛Neue Burg Heldenplatz Ⓤ Volkstheater, Herrengasse 🚋D, 1, 2, 71 🕙10am-6pm Wed-Sun 🌐khm.at

This massive, curved structure situated on Heldenplatz was added to the Hofburg Complex between 1881 and 1913. The Neue Burg wing of the Hofburg embodies the last gasp of the Habsburg Empire as it strained under aspirations of independence from its domains, when the personal prestige of Emperor Franz Joseph was all that seemed able to keep it intact. It was not quite the perfect moment to embark on an extension to the Hofburg, but the work was undertaken nevertheless, and the Neue Burg was built to designs by the Ringstrasse architects Karl von Hasenauer (1833–94) and Gottfried Semper (1803–79). Five years after its completion, the Habsburg Empire ended.

In 1938, Adolf Hitler stood on the terraced central bay to proclaim the Anschluss (the union of Austria and Germany) to tens of thousands of Viennese people.

Today the Neue Burg is home to the reading room of the national library, and as well as a number of museums that are all under the direction of the KHM-Museumsverband. Ancient finds excavated from the Greek and Roman site of Ephesus in Turkey are on display at the **Ephesos Museum**. Also on show are finds from the Greek island of Samothrace, excavated in the 1870s. The **Sammlung Alter Musikinstrumente** houses impressive Renaissance musical instruments, with pianos that belonged to Beethoven, Schubert and Haydn, and the world's oldest surviving claviorgan (1596). The weapons collection at the **Hofjadg und Rüstkammer** is astonishing both in its size and the workmanship of its finest items: filigree inlay on swords, medieval ceremonial saddles and jewelled Turkish and Syrian maces. The core collection comprises the personal armouries of the Habsburgs. The **Weltmuseum Wien** galleries offer an exploration of travel, anthropology and ethnography, with exhibits from across the globe.

🔶 **Ephesos Museum**
🕙10am-6pm Wed-Sun
🌐khm.at

🔶 **Sammlung Alter Musikinstumente**
🕙10am-6pm Thu-Tue
🌐khm.at

🔶 **Hofjiagd und Rüstkammer**
🕙10am-6pm Thu-Tue (to 9pm Fri) 🌐khm.at

🔶 **Weltmuseum Wien**
🕙10am-6pm Thu-Tue (to 9pm Fri) 🌐weltmuseum wien.at

DRINK

Esterhazykeller
This ancient and characterful cellar offers a great selection of Austrian wines and hearty classic food.

📍F6 🏛Haarhof 1, 1010 🌐esterhazykeller.at

€€€

Palmenhaus
In a Jugendstil greenhouse overlooking the Burggarten, this brasserie is a perfect spot for a glass of wine after a long day of museums and palaces.

📍F7 🏛Burggarten 1, 1010 🌐palmenhaus.at

€€€

The Neue Burg wing of the Hofburg embodies the last gasp of the Habsburg Empire as it strained under aspirations of independence from its domains.

④
Prunksaal

Q F7 **A** Josefsplatz 1 **U** Herrengasse **🚌** 1A, 2A **🕐** 10am-6pm daily (to 9pm Thu) **W** onb.ac.at

Commissioned as the court library by Karl VI, the State Hall, or Prunksaal, of the National Library was designed by Johann Bernhard Fischer von Erlach (*p168*) in 1719, and is the largest Baroque library in Europe today. The vast collection includes the personal library of Prince Eugene (*p86*), as well as tomes taken from monastic libraries closed during the religious reforms of Joseph II (*p56*). Paired marble columns frame the domed main room, and walnut bookcases line the walls. Spanning the vaults are frescoes by the Baroque painter Daniel Gran (1730), restored by Franz Anton Maulbertsch (1769). The fine statues, including the likeness of Karl VI in the hall, are the work of Paul Strudel (1648–1708) and his brother Peter (1660–1714). The National Library also spans the **Papyrus Museum**, which documents ancient Egyptian life, and at the nearby Mollard Clary Palace are the Esperanto and Globe Museums (*p108*).

⊛ Papyrus Museum
A Neue Burg, Heldenplatz, 1010 **W** onb.ac.at

◎ PICTURE PERFECT
Prunksaal

One of Vienna's best ceiling frescoes can be found in the dome of the Prunksaal within the Austrian National Library. You might have to lie on the floor to get the best shot.

The marble and gilded walnut interior of the Baroque Prunksaal ↑

Visitors enjoying
modern art in
the Albertina

⑤

Augustinerkirche

📍F7 🏛Augustinerstrasse 3
📞5337099 Ⓤ Stephansplatz 🚌1A, 2A 🕐7am-6pm Mon-Fri, 8am-7pm Sat & Sun

This church has one of the best-preserved 14th-century Gothic interiors in Vienna; only the modern chandeliers strike a jarring note. Its Loreto Chapel, dating back to 1724, contains the silver urns that preserve the hearts of the Habsburg family. Here too are the tombs of Maria Christina, favourite daughter of Maria Theresa, and Leopold II. Both lie empty; the royal remains are in the Kaisergruft (p108). The church is also celebrated for its music, including Masses by Schubert or Haydn held here on Sundays.

⑥ 🔧 📷 🍴 🛍

Albertina

📍F7 🏛Augustinerstrasse 1 Ⓤ Karlsplatz, Stephansplatz 🕐10am-6pm daily (to 9pm Wed & Fri) 🌐albertina.at

Once hidden away at the Opera end of the Hofburg is the Albertina, now a very distinctive, modern landmark. Its raised entrance boasts a controversial freestanding diving-board roof by Austrian architect Hans Hollein (p81). The palace once belonged to Maria Theresa's daughter, Maria Christina, and her husband the Duke Albert of Sachsen-Teschen, after whom the gallery is named. Today the Albertina houses a collection of priceless prints, over 65,000 water-colours and drawings, and some 70,000 photographs. Highlights include works by Dürer, with Michelangelo and Rubens also well represented. Picasso heads a fine 20th-century section. Other temporary exhibitions feature paintings on loan along with works owned by the Albertina. The permanent Batliner Collection is one of the most significant collections of Modernist art in Europe, comprising over 500 works including pieces by Monet, Degas, Cézanne and Picasso along with great works of Austrian expressionism by

Kokoschka and Egger-Lienze. The Albertina's extension on the Burggarten side houses study facilities and the largest of the three exhibition halls. Renovation has restored a number of features of the Albertina to their former glory, including the façades and the central courtyard. The Habsburg State Rooms are open to the public and a remarkable example of Neo-Classical architecture and interior decoration.

---

⑦
Burggarten

📍F7 🚌Burgring/Opernring ⓊKarlsplatz 🚋D, 1, 2, 71 🕐Apr-Oct: 6am-10pm daily; Nov-Mar: 6:30am-7pm daily

Before leaving Vienna, Napoleon showed his contempt for the Viennese by razing part of the city walls that had proved so ineffective at preventing his entry. Some of the space left around the Hofburg was later transformed by the Habsburgs into lovely landscaped gardens, planted with a variety of trees and wide herbaceous borders. The imperial garden was opened to the public in 1918, and today makes for a pleasant place to relax after exploring the surrounding palaces.

Overlooking the garden are Jugendstil greenhouses (1901–7) by the architect Friedrich Ohmann, and near the Hofburg entrance is a small equestrian statue (1780) of Emperor Franz I by Balthasar Moll. Closer to the Ringstrasse is the white marble Mozart Memorial (1896) by the Austrian sculptor Viktor Tilgner.

← The Burggarten's vast Jugendstil glasshouses

⑧ 🛍️
Schmetterlinghaus

📍F7 🚌Hofburg ⓊKarlsplatz 🚋D, 1, 2, 71 🕐Times vary, check website 🌐schmetterlinghaus.at

Enter the hot, humid air of the Hofburg's butterfly house, which occupies a spectacular Jugendstil glasshouse directly behind the Neue Burg. The former greenhouse is home to around 400 live butterflies, which can be seen flitting around in re-created natural tropical habitats.

Children will enjoy spotting the colourful creatures and learning about the various stages of metamorphosis: the whole life cycle of the butterfly is on display here. The pleasant gift shop sells a range of butterfly paraphernalia.

SPANISH RIDING SCHOOL

📍F6 🏛Michaelerplatz 1, A-1010 🚇Herrengasse 🚌1A, 2A to Michaelerplatz
🕐Times and performances vary, check website 🌐srs.at

Vienna's famous Lipizzaners are perhaps the only horses in the world to live in an emperor's palace. It's a fitting home for these noble creatures, whose performances are a timeless delight for visitors.

The origins of the Spanish Riding School are obscure, but it is believed to have been founded in 1572 to cultivate the classic skills of *haute école* horsemanship. By breeding and training horses from Spain, the Habsburgs formed the Spanische Reitschule. Today, 70- or 90-minute demonstrations ranging across three levels of complexity and formality, some accompanied by Viennese music, are performed in the opulent Winter Riding School, which dates from 1729. The gracious interior is lined with 46 columns and adorned with elaborate plasterwork, chandeliers and a coffered ceiling. At the head of the arena is the court box. Spectators sit here or watch from upper galleries.

↑ One of the riders, as immaculately turned out as his horse

THE LIPIZZANER HORSES

The stallions that perform their athletic feats on the sawdust of the Winter Riding School take their name from the stud farm at Lipizza near Trieste in Slovenia, which was founded by Archduke Karl in 1580. Today the horses are bred on the Austrian National Stud Farm at Piber near Graz. Lipizzaner horses were originally produced by crossing Arab, Berber and Spanish horses, and are renowned for their grace and stamina. They begin learning the complex sequences of steps at the age of three.

① The Riding School occupies the former residence of the Emperor Maximilian.

② The emperor Karl VI commissioned the Winter Riding School building.

③ Equestrian statue of Josef II in the school courtyard.

Did You Know?

Riders entering the arena must always doff their hats to the portrait of Karl VI, to show respect.

Horses and riders in ↑
perfect step, ready to
go through their paces

STATE APARTMENTS AND TREASURY

📍F6 🏛State Apartments, Sisi Museum & Silberkammer: Michaelerkuppel; Imperial Treasury: Schweizerhof ⏰State Apartments, Sisi Museum & Silberkammer: 9am–5:30pm daily (to 6pm Jul & Aug); Imperial Treasury: 9am–5:30pm Wed–Mon 🌐hofburg-wien.at; kaiserliche-schatzkammer.at

The Hofburg's State Apartments complex is a treasure trove, both literally and historically. From crowns to crucifixes, the priceless trappings of supreme power can be seen here, but there are also displays and well-preserved room settings that give a rare insight into daily imperial life.

The State Apartments are housed in the Reichskanzleitrakt and the Amalienburg, two separate sections of the Hofburg, and include rooms occupied by Franz Joseph I from 1857 to 1916, the apartments of Empress Elisabeth from 1854 to 1898, and the rooms where Tsar Alexander I lived during the Congress of Vienna in 1815. The rooms belonging to Elisabeth (or "Sisi") are the prettiest and most interesting, full of her belongings; there is also her death mask, created after her assassination. The Imperial Treasury holds treasures amassed during centuries of Habsburg rule, including the crown of the Holy Roman Emperor, a "unicorn" horn and religious objects.

EXPERIENCE Hofburg Quarter

1 The entrance to the museums are below the great copper dome known as the Michaelerkuppel.

2 Sisi was a slave to fitness and beauty regimes: her dressing room was fitted with a set of wall bars on which she exercised.

3 Sisi's dresses show her waistline of 45 cm (18 in), which she achieved through corsetry and fasting.

THE SILBERKAMMER

So extravagant were Habsburg banquets that a dedicated Silver Chamberlain was appointed to take responsibility for all the imperial tableware and linens, and ensure a perfect setting for the diners. In the five rooms of his Silver Chamber, or Silberkammer, a dazzling array of some 7,000 of the items that were in his care - gold, silver and the finest porcelain and glassware - are now on display. The highlights include a 33-m- (100-ft-) long gilded bronze centrepiece with accompanying candelabra from around 1800. Visitors can also admire the mid-18th-century Sèvres dinner service that was a diplomatic gift from Louis XV to Maria Theresa.

↑ The exterior of the Hofburg's State Apartments

Art on display at the Dorotheum auction house on Dorotheergasse ↑

EXPERIENCE MORE

2 Dorotheergasse

⊙ G6 Ⓤ Stephansplatz
🚌 1A, 2A, 3A

At No 11 on this street is the Eskeles Palace, now home to the **Jüdisches Museum** (Jewish Museum) which, along with its extension in Judenplatz (p70), chronicles the city's rich Jewish heritage. At No 17 is the Dorotheum,

built in the 17th century. A pawnbrokers and auction house, it has branches all over Vienna. Halfway along the street is the Evangelical Church (1783–4), originally by Gottlieb Nigelli. Close to where the street joins Graben are two popular Viennese gathering places, Café Hawelka at No 6 (p109) and Trzesniewski sandwich buffet at No 1. There are many art and antique dealers in this area.

Jüdisches Museum
⊙ G6 ⌂ Dorotheergasse 11
🕐 10am–6pm Sun–Fri
🌐 jmw.at

3 Kohlmarkt

⊙ F6 Ⓤ Herrengasse
🚌 1A, 2A

Leading directly up to the Hofburg Palace, the pedestrianized Kohlmarkt is lined with some of Vienna's most exclusive shops and remarkable shopfronts. No 9, the

Jugendstil Artaria Haus (1901), is the work of Max Fabiani (1865–1962), a protégé of Otto Wagner. No 16, the bookshop and publisher Manz, boasts a characteristic portal from 1912 by Adolf Loos. The striking abstract shopfront of jewellers Schullin (1982) was designed by the architect Hans Hollein.

4 Graben

⊙ G6 Ⓤ Stephansplatz
🚌 1A, 2A

Facing No 16 on this pleasant pedestrianized street is the Joseph Fountain by Johann Martin Fischer. Further along is his identical Leopold Fountain (both 1804). No 13, the clothing shop Knize, is by Adolf Loos. The Ankerhaus by Otto Wagner, at No 10, is topped by a studio once used by Wagner himself and, in the 1980s, by Friedensreich Hundertwasser (p184). Alois Pichl's Spar-Casse Bank from

---

THE DOROTHEUM

Vienna's answer to Christies of London, the Dorotheum is one of the world's oldest and most exclusive auction houses, its Vienna headquarters the biggest in continental Europe. It traditionally specialized in antiques, most notably paintings by some of the biggest names in European art history, but today also handles classic cars and stamps, among other things. To see what you might pick up with a spare hundred thousand euros, visit their website (www. dorotheum.com).

> **Leading directly up to the Imperial Palace, the pedestrianized Kohlmarkt is lined with some of Vienna's most exclusive shops and remarkable shopfronts.**

the 1830s is at No 21. Just off the Graben at No 19 Tuchlauben is the **Neidhart Fresco House**, a charming exhibition space which displays medieval frescoes.

Neidhart Fresco House

📍 Tuchlauben 19 🕐 1-6pm Tue-Sun Ⓦ wienmuseum.at

5

Pestsäule

📍 G6 🚇 Graben Ⓤ Stephansplatz 🚌 1A, 2A

During the plague of 1679, Emperor Leopold I vowed that he would commemorate Vienna's eventual deliverance. The plague over, he commissioned the architects and artists Lodovico Burnacini, Matthias Rauchmiller and the young Johann Bernhard Fischer von Erlach to build this Baroque plague column.

Devised by the Jesuits, its most striking image shows a saintly figure and an angel supervising the destruction of a hag, representing the plague, while the Emperor prays above.

6

Neuer Markt

📍 G7 Ⓤ Stephansplatz

Known as the Mehlmarkt, or flour market, until around 1210, the Neuer Markt was also used as a jousting area. Of these origins nothing is left, though a few 18th-century houses remain. In the middle of the Neuer Markt is a grand bronze replica of the Baroque Donnerbrunnen (Donner Fountain), created between 1737 and 1739 by the prolific Austrian sculptor Georg Raphael Donner. This is a symbolic celebration of the

role played by rivers in the economic life of the Habsburg Empire. The four figures denote tributaries of the Danube, while the central figure represents the Roman goddess Providentia, a deity that oversaw destiny – the fountain is also known as the Providentiabrunnen. The original figures are in the Lower Belvedere (*p172*).

In the 1980s this was a favourite gathering point for Vienna's various subcultures, most notably its mods.

The elaborate Pestsäule monument standing prominently on the Graben ↑

7

Michaelerplatz

F6 **Herrengasse, Stephansplatz** **1A, 2A**

Michaelerplatz faces the impressive Neo-Baroque Michaelertor (Michael's Gate), which leads through the Michaelertrakt to the Hofburg's inner courtyard (p94). On both sides of the doorway are 19th-century fountains, by Rudolf Weyer.

Opposite is the grand **Michaelerkirche**, once the parish church of the court and one of the oldest Baroque churches in the city. Its earliest parts were built in the 13th century; according to legend the church was built in 1221, but its present form dates from 1792. The porch is topped by Baroque sculptures (1724–5) by Italian sculptor Lorenzo Mattielli, and depicts the Fall of the Angels. Inside are

---

Did You Know?

Michaelerkirche's fine gilded pipe organ is the largest in Vienna.

Renaissance and 14th-century frescoes, and a vividly carved and gilded organ (1714) by Johann David Sieber, once played by Joseph Haydn. The main choir (1782), replete with cherubs and sunbursts, is by Karl Georg Merville.

Off the north choir is the crypt entrance. In the 17th and 18th centuries parishioners were often buried beneath their church. Well-preserved bodies clothed in their burial finery can still be viewed in open coffins.

Beside the Michaelerkirche is the domed Michaelertrakt, an extravagant wing of the palace. An old design by Joseph Emanuel Fischer von Erlach was used as the basis for a new design by Ferdinand Kirschner (1821–96). It was finished in 1893, complete with gilt-tasselled cupolas and statuary representing imperial Austria's land and sea power.

At the centre of the famous square there is a viewing spot for an excavation of a Roman encampment, as well as medieval foundations.

Michaelerkirche

Michaelerplatz 1 **7am–10pm Mon–Sat, 8am–10pm Sun & public hols** **michaelerkirche.at**

ADOLF LOOS

Pioneering architect Adolf Loos (1870–1933) loathed ornament included for its own sake – this is evident in his Modernist works. The lack of "eyebrows" (window hoods typical of Vienna's architecture) on the façades of Loos' buildings scandalized polite Viennese society. Surviving Loos interiors include Knize and the American Bar (p109), as well as the controversial, functionalist Looshaus.

8

Looshaus

F6 **Michaelerplatz 3** **Herrengasse** **1A, 2A** **9am–3pm Mon–Fri, (to 5:30pm Thu)**

Designed by Adolf Loos and erected in 1910–12 opposite the Michaelertor, this building so outraged the Emperor Franz Joseph that he declared that he would never use the Michaelertor again. The source of the emperor's indignation was the building's starkly functional upper façade, which contrasts dramatically with

→

The restored Gothic interior of the Minoritenkirche

the fine ornate Baroque architecture of the imperial square in which it is located.

Today, the Looshaus is a working bank, but visitors can still enter the lobby to view the elegant interior, which is richly clad in polished timber, green marble and mirrors.

9

Minoritenplatz

📍F6 Ⓜ Herrengasse

At No 1 Minoritenplatz is the Baroque-style State Archives building (although today the archives are no longer housed here), built onto the back of the Bunderskanzleramt in 1902. There are a number of palaces around the square. At No 3 is the grand former Dietrichstein Palace, dating from 1755, an early building by Franz Hillebrand. It now contains the offices of the Federal Chancellor and the Foreign Office. No 4 is the side of the Liechtenstein Palace, which has its frontage on Bankgasse, and the mid-17th-century Starhemberg Palace is at No 5. Now housing ministry offices, it was the residence of Count Ernst Rüdiger von Starhemberg, a hero of the 1683 Turkish siege.

At No 2 is the ancient **Minoritenkirche**, established here by the Minor friars in around 1224, although the present structure dates from 1339. The tower was given its odd pyramidal shape during the Turkish siege of 1529, when shells sliced the top off the steeple. During the 1780s the Minoritenkirche was restored to its original Gothic style, when Maria Theresa's son, Joseph II, made a gift of the church to Vienna's Italian community. The church retains a fine west portal (1340) with statues beneath traceried canopies; the carvings above the doorway are modern. The church interior is unexpectedly bright and airy, containing a mosaic copy of Leonardo da Vinci's *Last Supper*. Napoleon Bonaparte commissioned the Italian artist Giacomo Raffaelli to execute this work, and it was his intention to substitute it for the original in Milan and remove the real painting to Paris. Following Napoleon's downfall at Waterloo in 1815, Raffaelli's version was bought by the Habsburgs. In the south aisle is a painted statue of the Madonna and Child, dating from around 1350, while at the same spot in the north aisle is a faded fragment of a 16th-century fresco of St Francis of Assisi.

Minoritenkirche
🕐 9am–6pm daily
🌐 minoritenkirche-wien.info

↑ Gothic Michaelerkirche and the Hofburg's Michaelertrakt and Michaelertor

10

Mollard-Clary Palace

**⌖F6 ⌂Herrengasse 9
Ⓤ Herrengasse 🚌1A, 2A**

This magnificent Baroque palace dating from 1686 owes its name to two aristocratic tenants, Mollard and Clary. It is famous for its reforming cultural soirées presided over by Emperor Joseph II.

Today it forms part of the Austrian National Library, and is home to the world's only museum devoted solely to globes, the interesting **Globenmuseum**, which contains over 250 exhibits of celestial and terrestrial globes. A special chamber houses the huge globes of Venetian Vincenzo Coronelli and the giant 16th-century globes by Gerard Mercator.

Globenmuseum
♿ 🕐10am–6pm Tue–Sun (to 9pm Thu) Ⓦonb.ac.at

↑ Traffic-free Kärntner Strasse, full of shoppers and coffee-seekers

---

> 💬 **INSIDER TIP**
> **Combi Tickets**
>
> Combination tickets for the Literature, Papyrus, Globe and Esperanto Museums, and for the splendid Prunksaal (p95) - all part of the Austrian National Library - can be bought in advance online (eticket.onb.ac.at).

11

Kapuzinerkirche

**⌖G7 ⌂Tegetthoffstrasse 2
Ⓤ Stephansplatz 🕐6am–6pm daily**

Set back from the pleasant pedestrianized shopping street of Kärtner Strasse, Neuer Markt square (p105) is home to the Kapuzinerkirche. Featuring an impressive red façade, it was consecrated in 1632. Beneath the church and monastery are the vaults of the **Kaisergruft**, the imperial crypt, founded in 1619 by the Catholic Emperor Matthias. Here lie the remains of 145 Habsburgs, including Maria Theresa and her husband Franz Stephan in a large tomb by Balthasar Moll (1753).

The poignant tomb of Franz Joseph is flanked by those of his wife Elisabeth and their son Rudolf. The last reigning Habsburg, Empress Zita, died in 1989 and her remains are also buried here. The crypt is tended by resident guardians, the Capuchin monks.

Kaisergruft
🕐10am–6pm daily (to 9pm Thu) Ⓦkapuzinergruft.at

12

Kärntner Strasse

⌖G7 ⓊStephansplatz

This pedestrianized street was the main road to Carinthia in medieval times. Now it is the

↑ Visitors studying the many depictions of the planet at the Globenmuseum

old city's principal retail street. Day and night, it is packed with people shopping, buying fresh fruit juice from stands, pausing in cafés or listening to the street musicians.

No 37 on the street is the **Malteserkirche**. This church was founded by the Knights of Malta, who were invited to Vienna early in the 13th century by Leopold VI. The interior retains lofty Gothic windows and vaults.

At No 26 is **J&L Lobmeyr**, a unique shop founded in 1823 which houses handcrafted glassware designed for the Viennese Lobmeyr firm. There is a small museum on the third floor, with pieces on display by Josef Hoffmann, the founder of the Arts and Crafts studio, Wiener Werkstätte (p73).

Around the corner at No 5 Johannesgasse is the superb Questenberg-Kaunitz Palace, which dates from the early 18th century. Its design has been attributed to Johann Lukas von Hildebrandt.

Malteserkirche
🕐 7am–7pm daily

J&L Lobmeyr
🕐 9am–5pm Mon–Fri
🌐 lobmeyr.at

↑ Peter von Nobile's Temple of Theseus amid flowers in the Volksgarten

the first instance of rampant architectural Modernism. Loos drew inspiration from a sojourn studying the buildings of New York between 1893 and 1896. Today, the bar is an atmospheric place to enjoy a classic cocktail.

Volksgarten

📍 E6 🏛 Dr-Karl-Renner-Ring Ⓤ Herrengasse 🚋 D, 1, 2, 71 🕐 Apr–Oct: 6am–10pm daily; Nov–Mar: 6:30am–7pm daily

Like the lovely landscaped Burggarten, the elegant Volksgarten was created after Napoleon's destruction of the city walls, and was opened to the public soon after its completion in 1820. Its splendid formal and rose gardens are matched in grandeur by statuary and monuments, notably the Temple of Theseus (1823) by Peter von Nobile. Other highlights include Karl von Hasenauer's monument to the Austrian poet Franz Grillparzer and the fountain memorial to the assassinated Empress Elisabeth (1907) by architect Friedrich Ohmann and the Viennese sculptor Hans Bitterlich.

American Bar

📍 G6 🏛 Kärntner Strasse 10 Ⓤ Stephansplatz 🕐 Noon–4am daily 🌐 loos bar.at

Beneath a garish depiction of the Stars and Stripes is this tiny bar designed by Adolf Loos (p106) in 1908. The restored interior is impressive, with every detail carefully constructed by Loos, such as under-lit tables, exquisite glass cabinets and Loos' signature mahogany panelling. Mirrors create an illusion of a spacious interior, and onyx and marble panels reflect the soft lighting used throughout. The Loosbar is often cited as

EAT

Café Hawelka
The archetypal Central European café, with bentwood chairs, newspapers, excellent coffee and cakes.

📍 G6 🏛 Dorotheergasse 6 🌐 hawelka.at

€€€

Café Central
Enjoy a Grand Café experience at this Vienna institution where the likes of Freud and Loos once sipped their coffee. Opens early for breakfast.

📍 F5 🏛 Herrengasse 14 🌐 cafecentral.wien

€€€

Herrlich
This upmarket restaurant in the Steigenberger Hotel serves well-crafted Austrian and international dishes in formal surrounds.

📍 F6 🏛 Herrengasse 10 🌐 steigenberger.com

€€€

A SHORT WALK

IMPERIAL VIENNA

Distance 2 km (1 mile) **Nearest U-Bahn**
Herrengasse **Time** 30 minutes

The streets around the Hofburg are no longer
filled with the carriages of the nobility. Most
palaces have become offices, embassies or
apartments, but a pleasant stroll around the
quarter will still give visitors a sense of the city's
imperial past. This district remains the most
fashionable in Vienna, crammed with elegant
shops, art galleries and coffee houses, which
offer enjoyable interludes between visits to
the many museums and churches here.

*Herrengasse
U-Bahn*

HAARHOF

WALLNERSTRASSE

START

HERRENGASSE

*Home to the Mollard-Clary
Palace (p108),* **Herrengasse**
*was a prime site for the
palaces of the nobility.*

KOHL

*The unadorned design of the
Looshaus caused outrage. when it
was erected in 1912 (p106). It
overlooks Michaelerplatz, where
Roman ruins have been excavated.*

MICHAELERPLATZ

*Composer Joseph Haydn
once lived in rooms
overlooking the hand-
some courtyard of the
Grosses Michaelerhaus.*

*The crypt of **Michaelerkirche**
contains well-preserved
corpses from the late
18th century (p106).*

*An equestrian statue of
Joseph II stands at the
centre of elegant
Josefsplatz (p96).*

FINISH

←

Michaelerkirche's
interior, replete with
Renaissance frescoes

Naglergasse has some of the finest Baroque façades in the city.

On **Kohlmarkt** (p104) there are a number of shops by Hans Hollein, one of Austria's best-known architects.

The Spar-Casse Bank, with its gilt bee on the pediment, is just one of many fine buildings on pedestrianized **Graben** (p104).

GRABEN

↑ The Pestäule plague column on the busy Graben shopping street

Built after the plague of 1679, the grand gilded **Pestsäule** is the most imposing of Vienna's Baroque plague columns (p105).

Lining this narrow lane are art galleries and auction houses, including the **Dorotheum** (p104) and the much-loved **Café Hawelka** (p109).

Once a royal residence, the Stallburg now houses the **Spanish Riding School** stables and the Lipizzaner Museum (p100).

| 0 metres | | 40 |
| 0 yards | | 40 |

N ↑

SCHOTTENRING AND ALSERGRUND

At the core of this elegant part of the city is the 12th-century Schottenkirche. The former medieval complex, which gives the area its name, was actually established by Irish, not Scottish, Benedictine monks, who came to Vienna in Babenberg times to disseminate Christianity throughout Continental Europe.

Occupying the northern section of the city centre, the leafy Schottenring and Alsergrund comprise several former suburbs, quiet areas where nobility once built their summer palaces; the Baroque Ferstel Palace and 18th-century Kinsky Palace are among several on Freyung square. Later rulers of Austria were responsible for the area's other monuments: Habsburg Emperor Joseph II founded a vast public hospital, now the Josephinum, in 1785, and Franz Joseph I built the Votivkirche as a way of giving thanks after escaping assassination in 1853.

Known for its resident student and medic population, with the University of Vienna and AKH hospital nearby, it is perhaps not surprising that this area was where Sigmund Freud lived and worked during the 20th century.

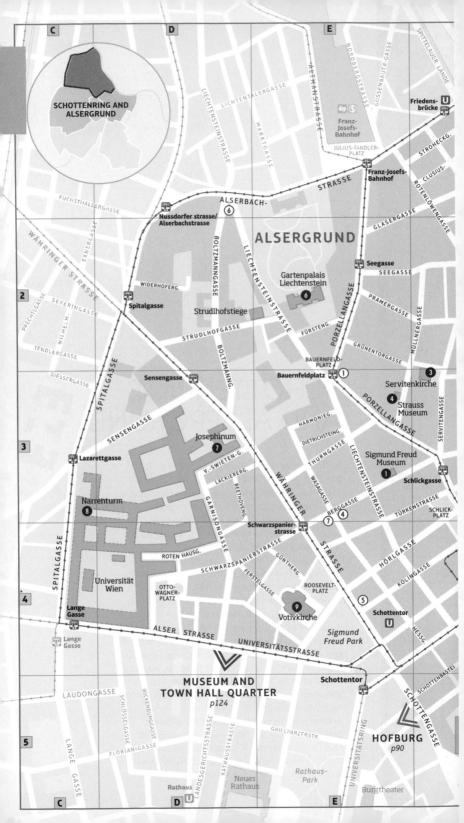

SCHOTTENRING AND ALSERGRUND

C D E

2

FUCHSTHALLERGASSE

WÄHRINGER STRASSE

PRECHTLGASSE
SEVERINGASSE
WILHELM-
TENDLERGASSE

Spitalgasse

Widerhoferg.

LICHTENTALERGASSE
LICHTENSTEINSTRASSE
MARKTGASSE

ALSERBACH-

Nussdorfer strasse/
Alserbachstrasse ⑥

ALTHANSTRASSE

NORDBERGSTRASSE
GUSSENBAUERGASSE
SPITTELAUER LÄNDE

Franz-
Josefs-
Bahnhof

JULIUS-TANDLER-
PLATZ

STRASSE

Friedens-
brücke Ⓤ

STROHECKG.

CLUSIUS-

Franz-Josefs-
Bahnhof

ROTENLÖWENGASSE

GLASERGASSE

ALSERGRUND

Seegasse

SEEGASSE

PRAMERGASSE

MÜLLNERGASSE

BOLTZMANNGASSE
LIECHTENSTEINSTRASSE
PORZELLANGASSE

Gartenpalais
Liechtenstein ⑥

FÜRSTENG.

GRÜNENTORGASSE

Strudlhofstiege

STRUDLHOFGASSE

BOLTZMANNG.

3

GIESSERGASSE

SPITALGASSE

SENSENGASSE

Sensengasse

Josephinum ⑦

V.-SWIETEN-G.

LACKIERERG.

BEETHOVENG.

GARNISONGASSE

BAUERNFELD-
PLATZ

Bauernfeldplatz ①

HARMONIEG.

DIETRICHSTEING.

THURNGASSE

WASAGASSE

BERGGASSE

WÄHRINGER

Servitenkirche
④
Strauss
Museum

③

PORZELLANGASSE

SERVITENGASSE

Sigmund Freud
Museum
①

Schlickgasse

LIECHTENSTEINSTRASSE

TÜRKENSTRASSE

SCHLICK-
PLATZ

⑦
④

Lazarettgasse

Narrenturm
⑧

Universität
Wien

OTTO-
WAGNER-
PLATZ

ROTEN HAUSG.

SCHWARZSPANIERSTRASSE

Schwarzspanier-
strasse

FERSTELGASSE

GÜNTHERG.

STRASSE

ROOSEVELT-
PLATZ

Votivkirche ⑨

HÖRLGASSE

KOLINGASSE

Schottentor
Ⓤ

HESSG.

Sigmund
Freud Park

⑤

4

SPITALGASSE

Lange
Gasse

Lange
Gasse

ALSER STRASSE

UNIVERSITÄTSSTRASSE

Schottentor Ⓤ

SCHOTTENBASTEI

SCHOTTENGASSE

5

LAUDONGASSE

SCHLÖSSELGASSE
WICKENBURGGASSE
LANDESGERICHTSSTRASSE
RATHAUSSTRASSE

FLORIANIGASSE

LANGE GASSE

**MUSEUM AND
TOWN HALL QUARTER**
p124

GRILLPARZERSTR.

UNIVERSITÄTSRING

HOFBURG
p90

Rathaus
Ⓤ

Neues
Rathaus

Rathaus-
Park

Burgtheater

C D E

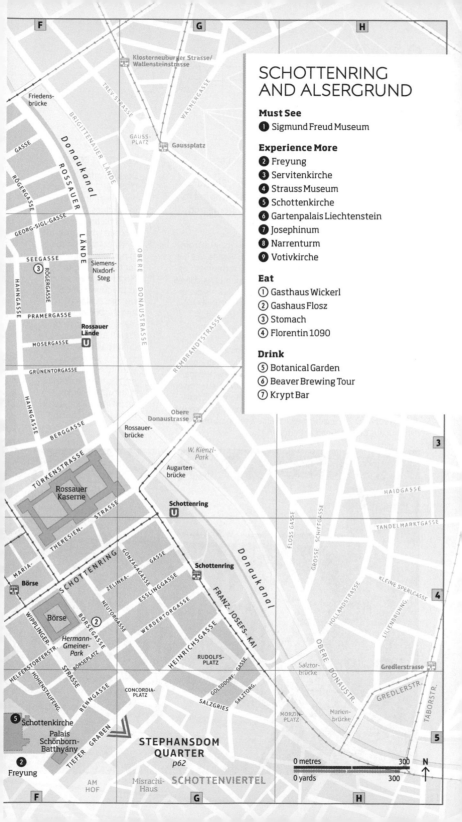

SCHOTTENRING AND ALSERGRUND

Must See
1 Sigmund Freud Museum

Experience More
2 Freyung
3 Servitenkirche
4 Strauss Museum
5 Schottenkirche
6 Gartenpalais Liechtenstein
7 Josephinum
8 Narrenturm
9 Votivkirche

Eat
1 Gasthaus Wickerl
2 Gashaus Flosz
3 Stomach
4 Florentin 1090

Drink
5 Botanical Garden
6 Beaver Brewing Tour
7 Krypt Bar

❶ 🖼️ Ⓜ️ 🏛️

SIGMUND FREUD MUSEUM

📍E3 🏠Bergasse 19 Ⓤ Schottentor 🚋D
🚌40A 🕙10am–6pm daily 🌐freud-museum.at

A Vienna resident for more than 50 years, Sigmund Freud is as synonymous with the Austrian capital as coffee houses and the waltz. His former home and surgery is now a fascinating museum.

Freud's former apartment at Berggasse 19 differs little from any other 19th-century apartment building in Vienna, yet it is now one of the city's most famous addresses and something of a shrine. The father of psychoanalysis, Sigmund Freud lived, worked and received patients here from 1891 until his departure from Vienna in 1938. There are more than 420 items of memorabilia on display, including letters and books, furnishings, photographs documenting Freud's long life, and various antiquities. Unique film material depicting the Freud family in the 1930s is shown in a video room with a commentary by Anna Freud. The flat was quickly abandoned when the Nazis forced Freud and his family to leave Vienna, but it has fortunately been successfully preserved as a museum to his life and work, and is also home to an extensive library.

The museum is closed for major refurbishment from spring 2019 to summer 2020, during which time a temporary exhibition is being staged at Bergasse 13.

FREUD'S LEGACY

Doctor Sigmund Freud (1856–1939) was not only the founder of the techniques of psychoanalysis, but a prolific theorist who wrote many essays and books expounding his often contentious ideas. Modern concepts such as the subconscious, the ego, sublimation and the Oedipus complex all evolved from Freudian theories. Freud posited different structural systems within the human psyche that, he posed, if disrupted, could result in emotional or mental disturbance.

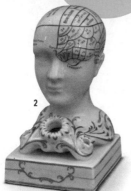

① Photographic displays illustrating Freud's career give an insight into contemporary Viennese life.

② A phrenology head with inkwell is among the Freud memorabilia.

③ The entrance to the exhibition space on the ground floor of the museum

←

The manuscript room, containing a model of Freud's famous couch

EXPERIENCE MORE

② Freyung

📍F5 Ⓤ Herrengasse

The Freyung is a curiously shaped "square". Its name derives from the right of sanctuary granted to the monks of the Schottenkirche. Fugitives from persecution who entered the area were safe from arrest. No 4 is the **Kinsky Palace** (1713–16), by Johann Lukas von Hildebrandt. Next door is the Porcia Palace of 1546, one of the oldest in Vienna, though much altered. At No 3 is the Harrach Palace; which has fine Rococo doors.

📷 PICTURE PERFECT
Freyung Passage

This elegant 19th-century shopping arcade provides some atmospheric camera fodder, its beautifully illuminated, barrel-ceilinged passages an impressive sight in the evening. The lovely seasonal decorations will add an extra dimension to your shot.

Opposite is the grand Austria Fountain: it has four figures to symbolize the major rivers of the Habsburgs' lands. Behind is the former Schottenkirche priory, unkindly known as the chest-of-drawers house.

Facing the Freyung is the Palais Ferstel, which dates from 1860 and takes its name from the architect, Heinrich von Ferstel. This Italian-style palazzo is home to the spectacular glass-roofed Freyung Passage. Lined with elegant shops and restaurants this luxury arcade presents a fine example of a civilized urban amenity. Enter the arcade from the Freyung side, and follow the passage to a small courtyard, to catch a glimpse of a many-tiered statue of the lissome mermaid of the Danube. The passage also has a secret entrance into one of Vienna's grandest coffee houses, the iconic Café Central (p109).

Kinsky Palace
🕙 10am–5pm Mon–Fri

③
Servitenkirche

📍F3 🏠 Servitengasse 9
📞 31761950 Ⓤ Rossauer Lände 🕙 7–9am & 6–7pm Mon–Fri, 7–9am & 5–8pm Sat & Sun

Although off the main visitor track, this church (1651–77) is worth a visit. Inside, a riot of Baroque decoration includes elaborate stucco ornamentation, a fine wrought-iron screen near the entrance and an exuberant pulpit (1739), partly by Balthasar Moll.

---

④
Strauss Museum

📍E3 🏠 Müllnergasse 3
🕙 2–6pm Wed–Sat
🌐 strauss-museum.at

No family quite sums up Vienna like the Strausses, a dynasty of composers that gave the world its most famous waltzes.

> **No family quite sums up Vienna like the Strausses, a dynasty of composers that gave the world its most famous waltzes.**

← People enjoying open-air refreshment on a summer day in the Freyung

This charming museum celebrates various members of this family of prodigies, with special prominence given to the "Waltz King", Johann Strauss Jr (1825–99), the composer of over 500 dance pieces, among them the *Blue Danube Waltz* (1876), which became Austria's unofficial national anthem. The influence of the Strauss family's music on Viennese social and political affairs is explored through 14 themed exhibitions, and audio stations accompany each. The venue also hosts Strauss-related events, for which tickets must be booked in advance.

⑤
Schottenkirche

📍F5 🏛Schottenstift, Freyung 6 Ⓤ Schottentor, Herrengasse 🚌1A
🌐schottenstift.at

Despite its name (Scottish Church), this 1177 monastic foundation was established by Irish Benedictines. The adjoining buildings have a fine medieval art collection, the **Museum in the Scots Abbey**, that includes the famous Schotten altarpiece (1475). The church has been altered repeatedly and has undergone extensive renovation. Today it presents a rather drab Neo-Classical façade, but inside a rich Baroque interior awaits.

Museum in the Scots Abbey

🏛Freyung 6 🕐11am–5pm Tue-Sat 🚫Sun & hols

Sumptuous decoration of the Schottenkirke's interior, and a statue adorning its exterior *(inset)* ↓

DRINK

Botanical Garden
Sip classy cocktails from a lengthy menu at this trendy basement bar. The atmosphere is cosy and the staff are friendly.

📍E4 🏛Kolingasse 1
🌐botanicalgarden.at

Beaver Brewing Tour
The craft beer trend has reached Vienna and this modern, hipster place serves some of the best.

📍D1 🏛Liechtensteinstrasse 69
🌐beaverbrewing.at

Krypt Bar
This vaulted cellar bar is just a hop and a skip from the Votivkirche, and attracts a hip crowd with its cool cocktails.

📍E3 🏛Wasagasse 17
🌐krypt.bar

⑥

Gartenpalais Liechtenstein

📍E2 🏠Fürstengasse 1
Ⓤ Friedensbrücke 🚌40A
🚋D ⏱For guided tours
only (by appt) 🌐palais
liechtenstein.com

Designed by Domenico
Martinelli and completed in
1692, the summer palace of
the Liechtenstein family now
houses the art collection of
Prince Hans-Adam II von und
zu Liechtenstein. Behind the
imposing Palladian exterior,
notable features include the
Neo-Classical library, and the
Hercules Hall and grand staircase, with their magnificent
frescoes. The art collection
centres on the Baroque, with a
special focus on Rubens, and
numerous paintings and
sculptures by German, Dutch
and Italian masters from the
Renaissance through to the
19th century. The palace is
situated in an extensive
garden in the English-style,
designed in the 19th century.

---

⑦

Josephinum

📍D3 🏠Währinger Strasse
25/1 Ⓤ Schottentor 🚋37,
38, 40, 41, 42 ⏱4–8pm
Wed, 10am–6pm Fri & Sat
🔒Public hols 🌐joseph
inum.ac.at

Emperor Joseph II, an ardent
reformer, established this
military surgical institute. Now
part of the Medical University
of Vienna, it also houses the
university's historic medical
collections, including exhibits
of 19th-century medical
research memorabilia. The
main attraction here is the
collection of anatomical wax
models commissioned by the
Emperor from Tuscan artists,
once used to train surgeons.

⑧

Narrenturm

📍C3 🏠Spitalgasse 2
📞52177606 Ⓤ Schotten-
tor 🚋5, 33 ⏱10am–6pm
Wed, 10am–1pm Sat
🔒Public hols

Once the Allgemeines
Krankenhaus, founded by
Joseph II, the Narrenturm
(Fools' Tower) is a former
asylum designed by Isidor
Canevale. The circular tower
now houses a Museum for
Pathological Anatomy, with a
reconstructed apothecary's
shop and models. The few
rooms open to the public
show only a fraction of what is

 ←
The interior of the
Votivkirche, bathed in
coloured light

one of the world's most comprehensive pathology and anatomy collections, but tours explore further areas.

9
Votivkirche

📍E4 🏛Rooseveltplatz 8
📞4061192 Ⓜ Schottentor
🚋D, 1, 71 🕐9am–1pm daily,
4–6pm Tue–Sat

After a Hungarian nationalist tried to assassinate Emperor Franz Joseph I on 18 February 1853, a collection was made to fund the construction of a new church opposite the Mölker-Bastei, where the attempt had been made. The architect was Heinrich von Ferstel and work on the church began in 1856. Many of the chapels are dedicated to Austrian regiments and military heroes. The finest monument is the Renaissance sarcophagus of Niklas Salm, who commanded Austria's forces during the 1529 Turkish siege. It is located in the chapel just west of the north transept. The church is topped with lacy steeples and spires.

↑ The 17th-century Gartenpalais Liechtenstein, overlooking colourful floral displays

---

EAT

Gasthaus Wickerl
A welcoming and cosy *beisl* serving seasonal Austrian favourites like schnitzel and *tafelspitz*.

📍E3 🏛Porzellangasse 234a
🌐wickerl.at

€€€

Gashaus Flosz
High-ceilinged brasserie serving only the freshest of Austrian food including schnitzel and *tafelspitz*, with around 100 Austrian wines to choose from.

📍F4 🏛Börseplatz 3
🌐flosz.at

€€€

Stomach
Enjoy wholesome Central European food and vegetarian dishes at this authentic and friendly restaurant.

📍F2 🏛Seegasse 26
📞01 310 2099
🕐Mon & Tue

€€€

Florentin 1090
The successor to the famous Café Berg, this LGBT+ friendly restaurant serves wholesome Israeli-influenced dishes.

📍E3 🏛Berggasse 8
🌐florentin1090.com

€€€

A SHORT WALK
AROUND THE FREYUNG

Did You Know?

Schottenkirche's shape lends it the name *Schubladkasten-haus* or "chest of drawers house".

Distance 1.5km (1 mile) **Time** 25 minutes
Nearest U-Bahn Herrengasse

At the core of this elegant part of the city is the former medieval complex of the Schottenkirche, courtyards and school. On the other side of the Freyung square are some beautiful Baroque palaces, including Hildebrandt's Kinsky Palace (1713–16) and the Palais Ferstel. The Freyung Passage links the Freyung with Herrengasse, which is lined with Baroque mansions and boasts the city's first skyscraper. Backing onto the Schottenring is the Italianate Börse stock exchange.

↑ The Baroque façade of the Schottenkirche

HELFERSTORFERSTRASSE

Founded in 1177 and redecorated in the Baroque period, this **Schottenkirche** has an adjoining museum (p119).

FINISH

The **Freyung** square is overlooked by fine buildings, including the former Schottenkirche priory, originally founded in 1155, then rebuilt in 1744.

FREYUNG

HERRENGASSE

The Freyung and Herrengasse are connected by the elegant **Freyung Passage** (p118).

Café Central (p109) has a papier-mâché statue of the poet Peter Altenberg, who frequented coffee houses around the city.

START

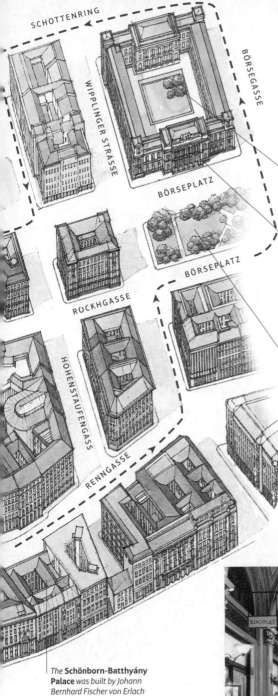

SCHOTTENRING

BÖRSEGASSE

WIPPLINGER STRASSE

BÖRSEPLATZ

BÖRSEPLATZ

ROCKHGASSE

HOHENSTAUFENGASSE

RENNGASSE

Locator Map
For more detail see p114

A central courtyard lies hidden within the former stock exchange buildings.

The Börse *(stock exchange) was commissioned when the Ringstrasse was first conceived. Designed by Theophil Hansen, it was completed in 1877 and today houses offices, a garden centre and a restaurant.*

The **Hermann Gmeiner Park** *includes a playground and commemorates the life and work of Hermann Gmeiner (1919–86). Gmeiner founded SOS Children's Villages, a worldwide organization that cares for orphans.*

| 0 metres | 50 |
| 0 yards | 50 |

N
↑

The **Schönborn-Batthyány Palace** *was built by Johann Bernhard Fischer von Erlach between 1699 and 1706.*

→

Rococo arches of the Freyung Passage, a luxury shopping arcade

The Kunsthistorisches Museum's elegant Cupola Hall

MUSEUM AND TOWN HALL QUARTER

This quarter is bordered by the wide imperial boulevard of the Ringstrasse, linking the city's most important cultural and political institutions. Comissioned by Franz Joseph and completed in the 1880s, the Ringstrasse's construction hailed a new age of grandeur in Vienna, despite the dwindling power of the Habsburgs. It was around this time that the Kunsthistorisches and Naturhistorisches museums, which house vast collections amassed by generations of Habsburg monarchs, were opened to the public. The Burgtheater, originally constructed in 1741 by Maria Theresa, who wanted to have a theatre next to her palace, was also restored in Renaissance style. The former imperial stables, commissioned in 1713 by Emperor Charles VI, were transformed into exhibition spaces in 1918 after the fall of the Habsburg Empire.

In 2001, the MuseumsQuartier opened on this site, after an investment of €150 million, and is today a contemporary equivalent of the Habsburgs' fine cultural institutions, with its superb collection of modern art and architecture.

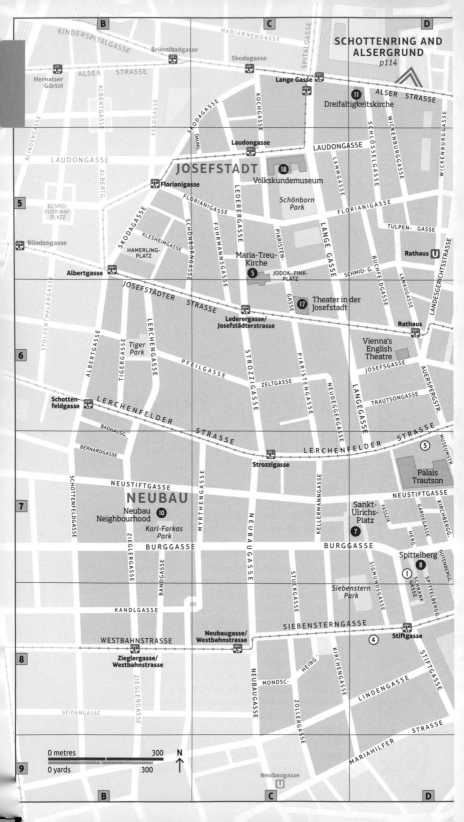

B   C   D

KINDERSPITALGASSE

MARIANNENGASSE

SPITALGASSE

Brünntbadgasse

Skodagasse

Hernalser Gürtel

ALSER STRASSE

Lange Gasse

ALSER STRASSE

11 Dreifaltigkeitskirche

ALBERTGASSE

FELDGASSE

BLINDENGASSE

KOCHGASSE

SKODAGASSE

DAUNG.

Laudongasse

LAUDONGASSE

LAUDONGASSE

SCHLÖSSELGASSE

WICKENBURGGASSE

JOSEFSTADT

Florianigasse

18 Volkskundemuseum

LAMMGASSE

5

LAUDONGASSE

ALBERTG.

BENNO-
FLORIANI-
PLATZ

SKODAGASSE

SCHÖNBORNGASSE

FLORIANIGASSE

LEDERERGASSE

FUHRMANNSGASSE

PIARISTEN-

Schönborn
Park

LANGE GASSE

FLORIANIGASSE

BUCHFELDGASSE

TULPEN- GASSE

Rathaus U

LANDESGERICHTSSTRASSE

Blindengasse

KLESHEIMGASSE

HAMERLING-
PLATZ

Maria-Treu-
Kirche
5

JODOK-FINK-
PLATZ

SCHMID-G.

LENAUGASSE

Albertgasse

JOSEFSTÄDTER STRASSE

Lederergasse/
Josefstädterstrasse

GASSE

17 Theater in der
Josefstadt

Rathaus

STOLZENTHALERGASSE

ALBERTGASSE

LERCHENGASSE

TIGERGASSE

Tiger
Park

PFEILGASSE

STROZZIGASSE

ZELTGASSE

PIARISTENGASSE

NEUDEGGERGASSE

Vienna's
English
Theatre

JOSEFSGASSE

LANGEGASSE

TRAUTSONGASSE

AUERSPERGSTR.

6

Schotten-
feldgasse

LERCHENFELDER

BADHAUSG.

BERNARDGASSE

STRASSE

Strozzigasse

LERCHENFELDER STRASSE

MUSEUMSTR.

5

Palais
Trautson

SCHOTTENFELDGASSE

NEUSTIFTGASSE

NEUBAU

Neubau
Neighbourhood **10**

Karl-Farkas
Park

BURGGASSE

MYRTHENGASSE

NEUBAUGASSE

KELLERMANNGASSE

Sankt-
Ulrichs-
Platz **7**

BURGGASSE

NEUSTIFTGASSE

FASSZIE...

GARDEGASSE

KIRCHBERGG.

Spittelberg

HERG...

GUTENBERGG...

8

1

SCHRANK-GASSE

SPITTELBERG...

7

ZIEGLERGASSE

BANDGASSE

STUCKGASSE

SIGMUNDSGASSE

Siebenstern
Park

KANDLGASSE

SIEBENSTERNGASSE

Stiftgasse

4

STIFTGASSE

WESTBAHNSTRASSE

Neubaugasse/
Westbahnstrasse

HEING...

KIRCHENGASSE

8

Zieglergasse/
Westbahnstrasse

ZIEGLERGASSE

NEUBAUGASSE

MONDSC-

ZOLLERGASSE

LINDENGASSE

SEIDENGASSE

MARIAHILFER STRASSE

0 metres   300
0 yards   300

N

Neubaugasse
U

9

B   C   D

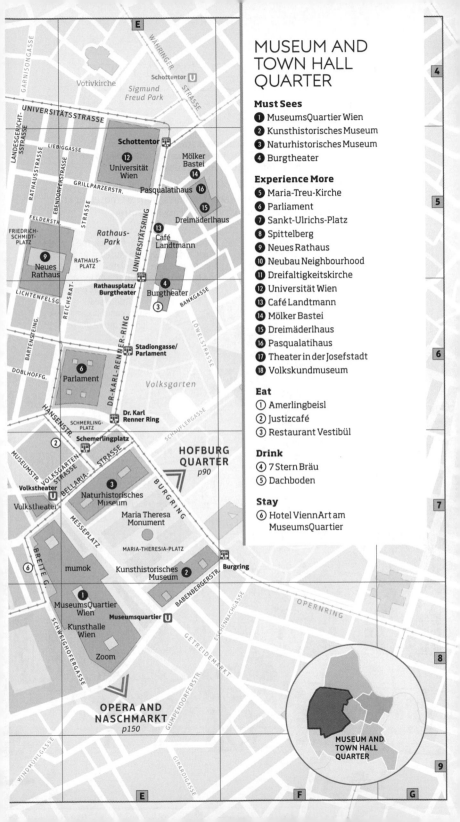

MUSEUM AND TOWN HALL QUARTER

Must Sees

1. MuseumsQuartier Wien
2. Kunsthistorisches Museum
3. Naturhistorisches Museum
4. Burgtheater

Experience More

5. Maria-Treu-Kirche
6. Parliament
7. Sankt-Ulrichs-Platz
8. Spittelberg
9. Neues Rathaus
10. Neubau Neighbourhood
11. Dreifaltigkeitskirche
12. Universität Wien
13. Café Landtmann
14. Mölker Bastei
15. Dreimäderlhaus
16. Pasqualatihaus
17. Theater in der Josefstadt
18. Volkskundmuseum

Eat

1. Amerlingbeisl
2. Justizcafé
3. Restaurant Vestibül

Drink

4. 7 Stern Bräu
5. Dachboden

Stay

6. Hotel ViennArt am MuseumsQuartier

MUSEUMSQUARTIER WIEN

♀ E8 🏛 Museumsplatz 1 Ⓤ Museumsquartier, Volkstheater 🚊 49 to Volkstheater 🚌 48A to Volkstheater 🕐 Visitor and Ticket Centres: 10am–7pm daily; for individual museum opening times check website ⓦ mqw.at

The vibrant MuseumsQuartier Wien is one of the largest cultural centres in the world. The district houses a diverse array of facilities, from art museums to a venue for contemporary dance to a children's creativity centre.

The MuseumsQuartier once housed the stables for Emperor Franz Joseph's horses. In 1918, after the fall of the Habsburg Empire, the buildings were transformed into an exhibition space to house the Wiener Messe's trade fairs. In 1986, modern and contemporary art galleries were constructed, including mumok, the Kunsthalle Wien and the Leopold Museum, and further renovations were completed in 2001. Today, the MQ, as it is called, hosts 60 institutions, and its courtyard offers pleasant cafés and outdoor seating where visitors can relax and soak up the atmosphere.

If you're visiting with children, then the MQ has plenty to keep them entertained. Head first to ZOOM *(p131)* for arts and crafts and an ocean-themed adventure playground. Dsungel hosts puppet shows and kids' film and opera events, while wienXtra has a diverting play area for under-13s.

1. Modern art is the focus of the collection at mumok.

2. ZOOM offers interactive creative workshops for kids.

3. The Leopold Museum houses an outstanding array of modern Austrian art.

Did You Know?

Every summer, the MQ's courtyards host live concerts and open-air festivals.

← Relaxing and socializing in the MQ's impressive main courtyard

The bright, airy interior of ↑
mumok with fine works
of modern art on display

Exploring the MuseumsQuartier Wien

More than 60 different cultural institutions are gathered together in the MuseumsQuartier Wien, together with restaurants, cafés and shops. The vast complex, with its grand main plaza and maze of passageways opening into art-filled courtyards, attracts more than four million visitors a year.

This is an ideal starting point for any trip to Vienna, since many other attractions are also nearby. It is advisable to stop off first at the MQ Point Info-Tickets-Shop, in the Fischer von Erlach Wing, to obtain a programme detailing all events and exhibitions currently taking place throughout the complex. Tours of the MQ offer visitors different perspectives on the centre: the KaiserQuartier Tour explores the Habsburg history of the complex; the weekly Site Tour grants an insight into the creation and evolution of the district; and the Backstage Tour takes visitors on a journey through the Q21 creative cluster to see behind the scenes in the studios and, if they're lucky, to meet the artists in residence there.

> **More than 60 different cultural institutions are gathered together in the MuseumsQuartier Wien.**

↑ Photography exhibited at
creative cluster Q21's gallery

↑ The bright limestone façade
of the Leopold Museum

Museum Guide

ZOOM Kindermuseum

▷ This lively centre offers an unconventional approach to the world of the museum for kids - its aim is to encourage learning through play and exploration for children aged 12 and under. The ZOOM Lab is for older children, while younger ones can take a dip in the ZOOM Ocean with their parents.

Q21

Over 50 cultural initiatives have turned Q21 into Vienna's centre for contemporary applied arts. The attractions for the public, which are on the ground floor, include fashion, design, book and music shops, an exhibition space for art schools, and large event halls.

Tanzquartier Wien

The Tanzquartier Wien is Austria's first dedicated performance and study venue focusing solely on modern dance. It offers facilities for dancers and hosts dance and other shows for the public.

mumok (Museum of Modern Art Ludwig Foundation Vienna)

◁ Containing one of the largest European collections of modern art, mumok's range of acquisitions include American Pop Art, Fluxus, Nouveau Réalism, Viennese Actionism, Arte Povera, Conceptual Art and Minimal Art. Galleries are split chronologically over five levels, two underground. There is also a cinema, a library and a studio.

Architekturzentrum Wien

This centre is committed to showcasing new architectural work to the public. Its permanent exhibition's focus is diversity in 20th-century architecture. Each year, four to six temporary exhibitions examine links between modern architecture and architecture throughout history.

EGON SCHIELE AT THE LEOPOLD MUSEUM

The Leopold Museum's collection of works by the artist Egon Schiele (1890–1918) is the largest in the world. Comprising over 40 paintings and around 180 drawings, it spans the artist's entire creative output, including self-portraits and landscapes, as well as some of the more controversial nudes. The Leopold Museum also houses famous works by Schiele's mentor, Secessionist master Gustav Klimt.

Leopold Museum

▷ The vast Leopold Collection of Austrian Art was compiled over five decades by Rudolf Leopold. Highlights of the exhibition space, which spans five floors, include the Egon Schiele collection and many fine Expressionist Austrian paintings. On the ground level, an exhibition on Secessionism and Art Nouveau includes pieces by Gustav Klimt, Richard Gerstl and Oskar Kokoschka.

Kunsthalle Wien

This striking red-brick building is a home for innovation and creativity, showing international and contemporary art. Exhibits emphasize cross-genre and cross-border arts, including experimental architecture, video, photography and film, plus new media.

② ⬡ ⬡ ⬡ ⬡ ⬡

KUNSTHISTORISCHES MUSEUM

📍E7 🏛Maria-Theresien-Platz, A-1010 🚇Museumsquartier, Volkstheater
🚋D, 1, 2, 71 🚌57A ⏰10am–6pm Tue–Sun (to 9pm Thu) 🌐khm.at

This astonishing institution attracts over 1.5 million visitors each year. Its opulent galleries house vast collections of fine art and antiquities, based largely on those accumulated over the centuries by generations of Habsburg monarchs.

When the Ringstrasse was built by Emperor Franz Joseph (p142), a pair of magnificent buildings, designed by architects Karl von Hasenauer and Gottfried Semper, were erected in Italian Renaissance style. The symmetrical Kunsthistorisches Museum (KHM) and Naturhistorisches Museum (p136) would house the collections of imperial art and natural history which, until the late 19th century, had been held in the Belvedere and Hofburg palaces. The KHM's lavishly decorated interiors, with ornate cupolas and sweeping Neo-Classical stairways, create a fitting setting for the treasures housed here. The Habsburg monarchs were enthusiastic patrons and collectors, and many of the works on display here, particularly the Old Masters, are among the most spectacular in the world.

1891
—
The KHM was opened, displaying the Habsburg's private treasures to the public.

THE APOTHEOSIS OF THE RENAISSANCE

Part of the museum's extravagant decorative scheme, a fabulous trompe l'oeil ceiling painting above the main staircase depicts *The Apotheosis of the Renaissance* (1890). The work of Hungarian painter Michael Munkácsy, it shows Leonardo, Michelangelo and Titian, all presided over by Pope Julius II.

↑ Fine classical statuary exhibited in the collection of Greek and Roman antiquities

→

Visitors admiring Renaissance paintings in the Picture Gallery

↑ The Italian Renaissance-style KHM overlooking Maria-Theresien-Platz

Exploring the Kunsthistorisches Museum

The museum's displays are spread over three floors, and are so large that they cannot be fully appreciated in one visit. On the ground floor, the ancient civilizations of Egypt, Greece and Rome are chronicled in their full splendour. The Kunstkammer, or Viennese chamber of curiosities, also on the ground floor, is known as a "museum within a museum", with its collection of rare Renaissance and Baroque treasure. The first floor contains the Picture Gallery, a unique collection of 16th-, 17th-, and 18th-century European paintings amassed by Habsburg monarchs, with masterworks of Renaissance and medieval art including pieces by Pieter Bruegel the Elder, Rembrandt and Dürer. On the second floor is one of the largest coin collections in the world.

Visitors can seek refreshment in the café in the central Cupola Hall, which is decorated in spectacular Renaissance fashion, with marble archways and a fine mosaic floor. Many prominent artists were employed to decorate the museum's interior. Keep an eye out for the especially ornate gilded frescoes by Gustav Klimt, which adorn the archways of the grand central staircase.

> **The ancient civilizations of Egypt, Greece and Rome are chronicled in their full splendour.**

↑ Caravaggio's *Madonna of the Rosary* (1601) hanging in the Picture Gallery

↑ An ancient faïence hippopotamus from the Egyptian Collection

→ Inspecting displays of sarcophagi and mummies in the Egyptian Collection

THE OLD MASTERS

The fine collection of Old Masters at the KHM is near unparalleled. The extensive Picture Gallery is filled with works by the Flemish masters, including about a third of all surviving pieces by Pieter Bruegel the Elder, including his renowned painting *Tower of Babel*. The Italian masters are well represented here too, with staggering works by Caravaggio, Titian and Tintoretto.

Picture Gallery

▷ The collection focuses on Old Masters from the 15th to the 18th centuries and largely reflects the personal tastes of its Habsburg founders. Venetian and 16th- and 17th-century Flemish paintings are particularly well represented, and there is an excellent display of works by Dutch and German artists.

Egyptian and Near Eastern Collection

Five specially decorated rooms adorned with Egyptian friezes and motifs provide the perfect setting for the bulk of the museum's collection of Egyptian and Near Eastern antiquities. The collection was founded by the Habsburg monarchs, though most of the items were acquired in the 19th or 20th century. This collection holds over 17,000 objects, with funerary art from Ancient Egypt and treasures from Babylon and Arabia.

Greek and Roman Antiquities

▷ Part of the museum's Greek and Roman collection is housed in the main building, with other finds displayed in the Hofburg (*p96*). The main gallery at the KHM (Room XI) is decorated in the style of an Imperial Roman villa, complete with a mosaic of Theseus and the Minotaur and ancient Greek and Roman statuary. Other rooms house stunning early Greek sculpture, the Austria Romana collection, and Eutruscan, Byzantine and Coptic pieces. There is also a very fine collection of Roman cameos, jewellery, pottery and glass.

Kunstkammer Wien

The curators call this "the cradle of the museum". Here, the personal prizes of Habsburg collectors Rudolf II and Archduke Leopold William are housed in their "wonder rooms". These were originally chambers of artifacts and natural wonders that were intended to represent the sum total of human knowledge of the day. In addition to sculpture, these princely treasuries contained precious items of high craftsmanship, exotic and highly unusual novelties, and scientific instruments.

Coins and Medals

▽ Tucked away on the second floor is one of the most extensive coin and medal collections in the world. Once again, the nucleus of the collection came from the former possessions of the Habsburgs, but it has been added to by modern curators and now includes many 20th-century items. Only a fraction of the museum's 600,000 pieces can be seen in the three exhibition rooms. Room I gives an overview of the development of money, including coins from Ancient Greece and Rome, examples of Egyptian, Celtic and Byzantine money, and medieval, Renaissance and European coins, as well as Austrian currency from its origins to the present.

3 🔸 🖥 🛍

NATURHISTORISCHES MUSEUM

📍E7 🏛Maria-Theresien-Platz, A-1010 Ⓤ Volkstheater 🚊 D, 1, 2, 46, 49, 71 🚌 48A 🕐 9am–9pm Wed, 9am–6:30pm Thu–Mon 🚫 Tue, 1 Jan, 25 Dec 🌐 nhm-wien.ac.at

Around 750,000 visitors every year come to see the frescoed ceilings and 39 grand halls of Vienna's Natural History Museum. Housing 30 million fascinating objects, its exhibits range from fossils of the very first life on Earth to a spectacular display on interstellar travel in its digital planetarium.

The museum's palatial home, built in the late 19th century, was purposely designed to be a splendid setting for vast royal collections, amassed to satisfy the imperial passion for discovery and knowledge. The institution remains one of Europe's foremost facilities for research in the earth and life sciences.

The museum displays cover two floors. To the right of the entrance on the ground floor are the rooms devoted to gemstones and mineralogy. Here can be found the world's largest and oldest collection of meteorites, as well as fabulous imperial jewellery pieces. To the left of the entrance hall are rooms housing artifacts that chart the evolution of humans and also the prehistoric collections. Some of the world's largest casts of dinosaur skeletons are on display there, as well as the museum's diminutive superstar, the carved Stone Age figurine known as the Venus of Willendorf.

The first floor is dedicated to the amazing diversity of animal life and includes specimens of now-extinct creatures such as Steller's sea cow. The collections of birds, butterflies and beetles from every corner of the globe are especially beautiful.

↑ A monument to Maria Theresa, who gave the museum to the state

↑ The richly decorated cupola above the grand staircase in the entrance hall

↑ Skeletons and taxidermy specimens arrayed in the Large Mammals hall

THE VENUS OF WILLENDORF

Found in Willendorf in 1908, this 11-cm (4-in) limestone figure is one of the most important prehistoric artifacts in the world. It is thought to be approximately 30,000 years old, and its purpose is unknown, although it has been speculated that the figure was used during ancient fertility rituals.

Must See

↑ Young visitors captivated by the displays in the Hall of the Dinosaurs

137

BURGTHEATER

④ 🚶 🅼🅱

📍E6 🏛 Universitätsring 2, A1014 Ⓤ Schottentor 🚊 D, 1, 71
🕐 For performances and guided tours ✕ 24 Dec & Good Friday,
Jul & Aug (except for guided tours) 🌐 burgtheater.at

A noted patron of the visual arts, the empress Maria Theresa also loved
music, plays and the opera. In the 1730s she commissioned a theatre
to be built conveniently next to her palace, and on 14 March 1741, the
Burgtheater, or Court Theatre, opened its doors for the very first time.

The Burgtheater is the most prestigious
theatrical institution in the German-speaking
world. Three of Mozart's operas, including
The Marriage of Figaro, were premiered here,
as was Beethoven's 1st Symphony. The original
building of Maria Theresa's reign adjoined the
Hofburg, but in the 19th century it was
decided to give the theatre a magnificent
new home among the architectural jewels
that stud the Ringstrasse *(p142)*, and today's
Italian Renaissance-style building by Karl von
Hasenauer and Gottfried Semper was completed in 1888. It stages a diverse range of plays
performed by its famed in-house ensemble.

← Emblems of music and the
dramatic arts hailing
visitors to the theatre

The grand façade, topped by
Apollo and the muses of ↑
comedy and tragedy

Timeline

1741
▽ Maria Theresa founds the Burgtheater in an empty ballroom at the Hofburg.

1874
Work on the present building begins on the Ringstrasse.

1955
Theatre reopens with Grillparzer's *King Ottokar*.

1750–76
△ Joseph II reorganizes the theatre and promotes it to the status of a national theatre.

1888
The Burgtheater opens on 14 October in the presence of the Emperor Franz Joseph and his family.

1945
△ World War II fire destroys the auditorium.

→

Thalia, Greek muse of comedy and idyllic poetry

International opera stars Anna Netrebko and Piotr Beczała on stage at the Burgtheater

💬 INSIDER TIP
Follow the Plot

Peformances at the Burgtheater are in German, but selected shows are surtitled in English. Check the website for details of what's on - it could be anything from modern classics by Arthur Miller to ancient Greek tragedies.

Exploring the Burgtheater

Daily guided tours (conducted in German and English) offer visitors a glimpse into the inner workings of the Burgtheater, or "Burg", as it is commonly known. The auditorium itself was completely remodelled just ten years after the theatre opened, to correct an original design flaw: some of the seats had no view of the stage. Forty-eight years later it was devastated again when a bomb fell on the building, leaving only the side wings containing the Grand Staircases intact. Subsequent restoration was so extraordinarily seamless that today its extent is hard to assess.

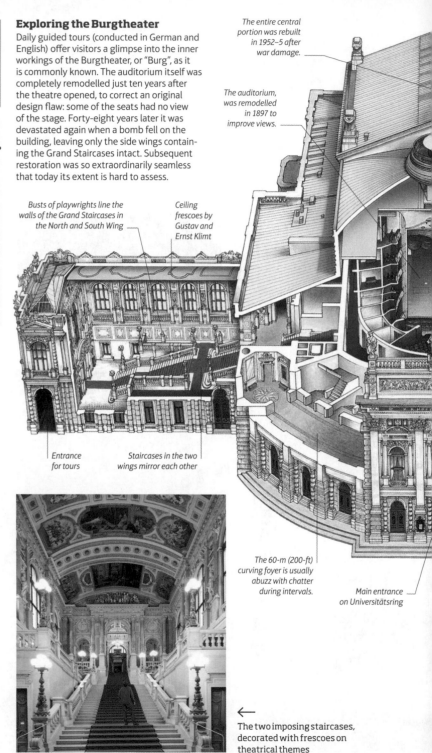

The entire central portion was rebuilt in 1952–5 after war damage.

The auditorium, was remodelled in 1897 to improve views.

Busts of playwrights line the walls of the Grand Staircases in the North and South Wing

Ceiling frescoes by Gustav and Ernst Klimt

Entrance for tours

Staircases in the two wings mirror each other

The 60-m (200-ft) curving foyer is usually abuzz with chatter during intervals.

Main entrance on Universitätsring

←

The two imposing staircases, decorated with frescoes on theatrical themes

→
The opulent red, cream and gold auditorium, a venue in which to see and be seen

Only the two wings survived bomb damage sustained in World War II.

Did You Know?

The Burg's revolving stage system, Europe's largest, enables sets to be changed in 40 seconds.

Frieze depicting Bacchus, god of drama, with his wife Ariadne and an energetic entourage

THE GRAND STAIRCASE FRESCOES

The Burg's elegant Grand Staircases are adorned with a series of marvellous frescoes painted in 1886 by Gustav and Ernst Klimt and Franz Matsch. The commission was the first for their Künstler-Compagnie (Artist's Company) association. Among the cycle of ten ceiling paintings exploring the history of theatre, four are by Gustav Klimt: the one depicting Shakespeare's Globe features the only known self-portrait of the artist.

EXPERIENCE MORE

⑤
Maria-Treu-Kirche

📍C5 🏛Jodok-Fink-Platz
Ⓤ Rathaus 🚌13A 🚊2
🕐For services and by
appointment 🌐maria
treu.at

Flanked by fine monastic
buildings, the Church of Maria
Treu was designed by Johann
Lukas von Hildebrandt in
1716, and later altered by
Matthias Gerl in the 1750s.
The church didn't acquire its
present form until the 19th
century, when the elegant
twin towers were added.

Inside is a vibrant Baroque
frescoed ceiling (1752–3) by
the great Austrian painter
Franz Anton Maulbertsch. A
chapel to the left of the choir
contains an altarpiece with a
Crucifixion dating from about
1774, also by Maulbertsch.

Did You Know?

Austria's Federal
President can veto bills
and dissolve
parliament - but to
date never has.

In front of the church, rising
up from the square is a pillar
with a statue of the Madonna,
with statues of saints and
angels below. Like many such
columns in Vienna, this commemorates delivery from
a plague, in this case the
epidemic of 1713.

---

⑥ Ⓜ
Parlament

📍E6 🏛Dr-Karl-Renner-
Ring 3 Ⓤ Volkstheater
🚊D, 1, 2, 71 🕐Times vary,
check website 🌐parla
ment.gv.at

Architect Theophil Hansen
gave the Parlament (parliament) building and neigh-
bouring Palais Epstein a strict
Neo-Classical style. The
building was constructed as
part of the Ringstrasse
development to act as the
Reichsrat (the parliament of
the Austrian part of the
Habsburg Empire). Work
began in 1874 and finished in
1884. At the foot of the
Parlament's grand
entrance steps are
the bronze *Horse
Tamers* (1901) by
sculptor Josef Lax
and marble figures of

RINGSTRASSE

The 5.3-km (3.3-mile)
Ringstrasse, ordered by
Emperor Franz Joseph
in 1857, took over 50
years to build. Lined
with palaces and
institutions such as
the Kunsthistorisches
Museum and Natur-
historisches Museum,
the boulevard was
intended as a grand
show of imperial power
in the capital of the
Habsburg Empire. A
spin around it is one of
the highlights of any
trip to the city.

Greek and Roman historians.
On the roof there are chariots
and impressive statues of
ancient scholars and states-
men. Before the central
portico, the Athenebrunnen
fountain, by Carl Kundmann,
is dominated by a figure of
Pallas Athene, Greek goddess
of wisdom. In this
splendid setting, on
11 November 1918,
after the collapse of
the Habsburg Empire,
parliamentary dep-
uties proclaimed the
formation of the

→ Historic buildings lining pleasant Spittelbergasse in the heart of Spittelberg

republic of Deutsch-Österreich. It was renamed the Republic of Austria in 1919.

---

❼
Sankt-Ulrichs-Platz

📍D7 🚇Between Neustiftgasse and Burggasse
Ⓤ Volkstheater 🚌48A

This tiny sloping square is an exquisite remnant of early Vienna. The dainty Baroque house at No 27 is worth a look, as is the adjoining house, which escaped destruction by the Turks during the sieges, most probably because their commander Kara Mustafa pitched his own tent nearby.

The Baroque **Ulrichskirche**, built by Josef Reymund in 1721–4, is where composer Christoph Willibald Gluck was married and Johann Strauss the Younger was christened. Handsome patrician houses encircle the square – the prettiest is No 2, the elaborately decorated Schulhaus, dating from the 18th century.

Ulrichskirche
🕐 For services only
🌐 stulrich.com

❽
Spittelberg

📍D7 Ⓤ Volkstheater

Often described as the "village in the city", the pedestrianized area of Spittelberg is the oldest and most colourful part of the district. In the 17th century, the cluster of streets between the charming Siebensterngasse and Burggasse, and around the Spittelberggasse, was Vienna's first immigrant worker district. Its inhabitants were mainly craftsmen, merchants and servants from Croatia and Hungary, brought to work in the court.

The area was rediscovered in the 1970s and the city authorities restored the buildings. Today, it is a district of restaurants, cafés and boutiques, all of which keep the cobbled streets buzzing into the early hours. It hosts a Christmas market, and a regular **Arts and Crafts Market** between April and November. The **Amerlinghaus** theatre at No 8 Stiftgasse serves as the area's cultural and community centre and provides a venue for exhibitions and events.

← The Athenebrunnen fountain in front of the Parlament building

Arts and Crafts Market
🕐Apr–Jun & Sep–Nov: 10am–6pm Sat; Jul & Aug: 2–9pm Sat
🌐spittelberg-markt.at

Amerlinghaus
🕐2–10pm Mon–Fri
🌐amerlinghaus.at

9 (M3)
Neues Rathaus

D5 **Friedrich-Schmidt-Platz 1** **Rathaus** **D, 1, 71** **For tours at 1pm Mon, Wed & Fri; groups by appointment** **wien.gv.at**

The New Town Hall is the seat of the Vienna City and Provincial Assembly. Built in 1872–83 to replace the Altes Rathaus (p80), its design is unashamedly Neo-Gothic in style. The architect, Friedrich von Schmidt, was chosen by the city authorities in a competition for the best design.

The huge central tower is 100 m (325 ft) high and is topped by a 3 m (10 ft) statue of a knight in armour with a lance, dominating the front façade. Known affectionately to locals as the Rathausmann, the figure was designed by Franz Gastell and made by the wrought-iron craftsman Alexander Nehr.

The most attractive feature of the building is the lofty loggia, with its delicate tracery and curved balconies. Around all four sides are Neo-Gothic arcades, together with statues of Austrian worthies. Inside, at the top of the first of two grand staircases, is the *Festsaal*, a ceremonial hall that stretches the length of the building.

In front of the Rathaus is the wide Rathausplatz Park and there are also several courtyards here, one of which is a popular concert venue. There is also an ice rink in the winter.

> INSIDER TIP
> ### Free Tours of the Rathaus
>
> Take a free tour of the Neues Rathaus, which reveals controversies and uncovers the city's lesser-known political secrets (*www.wien.gv.at/english/cityhall/tours.htm*).

10
Neubau Neighbourhood

B7 **Neustiftgasse, Burggasse & Lindengasse**

Vienna's 7th district is perfect for wandering, with bustling shopping streets adorned with murals and trendy bars setting a lively scene.

The area is peppered with independent vintage and interiors boutiques, and organic and ethnic food shops, plus plenty of hip cafés. Restaurant **Landia** offers pleasant vegan fare, and there's great coffee to be had at places like American diner-style **Café Espresso**, which turns into a bar in the evenings.

Neubau is known for its young, student population – it was the first constituency in Austria to vote in a council led by the Green Party in 2001. With an atmosphere comparable to the hipster parts of London or Berlin, a visit to this area makes a refreshing antidote to the respectful silence of the more noble MuseumQuartier institutions.

→

The arcaded courtyard of the historic and much revered University of Vienna

Landia
Ahornergasse 4 **landia.at**

Café Espresso
Burggasse 57 **espresso-wien.at**

11
Dreifaltigkeitskirche

D4 **Alser Strasse 17** **4057225** **Rathaus** **43, 44** **8-11:30am Mon-Sat, 8am-noon Sun**

Built between 1685 and 1727, the Church of the Holy Trinity contains an altarpiece (1708) in the north aisle by the painter Martino Altomonte, and a graphic Crucifix in the south aisle from the workshop of Veit Stoss. It was to this church that Beethoven's body was brought when he died in 1827. Following the funeral service, which was attended by many of his contemporaries, including Schubert and the poet Franz Grillparzer, the cortege bore his coffin to the cemetery at Währing on the

←

The stately Neues Rathaus building, viewed from Rathausplatz Park

city's outskirts. The following year, the church was given three fine new bells, for which Schubert composed a choral work *Glaube, Hoffnung und Liebe* (Faith, Hope and Love).

12

Universität Wien

📍E5 🏛Universitätsring 1 Ⓤ Schottentor 🕐Times vary, check website 🌐univie.ac.at

Founded in 1365 by Duke Rudolf IV, the University of Vienna now has over 90,000 students. The versatile architect Heinrich von Ferstel designed its present home in 1883, adopting an Italian Renaissance style.

From the entrance hall, huge staircases lead up to the university's ceremonial halls. In 1895, Gustav Klimt was commissioned to decorate the hall with frescoes, but the degree of nudity portrayed in some panels proved unacceptable to the authorities. Eventually, when no agreement could be reached, Klimt returned his fee to the government and took back the paintings; they were destroyed during World War II. A spacious arcaded courtyard,

lined with stern busts of the university's most distinguished professors, is located in the centre of the building. Among the figures on display are those of the founder of psychoanalysis Sigmund Freud *(p116)* and philosopher Franz Brentano. Nearby are the smoke-filled and poster-daubed corridors of today's university students.

13

Café Landtmann

📍E5 🏛Universitätsring 4 Ⓤ Schottentor, Herren-gasse 🚋D, 1, 71 🕐7am–midnight daily 🌐landt mann.at

If Café Central *(p109)* is the coffee house of Vienna's intelligentsia, Café Landtmann is surely the coffee house of Vienna's affluent middle classes. Established in 1873 by Franz Landtmann, this was once Sigmund Freud's favourite coffee house – it is still extremely popular. Inside, the walls are adorned with mirrors and elegant wood panelling, and there is a tempting cake display. The terrace is also an attractive setting for coffee and cake, schnitzel, or even cocktails.

EAT

Amerlingbeisl
This traditional *beisl* (bistro) is a well-kept secret, serving delicious seasonal mains, snacks and alpine breakfasts in a crisply designed dining room.

📍D7 🏛Stiftgasse 🌐amerlingbeisl.at

€€€

Justizcafé
A celebrated canteen perched high in the Palace of Justice. You'll need to pass through security to enter, then take the lift to the top – hearty mains and fabulous vistas await.

📍D7 🏛Schmerling-platz 10 🌐justizcafe.at

€€€

Restaurant Vestibül
This upmarket restaurant in the Burgtheater serves traditional dishes with a modern twist, like roasted *tafelspitz* with almond-garlic purée.

📍E6 🏛Universitäts-ring 2 🌐vestibuel.at

€€€

Museum and Town Hall Quarter

14 Mölker Bastei

◉E5 Ⓤ Schottentor
🚋D, 1, 71

Just paces from the bustling Schottentor is the quiet street of Mölker Bastei, built on a former bastion of the city walls. It is graced by some beautiful late-18th-century houses. Beethoven lived here, and the Emperor Franz Joseph nearly met his death on the bastion in 1853 when a tailor attempted to assassinate him.

No 10 is the house where the Belgian Prince Charles de Ligne lived during the Congress of Vienna in 1815. De Ligne wrote several cynical commentaries on the activities of the crowned heads of Europe who came to Vienna at that time. A ladies' man, he caught a fatal chill while waiting for a rendezvous on the bastion.

Did You Know?
In Vienna, Beethoven was a pupil of Wolfgang Amadeus Mozart and then Joseph Haydn.

15 Dreimäderlhaus

◉E5 Ⓐ Schreyvogelgasse
10 Ⓤ Schottentor 🚋D, 1, 71

Houses on one side of the cobbled Schreyvogelgasse are a reminder of Biedermeier Vienna, and the prettiest of all is the Dreimäderlhaus (1803). It is said that Schubert had three sweethearts *(drei Mäderl)* ensconced here, but it is more likely that the house was named after the 1920s operetta *Dreimäderlhaus*, which uses his melodies.

16 Pasqualatihaus

◉E5 Ⓐ Mölker Bastei 8
Ⓤ Schottentor ◷10am–1pm & 2-6pm Tue-Sun
🌐wienmuseum.at

The Pasqualatihaus is no different in appearance from any of the other houses along this lane, but it is the most famous of more than 30 places where Ludwig van Beethoven resided in Vienna.

STAY

Hotel ViennArt am MuseumsQuartier
This stylish 60-room design hotel puts you right in the heart of the MuseumsQuartier, mere steps from the main attractions.

◉D7 Ⓐ Breite Gasse 9
🌐austrotel.at

€€€

Named after its original owner, Baron Johann von Pasqualati, it was Beethoven's home between 1804 and 1808, and from 1810 to 1815. He composed many of his best-loved works here, including Symphonies 4, 5, 7 and 8, the wonderful opera *Fidelio*, Piano Concerto No 4, and numerous string quartets.

Today, the rooms on the fourth floor, which the composer occupied, house

→ Vistors explore Beethoven's life at the Pasqualatihaus museum

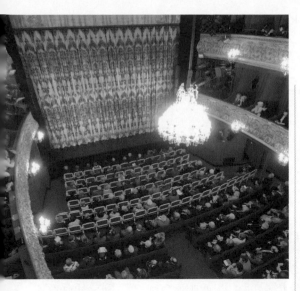

← The rich interior of the
19th-century Theater
in der Josefstadt

18 🔾 🍴

Volkskundemuseum

🔲 C5 🔲 Laudongasse 15-19
🔲 Rathaus 🚌 13A 🚊 3, 33
🕙 10am-5pm Tue-Sun (to
8pm Thu) 🔲 1 Jan, Easter
Mon, 1 May, 1 Nov, 25 Dec
🔲 volkskundemuseum.at

This charming folk museum is
a reminder that Vienna has a
history beyond imperialism.
With artifacts ranging from
the 17th to 19th centuries, the
museum's exhibits reflect the
culture and daily life of people
living in Austria and its neighbouring countries.

The museum is housed in
the 18th-century Schönborn
Palace, designed by Johann
Lukas von Hildebrandt as a
mansion and altered in 1760
by Isidor Canevale.

Today the museum has a
pleasant, reasonably priced
restaurant and a charming
park located to the rear
of the building.

a small museum. Various
intriguing memorabilia is
on display, such as a lock of
Beethoven's hair, a photo-
graph of his grave at Währing
cemetery, a rather gruesome
deathbed engraving and
early editions of his scores.
The museum also contains
busts and paintings of the
great composer, including a
famous portrait by Willibrord
Joseph Mähler, and a fine
painting of his patron Prince
Rasumofsky, the Russian
ambassador to Vienna.

17

Theater in der
Josefstadt

🔲 C6 🔲 Josefstädter
Strasse 26 🔲 Rathaus
🚌 13A 🚊 2 🔲 For perfor-
mances 🔲 josefstadt.org

This intimate theatre, one of
the oldest still standing in
Vienna, has enjoyed an illustrious history. Founded in
1788, it was rebuilt by Joseph
Kornhäusel in 1822, and has
been in operation ever since,
accommodating ballet, opera
and theatre performances.
Beethoven composed his
overture *The Consecration*

of the House for the reopening
of the theatre after its renovation, conducting it himself at
the reopening gala.

In 1924, the director Max
Reinhardt supervised the
further restoration of the
theatre, and introduced an
ambitious modern repertoire
of contemporary comedy,
classic plays and musicals.

THE VIENNESE BALL SEASON

There's nothing more quintessentially Viennese
than a ball, a Habsburg-era tradition that continues
to thrive to this day. Between November and February
more than 450 grand and elegant balls take place
across the city, although things reach a climax during
the carnival season in January and February. Some of
the most famous annual balls include the Vienna Red
Cross Ball in November, the New Year's Eve Ball at the
Hofburg and the Hunters' Ball in January.

A SHORT WALK
JOSEFSTADT

Distance 1.5 km (1 mile) **Nearest U-Bahn**
Rathaus **Time** 25 minutes

Tucked behind the grand museums of the Ringstrasse
is the 18th-century district known as Josefstadt, named
after Emperor Joseph I. Although outside the inner city,
Josefstadt has a vibrant cultural life, with a popular theatre,
many good restaurants, handsome churches and museums,
and is best seen by foot. Students from the university and
lawyers from the courthouses provide a varied clientele for
the district's many establishments.

*Founded by the fathers
of the Piarist order,
Maria-Treu-Kirche was
built from 1716 (p142).*

*The **Plague Column**
here commemorates
an epidemic that
occurred in 1713.*

↑ The elegant façade of the
Baroque Maria-Treu-Kirche

*Founded in 1788, **Theater in
der Josefstadt** has kept its
doors open continuously
since it was rebuilt by Josef
Kornhäusel in 1822.*

PIARISTENGASSE

JOSEFSTÄDTER STRASSE

0 metres   50
0 yards   50   N

START

ZELTGASSE

*Built for servants and workers
in the 18th century, the
cottages lining this courtyard
on Lange Gasse have changed
very little over the years.*

FINISH

Locator Map
For more detail see p126

LAUDONGASSE

KOCHGASSE

FLORIANIGASSE

MARIA TREU GASSE

LANGE GASSE

The **Volkskunde Museum** *in the Schönborn Palace houses exhibits examining folklore and rural life in Austria (p147).*

Schönborn Park *is a secluded, leafy retreat. Among the sculptures here is a bust (1974) of the composer Edmund Eysler by Leo Gruber.*

No 53 Lange Gasse *has handsome statuary on its gates. It was built in the early 18th century when Vienna was expanding beyond the old city walls.*

Alte Backstube *was a working bakery from 1701 to 1963.*

→
Theater in der Josefstadt, Vienna's oldest theatre

Ceramic façade patterning Otto Wagner's Majolikahaus

OPERA AND NASCHMARKT

This area has been home to the great sprawling Naschmarkt since the late 18th century, although the origins of the market are not entirely clear. It is thought that the bazaar derives its name from that of an earlier dairy market on this site, the Aschenmarkt, where milk was traded in containers made from ash wood *(asch)*. But the name more likely stems from the exotic fare lining the market stalls, ready to nibble *(naschen)*.

From the early 1800s this mercantile centre expanded as imported goods flowed in from across the empire, arriving on the Danube canal. In the 19th century, the Wien river, which cuts through Vienna, was paved over and the market sprawled further, extending along the bustling thoroughfare of the Linke Wienzeile.

In the north of the district, the Staatsoper was completed in 1869 in typical Neo-Renaissance style, the first building of Emperor Joseph II's opulent Ringstrasse boulevard. At the turn of the century, great and controversial monuments of *Jugendstil* architecture sprang up, including Joseph Maria Olbrich's Secession Building and Otto Wagner's richly embellished apartment blocks.

OPERA AND NASCHMARKT

Must Sees
1 Wiener Secession
2 Staatsoper

Experience More
3 Naschmarkt
4 Theater an der Wien
5 Hotel Sacher
6 Akademie der bildenden Künste Wien
7 Mariahilfer Strasse
8 Haus des Meeres – Aqua Terra Zoo
9 Wagner Apartments
10 Kaiserliches Hofmobiliendepot
11 Third Man Museum

Eat
① Heuer am Karlsplatz
② Café Sacher

Drink
③ Sekt Comptoir
④ Ebert's Cocktail Bar
⑤ Café Phil

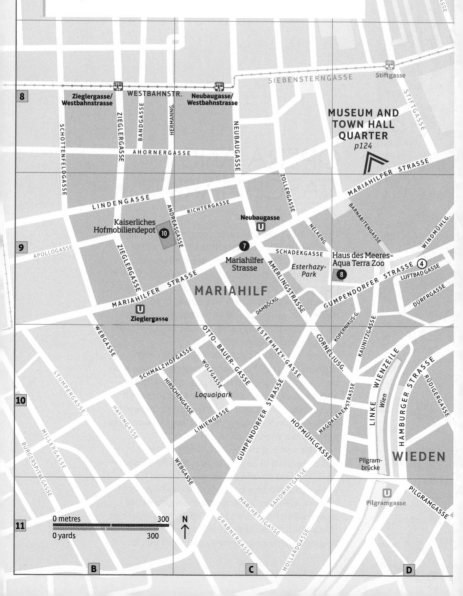

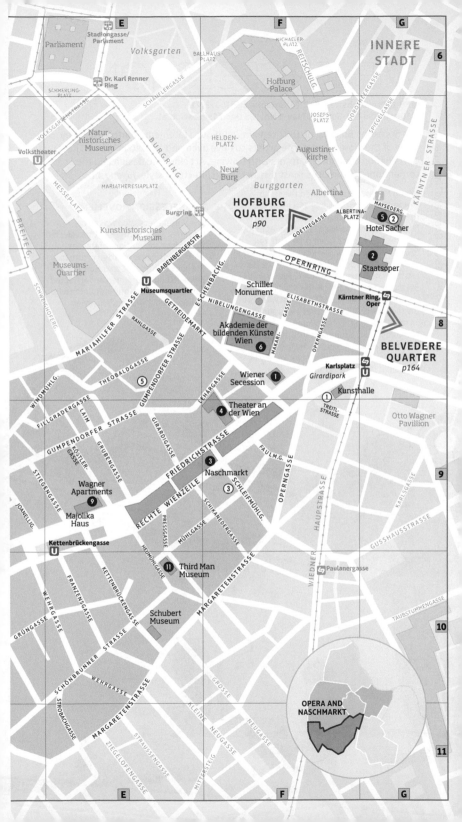

E · F · G

6 · INNERE STADT

Parliament
Stadiongasse/Parlament
Volksgarten
BALLHAUS-PLATZ
MICHAELER-PLATZ
Hofburg Palace

Dr. Karl Renner Ring
SCHENKENSTRASSE
SCHMERLING-PLATZ
VOLKSGARTENSTRASSE

Naturhistorisches Museum
BURGRING
HELDEN-PLATZ
Neue Burg
Burggarten

7

Volkstheater U

JOSEFS-PLATZ
Augustinerkirche

DOROTHEERGASSE
SPIEGELGASSE

KÄRNTNER STRASSE

MARIATHERESIAPLATZ
MESSEPLATZ

Albertina

BREITE G.
Museums-Quartier
Kunsthistorisches Museum
HOFBURG QUARTER *p90*
GOETHEGASSE
ALBERTINA-PLATZ
MAYSEDERG.
Hotel Sacher **5** **2**

SCHWEIGHOFERG.
Burgring
OPERNRING
Staatsoper **2**

BABENBERGERSTR.
ESCHENBACHG.
Schiller Monument
NIBELUNGENGASSE
ELISABETHSTRASSE
Kärntner Ring, Oper

8

Museumsquartier U
GETREIDEMARKT
Akademie der bildenden Künste Wien **6**
MAKARTI-GASSE
OPERNGASSE

MARIAHILFER STRASSE
RAHLGASSE
GUMPENDORFER STRASSE
LEHARGASSE
Wiener Secession **1**
Karlsplatz
Girardipark
BELVEDERE QUARTER *p164*

THEOBALDGASSE
(5)
Karlsplatz U
Kunsthalle (1)
TREITL-STRASSE

WINDMÜHLG.
FILLGRADERGASSE
GUMPENDORFER STRASSE
GIRARDIGASSE
Theater an der Wien **4**
FAULM.G.
Otto Wagner Pavillion

9

LAIM
KÖSTLER-GASSE
GRUBENGASSE
FRIEDRICHSTRASSE
Naschmarkt **3**
SCHIKANEDERGASSE
SCHLEIFMÜHLG.
OPERNGASSE
HAUPTSTRASSE
KARLSGASSE

STIEGENGASSE
Wagner Apartments **9**
RECHTE WIENZEILE
(3)
GUSSHAUSSTRASSE

JOANELLIG.
Majolika Haus
PRESSGASSE
MÜHLGASSE
WIEDNER

Kettenbrückengasse U
Paulanergasse

HEUMÜHLGASSE
Third Man Museum **11**
MARGARETENSTRASSE

10

WEHRGASSE
FRANZENSGASSE
KETTENBRÜCKENGASSE
Schubert Museum
TAUBSTUMMENGASSE

GRÜNGASSE
SCHÖNBRUNNER STRASSE
GROSSE NEUGASSE

WEHRGASSE
MARGARETENSTRASSE
KLEINE NEUGASSE
OPERA AND NASCHMARKT

11

STROBACHGASSE
ZIEGELOFENGASSE
STRAUSSENGASSE
MITTERSTEIG

E · F · G

WIENER SECESSION

📍F8 🏠 Friedrichstrasse 12 Ⓤ Karlsplatz 🚊D, 1, 2, 71
🕐10am–6pm Tue–Sun 🚫1 May, 1 Nov, 25 Dec 🌐secession.at

The Secession Building of 1897 remains a unique statement of intent made by some of the most avant-garde artists to have lived and worked in Vienna. Its combination of geometric forms with flowing, Art Nouveau design laid the cornerstone for the city's most distinctive architectural style, *Jugendstil*.

Joseph Maria Olbrich designed the striking, almost windowless building as a showcase for the Secession movement's artists. With its filigree globe of entwined laurel leaves on the roof, the building is a squat cube with four towers. The Secessionist motto, emblazoned in gold on the façade, states, "To every age its art, to art its freedom". Inside, Gustav Klimt's *Beethoven Frieze* of 1902 is the building's best-known feature and one of the finest works of the movement. It covers three walls and is 34 m (110 ft) long. It shows interrelated groups of figures and is a commentary on Beethoven's Ninth Symphony. Alongside the building there is an extraordinary statue of Mark Antony in his chariot (1899), by Arthur Strasser.

THE SECESSION MOVEMENT

The Vienna Secession was an art movement formed in 1897 that rejected the artistic conventions of the day, seeking to release creativity from the confines of academic tradition. Led by Gustav Klimt, the movement attracted painters, sculptors and architects who championed the *Jugendstil* style.

1 The storm god Typhon and his daughters stand amid images of misery and vice on Klimt's *Beethoven Frieze*.

2 Arthur Strasser's statue of Mark Anthony depicts a corpulent, lazy figure, perhaps symbolizing the complacency of old regimes.

3 Three Gorgons decorate the façade, representing Painting, Architecture and Sculpture.

TOP 4 FEATURES OF THE SECESSION BUILDING

Gorgons' heads
The mythical demons sit above the legend "Painting, Architecture and Sculpture".

Dome
The great dome is made from 2,500 gilt laurel leaves and 311 berries.

Planters
Look out for the turtles that support massive plant pots on either side of the entrance.

Owl Reliefs
Koloman Moser's wise birds can be found on the side of the building.

←

The Wiener Secession, as breathtaking today as when it first opened

② ⊘ Ⓜ ▭

STAATSOPER

📍 G8 🏛 Opernring 2, A-1010 Ⓤ Karlsplatz 🚋 D, 1, 2, 71 🕐 Check website for performances and guided tour timings 🌐 wiener-staatsoper.at

Within the lavish auditorium of this Viennese institution, traditional classical music, opera and ballet live on. With its exceptional accoustics and a vibrant programme of over 350 performances each season, the great, grand State Opera house is surely the finest performance space in the city.

The first of the buildings on the Ringstrasse (*p142*) to be completed, the Vienna State Opera House opened on 25 May 1869 to the strains of Mozart's *Don Giovanni*. Though built in elaborate, Neo-Renaissance style, it initially failed to impress the Viennese. Yet when it was hit by a bomb in 1945 and largely destroyed, the event was seen as a symbolic blow to the city. With a new auditorium and stage using the latest technology, the Staatsoper reopened on 5 November 1955 with a performance of Beethoven's *Fidelio*.

↑ The façade of the Staatsoper, uplit at night

Painted reliefs above the main staircase

The main staircase is embellished with statues of the seven liberal arts.

The Schwind Foyer, decorated with scenes by Moritz von Schwind.

Main entrance

Franz Joseph used to spend the intervals in this graceful tea room.

The Staatsoper, designed by ↑ architects Eduard van der Nüll and August Siccardsburg in 1861–9

Auditorium

The auditorium, rebuilt to original 1869 designs after its destruction in World War II ↑

> **INSIDER TIP**
> **Standing Room Tickets**
>
> Opera tickets can be very pricey and sell out far in advance. But if you're willing to queue on the day, there are often a limited number of standing tickets for as little as €2 to €4. Visit the Stehplätze (standing room) ticket office 80 minutes before the performance.

Terraces can be enjoyed during the intermission.

The Gustav Mahler salon is hung with modern tapestries of scenes from The Magic Flute.

Two graceful fountains by Josef Gasser stand on either side of the opera house.

VIENNA OPERA BALL

On the last Thursday of the Vienna Carnival *(p52)*, the stage is extended to cover the seats in the auditorium, creating space for the Opera Ball. This extravagant social event is opened by debutantes in white dresses and attended by around 5,000 guests, including international celebrities, who waltz the night away in opulent surrounds.

EXPERIENCE MORE

3

Naschmarkt

📍F9 Ⓤ Karlsplatz, Kettenbrückengasse
🕐6am-6:30pm Mon-Fri, 6am-6pm Sat ⓦnasch markt-vienna.com

↑ Buyers inspecting fresh produce at the lively Naschmarkt

Vienna's liveliest market has a huge variety of stalls and some of the best snack bars in the city. In the western section of the market, you'll find flowers, farm produce and wine, as well as cakes, bread and meats. Held each Saturday, the lively flea market mixes professional antique dealers with pure junk, and makes for a fun morning activity. There are certainly bargains to be had here, but it also pays to be aware – no returns are accepted.

At No 6 Kettenbrückengasse, by the U-Bahn, is the simple flat where Franz Schubert died in 1828. Today this is the **Schubert Museum** (it is signposted as the "Schubert Sterbewohnung"). This tiny two-room flat and music studio, housing an elaborate grand piano and a meagre scattering of personal effects, is perhaps the most haunting of all memorials to the great classical composer.

Schubert Museum
📞5816730 🕐10am-1pm, 2-6pm Wed & Thu

EAT

Heuer am Karlsplatz
Expect modern twists on Austrian classics, made with organic and locally sourced ingredients.

📍F8 🏠Treitlstrasse 2 ⓦheuer-amkarls platz.com

€€€

Café Sacher
This stylish venue offers exquisite coffees and high-quality traditional cuisine.

📍G7 🏠Philhar-monikerstrasse 4 ⓦsacher.com

€€€

4

Theater an der Wien

📍F9 🏠Linke Wienzeile 6
Ⓤ Karlsplatz 🚌59A
🕐For performances and occasional guided tours twice a month; call 588302015 for details
ⓦtheater-wien.at

Emanuel Schikaneder, a friend of Mozart, founded this theatre in 1801; a statue above the entrance shows him playing Papageno in Mozart's *The Magic Flute*. The premiere of Beethoven's *Fidelio* was staged here in 1805. The theatre remained closed for a number of years until it opened its doors once more in 2006, the 250th anniversary of Mozart's birth. Today it is the oldest standing theatre in the city and, following its rejuvenation, hosts popular

↑ The sumptuous auditorium of the Theater an der Wien

↑ The elegant Blaue Bar in the luxurious Hotel Sacher

360,000

"Original" Sachertorten are produced by the Hotel Sacher each year.

operas, dance performances and classical concerts along with lectures and symposiums.

---

5 Hotel Sacher

📍 G7 🏠 Philharmoniker-strasse 4 Ⓤ Karlsplatz
🌐 sacher.com

This grand five-star hotel and Viennese institution was founded by the son of Franz Sacher, who, according to some, was the creator of the "original" Sachertorte in 1832.

The hotel came into its own under Anna Sacher. The cigar-smoking daughter-in-law of the founder ran the hotel from 1892 until her death in 1930. During her time the Sacher became a venue for the extra-marital affairs of

the rich and noble. It is still a discreetly sumptuous hotel with a gorgeous café.

Akademie der bildenden Künste Wien

📍 F8 🏠 Schillerplatz 3
Ⓤ Karlsplatz 🚊 D, 1, 2, 71
🔒 Closed for renovations
🌐 akademiegalerie.at

Theophil Hansen built the Academy of Fine Arts between 1872 and 1876. The teaching academy is closed to visitors until 2020. Its small but exquisite painting collection, which includes late Gothic and early Renaissance works, and Hieronymus Bosch's *Last Judgment*, is in the meantime on display at the Hofburg Quarter's **Theatermuseum**.

Theatermuseum
🏠 Lobkowitzplatz 2, 1010
🕐 10am–6pm Wed–Mon
🌐 theatermuseum.at

TOP 5 **AUSTRIAN CAKES**

Sachertorte
The rich chocolate cake filled with apricot jam, allegedly invented by Franz Sacher in 1832.

Linzertorte
A crisp almond pastry filled with jam, hailing from the city of Linz.

Dobostorte
An eight-tiered sponge cake layered with chocolate buttercream and caramel.

Esterházy Torte
Named for the diplomat Prince Esterházy, this Hungarian dessert is popular in Vienna.

Apfelstrudel
Austria's simple buttery apple strudel is second to none.

7

Mariahilfer Strasse

📍 C9 Ⓤ Zieglergasse, Neubaugasse

This is one of Vienna's busiest pedestrianized shopping streets. On the corner of Stiftgasse is the **Stiftkirche.** The architect is unknown, but the church dates from 1739. The façade is an austere pyramidal structure, rising to a bulbous steeple, and has some lively Rococo reliefs set into the walls. Opposite, at No 45, is the house where the playwright Ferdinand Raimund was born in 1790. Its cobbled courtyard is lined with shops. Baroque-style **Mariahilfer Kirche**, dominated by two towers with large steeples, is named after a 16th-century cult of the Virgin Mary, which was founded at the Mariahilfer Kirche in Passau.

Stiftkirche
🕐 7:30am–6pm Mon–Fri, 7am–11pm Sat, 8:30am–9:30pm Sun

Mariahilfer Kirche
🕐 8am–7pm Mon–Sat, 8:30am–7pm Sun

8

Haus des Meeres – Aqua Terra Zoo

📍 D9 🏛 Fritz-Grünbaum-Platz 1 🕐 9am–6pm daily 🌐 haus-des-meeres.at

This aquarium and zoo, which is a sure-fire hit with kids,

occupies one of Vienna's *Flaktürme* – huge concrete towers built during World War II as anti-aircraft defence installations and air-raid shelters. Some 10,000 creatures call this place home. Terrariums house crocodiles and poisonous snakes, and sea water aquariums teem with sharks, sea turtles, stunning tropical fish and corals. Sea life such as urchins, crustateae and starfish from southern Europe dwell in the Mediterranean Sea section, and there is even a tropical house devoted to birds and monkeys. One of the most popular attractions is the 300,000-litre (66,000-gallon) shark tank, Austria's largest aquarium, which is home to blacktip, whitetip and bamboo sharks, and a rescued sea turtle. Feeding time reliably draws crowds.

 GREAT VIEW
Flak Tower

At the Haus des Meeres, take the lift to the top of this World War II defence tower for unique views across the city. It's particularly impressive when the sun is setting behind the mountains.

9

Wagner Apartments

📍 E9 🏛 Linke Wienzeile 38 & 40 Ⓤ Kettenbrückengasse

Overlooking the Naschmarkt are two remarkable apartment buildings. Designed by Otto Wagner in 1899, they represent the apex of Secessionist *Jugendstil*. No 38 has sparkling gilt ornamentation, mostly by Kolo Moser. No 40, known as the Majolikahaus after the glazed pottery used for surface decoration, is the more striking. The façade has subtle flower patterns in pink, blue and green. Even the sills are moulded and decorated. No 42 next door, in grand Historicist style, shows what the Secession architecture was reacting against.

> **Terrariums house crocodiles and poisonous snakes, and sea water aquariums teem with sharks, sea turtles, stunning tropical fish and corals.**

←

The richly decorated façades of the Wagner Apartments overlooking the Naschmarkt

10

Kaiserliches Hofmobiliendepot

📍B9 🏠Andreasgasse 7 🚇Zieglergasse 🕐10am–6pm Tue–Sun 🌐hof mobiliendepot.at

The imperial furniture collection, founded by Maria Theresa in 1747, provides an intimate portrait of the Habsburg way of life, as well as a detailed historical record of Viennese interior decoration and cabinet-making in the 18th and 19th centuries. Also included in the collection are pieces created by artists and designers of the early 20th century. Room after room is filled with outstanding furnishings and royal domestic objects, ranging from a faithful recreation of the Empress Elisabeth's Schönbrunn Palace apartments to a simple folding throne that was used while travelling. The exhibits, which range from the mundane to the priceless and often eccentric, provide a fascinating and evocative insight into the everyday lives of the imperial family.

11

Third Man Museum

📍E10 🏠Pressgasse 25 🕐2–6pm Sat 🚇Sun–Fri 🌐3mpc.net

The brainchild of two film enthusiasts, Gerhard Strassgschwandtner and Karin Höfler, this private museum must be the only one in the world to focus on a single film – the 1949 Oscar-winning classic *The Third Man*. Film buffs will find plenty to explore here, with 2,300 exhibits spread out over 13 rooms, including the zither used by Anton Karas to play the film's acclaimed soundtrack, and the cameras that shot famous scenes on the streets of Vienna. Displays explore the experience of life in post-World War II Vienna, a city divided between the four states of the USA, Great Britain, France and the USSR. The museum also hosts monthly zither concerts.

DRINK

Sekt Comptoir
Sample Austrian *sekt* (sparkling wine) from Burgenland's Szigeti vineyards at this bar by the Naschmarkt.

📍F9 🏠Schleifmühl-gasse 19 🕐Sun 🌐sektcomptoir.at

Ebert's Cocktail Bar
This stylish, minimalist cocktail bar is staffed by expert bartenders and mixologists from the bartending school next door.

📍D9 🏠Gumpendorfer Strasse 51 🕐Sun–Wed 🌐eberts.at

Café Phil
This hip bookshop-café comes alive after hours with good drinks and trendy DJs.

📍E8 🏠Gumpendorfer Strasse 10 🌐phil.info

↑ Visitors viewing imperial possessions in the Kaiserliches Hofmobiliendepot

A SHORT WALK
OPERNRING

Distance 2 km (1 mile) **Nearest U-Bahn**
Karlsplatz **Time** 30 minutes

Between the Opera House and Karlskirche, two
of the great landmarks of Vienna, lies an area that
typifies the varied culture of the city. Here, you'll pass
an 18th-century theatre, a 19th-century art academy
and the Secession Building. Mixed in with these
cultural monuments are emblems of the Viennese
devotion to good living: the Hotel Sacher, as
sumptuous today as it was a century ago; the
Café Museum, still as popular as it was in the early
20th century; and the hurly-burly of the colourful
Naschmarkt, where you can buy everything from
oysters and exotic fruits to second-hand clothes.

↑ The glittering dome
above the entrance to
the Secession Building

*The **Goethe Statue** was
designed by Edmund
Hellmer in 1890.*

*The **Schiller
Statue** stands
in the charming
park in front of
the Academy of
Fine Arts.*

*The Italianate
**Academy of Fine
Arts** building is
home to one of the
best collections of
Old Masters in
Vienna (p159).*

ELISA BETHSTRASSE

SCHILLERPLATZ

NIBELUN GENGASS

MAKARTGASSE

*Built in 1898 as a showroom
for the Secession artists, the
Secession Building houses
the Beethoven Frieze by
Gustav Klimt (p154).*

*The **Mark Anthony
Statue** (1899),outside
the Secession Building, is
a decadent bronze work
by Arthur Strasser.*

GETREIDEMARKT

*Today, the 18th-century
Theater an der Wien
is used as an opera
house (p158). It has
been the venue for many
premieres, among them
Beethoven's Fidelio.*

MILLÖCK ERGASSE

LINKE WIENZEILE

*The **Naschmarkt**
sells everything from
fresh farm produce
to bric-a-brac (p158).
It is liveliest early on
Saturday mornings.*

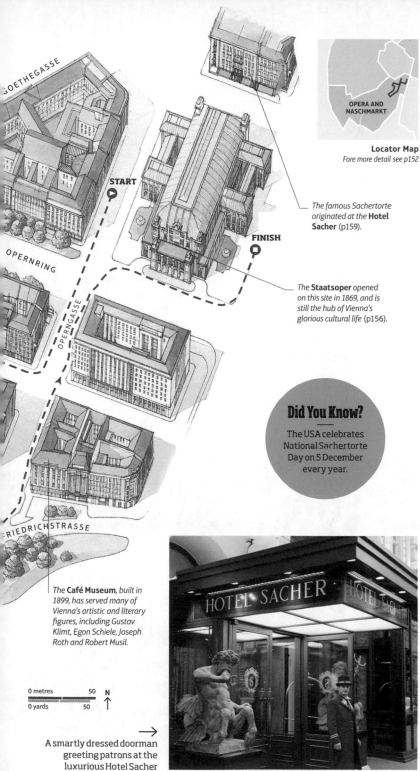

GOETHEGASSE

OPERNRING

OPERNGASSE

FRIEDRICHSTRASSE

START

FINISH

Locator Map
Fore more detail see p152

OPERA AND
NASCHMARKT

The famous Sachertorte
originated at the **Hotel
Sacher** (p159).

The **Staatsoper** opened
on this site in 1869, and is
still the hub of Vienna's
glorious cultural life (p156).

Did You Know?

The USA celebrates
National Sachertorte
Day on 5 December
every year.

The **Café Museum**, built in
1899, has served many of
Vienna's artistic and literary
figures, including Gustav
Klimt, Egon Schiele, Joseph
Roth and Robert Musil.

0 metres   50
0 yards   50

N ↑

→
A smartly dressed doorman
greeting patrons at the
luxurious Hotel Sacher

Fountains in front of the graceful Belvedere Palace

BELVEDERE QUARTER

The grandiose and extravagant Belvedere Quarter extends into the southeastern suburbs of the city. For decades, Vienna had been under threat and siege from the Ottoman Empire, but in 1683, the Turks were defeated at the Battle of Vienna by the Habsburgs' imperial forces. With the Ottoman threat abated, the imperial court turned its energy towards regeneration of the city, and as such the quarter is shaped by masterpieces of 18th-century Baroque architecture.

The palaces and beautiful gardens that lend this quarter its name were designed by the court architect Johan Lukas von Hildebrandt, and constructed from 1714 to 1723. The Belvedere was the summer residence for Prince Eugene of Savoy, the military commander whose strategies had helped vanquish the Turks. The richly Baroque Karlskirche was designed by von Hildebrandt's rival, Fischer von Erlach, and completed in 1737. It was commissioned by Emperor Karl VI to honour St Charles Borromeo, patron saint of the plague, following Vienna's deliverance from one of the last great outbreaks of disease which had decimated the city's population in 1713.

Maria Theresa had the palaces transformed into museums, installing the Imperial Picture Gallery with works from private Habsburg collections in the Upper Belvedere. The gardens first opened to the public in 1779 and the gallery in 1780.

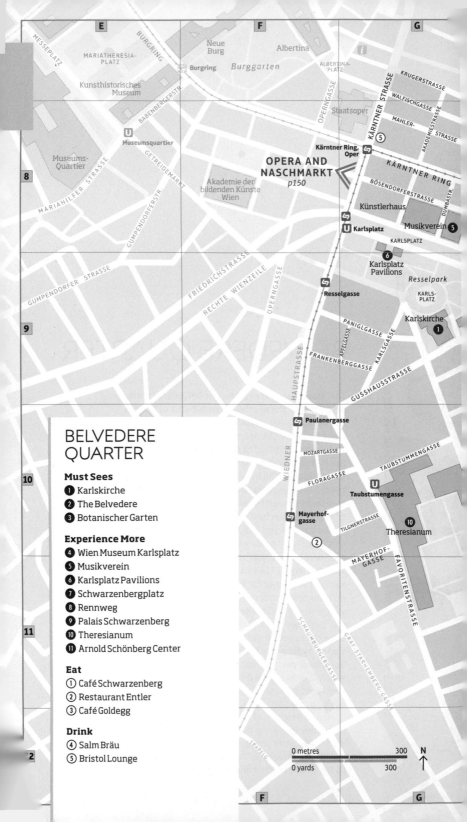

BELVEDERE QUARTER

Must Sees
1. Karlskirche
2. The Belvedere
3. Botanischer Garten

Experience More
4. Wien Museum Karlsplatz
5. Musikverein
6. Karlsplatz Pavilions
7. Schwarzenbergplatz
8. Rennweg
9. Palais Schwarzenberg
10. Theresianum
11. Arnold Schönberg Center

Eat
① Café Schwarzenberg
② Restaurant Entler
③ Café Goldegg

Drink
④ Salm Bräu
⑤ Bristol Lounge

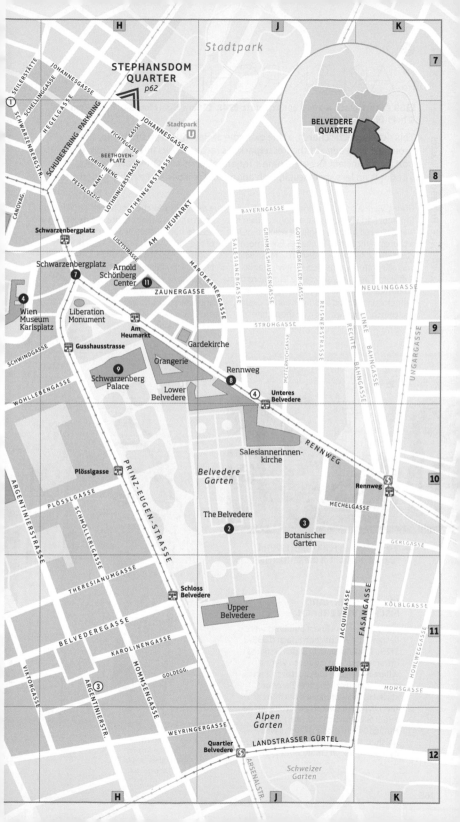

❶ ⚲ Ⓜ

KARLSKIRCHE

📍G9 🚇Karlsplatz, A-1040 ⓊKarlsplatz 🚌4A 🕐9am-6pm Mon-Sat, noon-7pm Sun & hols 🌐karlskirche.at

This richly eclectic church, a fine example of Baroque craftsmanship, sits proudly on the edge of the Resselpark. Its façade draws influence from the porticos of ancient Greece, Rome's Trajan columns and Oriental minarets. The interior is no less spectacular, with abundant frescoes and a richly gilded alter.

EXPERIENCE Belvedere Quarter

During Vienna's plague epidemic of 1713, Emperor Karl VI vowed that as soon as the city was delivered from its plight he would build a church dedicated to St Charles Borromeo (1538–84), a former Archbishop of Milan who was celebrated for the help he gave plague sufferers. The epidemic would claim more than 8,000 lives in Vienna. The following year, the Emperor announced a competition to design the church, which was won by the architect Johann Bernhard Fischer von Erlach. The result

was the Karlskirche (St Charles' Church). The church's two huge columns are decorated with scenes from the life of St Borromeo. A statue of the saint stands atop the Classical portico, designed by Lorenzo Mattielli. Building took almost 25 years, and the interior was embellished with carvings and altarpieces by leading architects Daniel Gran and Martino Altomonte.

↑ Henry Moore's *Hill Arches* (1973) in the pond in front of the Karlskirche

Internal stairway (closed to public)

Two Chinese pavilion-inspired gatehouses lead to side entrances.

JOHANN BERNHARD FISCHER VON ERLACH

Many of Vienna's finest buildings were designed by Fischer von Erlach (1656-1723). The Graz-born architect studied in Rome, and then moved to Vienna, where he became the court architect and a leading exponent of Baroque style. His designs include Karlskirche, the Salzburg university church and the initial plans for Schönbrunn Palace. He died before the Karlskirche was finished; the cathedral was completed by his son, Joseph Emanuel, in 1737.

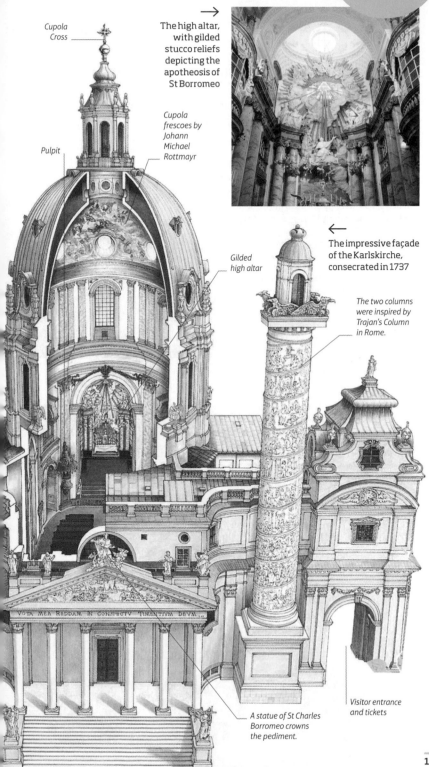

Cupola Cross

→ The high altar, with gilded stucco reliefs depicting the apotheosis of St Borromeo

Cupola frescoes by Johann Michael Rottmayr

Pulpit

Gilded high altar

← The impressive façade of the Karlskirche, consecrated in 1737

The two columns were inspired by Trajan's Column in Rome.

VOTA MEA REDDAM IN CONSPECTV TIMENTIVM DEVM.

Visitor entrance and tickets

A statue of St Charles Borromeo crowns the pediment.

② ⊗ ⊗ ⊗ ⊗ ⊗

THE BELVEDERE

📍 J10 🏠 Upper: Prinz-Eugen-Strasse 27, A-1030; Lower: Rennweg 6, A-1030 🚇 Upper: Quartier Belvedere Ⓤ Upper: Südtirolerplatz 🚊 Upper: D, O, 18; Lower: D, 71 🚌 Upper: 69A 🕐 10am–6pm daily (to 9pm Fri) 🌐 belvedere.at

The Belvedere was constructed by Johann Lukas von Hildebrandt as the summer residence of Prince Eugene of Savoy, the brilliant military commander whose strategies helped vanquish the Turks in 1683. Everything here reflects glory – from the magnificence of the palace interiors, through the carefully landscaped gardens, to the copper roofs in the shape of Turkish tents, a sly allusion to the great victory.

Situated on a gently sloping hill, the Belvedere consists of two palaces linked by a formal garden laid out in the French style by designer Dominique Girard. Standing at the highest point of the garden, the Upper Belvedere (completed in 1723) is the larger and grander of the two, with a more elaborate façade than the Lower Belvedere. In addition to the impressive interiors of the Sala Terrena with its sweeping staircase, Prince Eugene's sumptuous private chapel and the Marble Hall, the building now houses an Austrian art collection with works ranging from the Middle Ages to the present day. Here, works by Klimt are the star attractions, but look out, too, for paintings by fellow Austrians Egon Schiele and Oskar Kokoschka, and by Monet and van Gogh.

Building of the Lower Belvedere was completed first, in 1716. Now used for themed exhibitions, it has its own two-storey Marble Hall, where Eugene is depicted as Apollo. Other attractions include the state bedrooms, the Hall of Grotesques and the Marble Gallery. The Lower Belvedere incorporates the Orangery and the palace stables, both of which are also used for art exhibitions. Pieces are often loaned from galleries and museums worldwide, supplementing the Belvedere's collection

KLIMT AT THE BELVEDERE

A place of pilgrimage for Klimt fans, the Belvedere holds the largest collection of the Viennese artist's work, some 24 oil paintings, and one of his sketchbooks. The museum's undisputed highlight is the artist's most famous painting, *The Kiss (1907–8)*, an instantly recognizable gilded image from his Golden Period.

↑ Copper roofs of the Upper Belvedere echoing the immaculate lawns

↑ Prince Eugene basking in glory, being lauded by History and Fame, on the Marble Hall ceiling

Timeline

1723
Upper Belvedere completed.

1752
▽ Habsburgs acquire the Belvedere.

1897
▽ Archduke Franz Ferdinand, heir to the throne, moves to the Upper Belvedere.

1955
▽ The Austrian State Treaty signed in the Marble Hall.

↑ Klimt's perilously perched lovers, wrapped in an embrace for *The Kiss*

Exploring the Belvedere Gardens

From the imposing wrought iron gate at the top, with its "S" for Savoy and cross of Savoy, to the arch of triumph at the bottom, everything at the Belvedere trumpets Prince Eugene's glory. The flattering Classical and heroic references that pervade the two palaces continue into the gardens, which are a delight to explore. The garden's designer Girard, trained with André le Nôtre at Versailles, and the influence french formal garden style is evident here. The three levels each convey Classical allusions: the lower part of the garden represents the domain of the Four Elements, the centre is Parnassus and the upper section is Olympus, home of the gods.

The Baroque main gate (1728) by Arnold and Konrad Küffner

The lively façade of the Upper Belvedere, dominating the formal landscaped gardens

Water flows from an upper basin over five shallow steps in the Upper Cascade

Putti *(cherubs) representing the 12 months flank these steps*

Nymphs and goddesses in the Lower Cascade

Statues of the Eight Muses

Bosquet or hedge garden

Entrance to Lower Belvedere from Rennweg

Lower Belvedere north façade

Triumphal gate to Lower Belvedere

THE ORANGERY

Next door to the Lower Belvedere is the handsome Orangery building, originally used to shelter tender garden plants in winter and now transformed into an exhibition hall retaining its original character. It previously housed the Museum of Austrian Medieval Art but now has regularly changing temporary exhibitions. Next to the "White Cube", the southern side gallery corridor offers a spectacular view of the Privy Garden and the Upper Belvedere.

Entrance to Upper Belvedere and gardens from Prinz-Eugen-Strasse

① Girard, a master of hydraulics, designed the impressive cascades and fountains that divide the garden levels.

② Maria Theresa added gilded panelling to the Lower Belvedere's Gold Cabinet.

③ A guard of honour of clipped topiary on the approach to the Lower Belvedere.

Statues of sphinxes, their lion bodies representing strength and their human heads intelligence

Privy Garden, the prince's private space

Did You Know?

Literally meaning "beautiful views", a *belvedere* is a building that commands fine prospects.

Orangery

Palace Stables

Entrance to Orangery

↑ The Belvedere Palace and its geometrically designed gardens

Did You Know?
—
Vienna is a very bee-friendly city – close to 130 species have been recorded at the Botanical Garden.

③

BOTANISCHER GARTEN

📍 J10 🏛 Rennweg 14 🚇 Rennweg, Unterest Belvedere
🕐 10am–dusk daily 🌐 botanik.univie.ac.at/hbv

Home to over 12,000 plant species, Vienna University's beautifully landscaped Botanical Garden is a tranquil spot in the Austrian capital. This green retreat is far less busy than the neighbouring Belvedere gardens.

The Botanischer Garten der Universität Wien was created in 1754 by Maria Theresa and her physician Van Swieten for the cultivation of medicinal herbs. Extended and opened to the public in the 19th century, it remains a centre for the study of plant sciences as part of the University of Vienna's Institute of Botany. It is divided into a number of themed areas, including the Flora of Austria and an Alpine Garden. For many visitors the two huge sequoia trees are the undoubted highlight, while youngsters will be intrigued by the huge display of carnivorous plants. In all there are more than 12,000 different species on display from across six continents.

TOP 3 STRANGEST PLANTS

Vanilla Orchid
This beauty from Madagascar, with its trailing stems of greenish-yellow, flowers, can grow to 3 m (10 ft) in length.

Sacred Lotus
Lotus leaves are so resistant to water that water droplets maintain their shape on them, like bright jewels.

Giant Rhubarb
The Chilean *Gunnera tinctoria* may look much like common rhubarb, but it is in fact no relation. Its huge leaves can grow to a substantial 2.5 m (8 ft) across.

↑ Visitors exploring a display of weird and wonderful cacti and succulents in a desert setting

1 Red canna lilies in late summer take centre stage in an area of formal landscaping.

2 The petals of the sacred lotus gradually fall to reveal the stately flower's distinctive "pepperpot" seedhead.

3 Students rake up scythings from a wildflower meadow as part of the university's "Green Schools" initiative.

💬 INSIDER TIP
Art Courses

Fancy painting or drawing what you see? The gardens offer introductory courses to the basic techniques of botanical illustration, taught by painters from the Vienna Academy of Fine Arts. There are also regular exhibitions of botanical art in the Kalthaus greenhouse.

EXPERIENCE MORE

Wien Museum Karlsplatz

📍 G9 🚇 Karlsplatz 8
Ⓤ Karlsplatz 🕐 10am–6pm
Tue–Sun & hols 🚫 1 Jan,
1 May, 25 Dec 🌐 wien
museum.at

Permanent highlights at this museum include the large 3D scale models of city buildings, and paintings by Gustav Klimt and Egon Schiele, most notably his celebrated self-portrait. The museum is strongest on the 19th century – not only paintings but also furniture and clothing. Several reconstructed apartments show period life, including the homes of radical architect Adolf Loos (p106) and local poet Franz Grillparzer. The oldest room, decorated with painted silks and dating back to 1798, originates from the Caprara-Geymüller Palace.

Strolling through the rooms, visitors quickly get an overview of Vienna's history. Neolithic shards and spears lead on to the Roman military encampment of Vindobona (p86). In later periods, the planning of monuments and palaces is preserved, as are Johann Bernhard Fischer von Erlach's original plans for the Schönbrunn Palace (p188) and original stained-glass windows and sculptures from the Stephansdom, including the famous Fürstenfiguren, or figures of royalty.

Everything from the plague to celebrations of victory over the Turks is portrayed. Many objects are works of art in their own right, such as glassware by Josef Hoffmann, designs from the Wiener Werkstätte (p73), and 14th- and 15th-century gargoyles. Weapons and war are represented, including items from Turkish invaders.

DRINK

Salm Bräu
This hop-wreathed cellar and micro-brewery serves fine beers and lagers, including wheat and dark varieties brewed on site.

📍 J9 🚇 Rennweg 8
🌐 salmbraeu.com

Bristol Lounge
Expect live piano music, an open fireplace and one of the finest wine lists in Vienna. Proximity to the State Opera House draws a formal crowd.

📍 G8 🚇 Kärntner Ring 1
🌐 bristol-lounge.at

Vienna's fascination with music is also covered, with paintings chronicling opera and ballet. A room dedicated to Baroque painting in Vienna includes works by Franz Anton Maulbertsch, Johann Michael Rottmayr and Paul Troger.

An exciting plan has been announced to build a modern museum on top of the existing three-storey structure, and the museum may soon close for several years, starting sometime in 2019 or 2020. It will continue to schedule themed exhibitions on Viennese citizens and phases of Vienna's history.

←

Exterior of the 1950s building containing the collections of the Wien Museum Karlsplatz

Illumination highlighting ornate features on the Musikverein's façade at night ↑

Musikverein

📍G8 🏠Bösendorfer-strasse 12 Ⓤ Karlsplatz Ⓒ For concerts and guided tours (1pm Mon-Sat) 🌐 musikverein.at

The elegant Musikverein building – the headquarters of the Society of the Friends of Music – was designed in 1867–9 by Theophil Hansen, in a mixture of styles employing terracotta statues, capitals and balustrades. It is the home of the great Vienna Philharmonic Orchestra, which gives regular performances

NEW YEAR'S DAY CONCERT

Since the late 1930s, at 11:15am on every New Year's Day, families across Austria switch on the TV for one of the annual musical highlights: the Vienna Philharmonic Orchestra's New Year's Day concert at the Musikverein. It only features Austrian composers and music by the Strauss family is always included on the programme.

here. The concert hall seats almost 2,000. Tickets are sold by subscription to Viennese music-lovers, but some are also available on the day.

Karlsplatz Pavilions

📍G9 🏠Karlsplatz Ⓤ Karlsplatz Ⓒ Apr–Oct: 10am–6pm Tue–Sun & hols 🔒1 May 🌐 wienmuseum.at

The master of Jugendstil, Otto Wagner was responsible for much of Vienna's underground system in the late 19th century, including his stylish pair of underground railway exit pavilions (1898–9) next to Karlsplatz. The green copper of the roofs and the ornamentation complement the Karlskirche beyond. Gilt patterns are stamped on the white marble cladding and eaves, with repetitions of Wagner's sunflower motif. The greatest impact is made by the buildings' curving rooflines. The two pavilions face

Monument to the Prince of Schwarzenberg on Schwarzenbergplatz →

each other: one is now a café; the other hosts exhibitions.

Schwarzenbergplatz

📍H9 Ⓤ Karlsplatz 🚋D, 71

At the centre of this grand square is an equestrian statue (1867) of Prince Schwarzenberg, who led the Austrian and allied armies against Napoleon at the Battle of Leipzig (1813). The square comprises huge office blocks, the Ringstrasse and the Baroque splendours of the Schwarzenberg and Belvedere palaces. Behind the Hoch-strahlbrunnen (1873), at the corner of Prinz-Eugen-Strasse and Gusshausstrasse, a contentious monument recalls the Red Army's liberation of the city.

8

Rennweg

◉ J9 Ⓤ Karlsplatz

Rennweg stretches from Schwarzenbergplatz along the edges of the Belvedere palaces. Palais Hoyos at No 3, now a hotel, is one of three on the street built by Otto Wagner in 1890. Though the façade is shabby, the building is an interesting example of Wagner's work just as he was transitioning from Ringstrasse pomp to his later Jugendstil (Art Nouveau) phase.

Next door at No 5 is where the late-Romantic composer Gustav Mahler lived from 1898 to 1909. No 5a is the **Gardekirche** (1755–63) by Nikolaus Pacassi (1716–99), Maria Theresa's court architect. It was originally built as the church of the Imperial Hospital and since 1897 has served as Vienna's Polish church. Its fine interior is embellished with Rococo gilt detailing over the side chapels and between the ribs of the huge dome.

Did You Know?

Schwarzenberg played a starring role as James Bond's hotel in the 1987 film *The Living Daylights*.

Just beyond the Belvedere palace gates at No 6a stands a Baroque mansion. The forecourt at No 8 has formed part of the Hochschule für Musik since 1988.

At No 10, behind splendid wrought-iron gates, is the Salesianerinnenkirche of 1717–30. Its Baroque façade is flanked by monastic buildings in the same style. The upper storey has scrolled projections supporting statues. Like the Gardekirche, this church is domed, its design partly attributed to Joseph Emanuel Fischer von Erlach. Apart from the pulpit, the interior is of little interest.

At No 27, the Italian Embassy occupies the palace where

Habsburg Prince Metternich (1773–1859) lived until he was forced to flee the city in 1848.

Gardekirche
◉ 8am–8pm daily

9

Palais Schwarzenberg

◉ H10 Ⓐ Schwarzenberg-platz 9 Ⓒ To the public

The Schwarzenberg Palace was built by Johann Lukas von Hildebrandt in 1697 and then altered by the Fischer von Erlachs in the 1720s. Behind the palace are the lawns and shady paths of the park, centred around a pool and fountain designed by Joseph Emanuel Fischer von Erlach.

Today, one wing of the palace is occupied by the Swiss Embassy. The present head of the Schwarzenberg family served as an advisor to President Havel following the Velvet Revolution in Czechoslovakia in 1989 and was Czech foreign minister in 2007–2009 and 2010–13.

EAT

Café Schwarzenberg

Choose from a selection of teas and coffees. The pastry cabinet has a tempting array of sweet treats too.

📍G8 🚇Kärtner Ring 17 🌐cafe-schwarzen berg.at

€€€

Restaurant Entler

Enjoy modern Austrian cuisine in this cosy, informal restaurant.

📍F10 🚇Schlüssel-gasse 2 🌐entler.at

€€€

Café Goldegg

A lovely place for brunch and coffees, this place first opened in 1910, and is bedecked with velvet and Art Nouveau finery.

📍H11 🚇Argentinier-strasse 49 🌐cafegoldegg.at.

€€€

🔟 Theresianum

📍G10 🚇Favoritenstrasse 15 🚇Taubstummengasse 🚫To the public

The original buildings of this former imperial summer palace date from the early 17th century, but were essentially rebuilt in Baroque style after the Turkish siege of 1683 by the architect and theatre designer Lodovico Ottavio Burnacini (1636–1707) and others. Known as the Favorita, it became a favourite residence of Leopold I, Joseph I and Karl VI. In 1746, Maria Theresa, who had moved into Schönbrunn (p190), handed it over to the Jesuits. They established a college here for children from less well-off aristocratic families – the sons of these families were trained to be officials.

Today, the Theresianum is still a school and, since 1964, has also been a college for diplomats and civil servants. In the Theresianum park on Argentinierstrasse stands Radio House. It has a beautiful entrance hall, which was designed by architect Clemens Holzmeister in 1935.

⓫ Arnold Schönberg Center

📍H9 🚇Schwarzenberg-platz 6 (entrance at Zauner-gasse 1-3) 🚇Karlsplatz 🚌4A 🚋D, 71 🕙9am-5pm Mon-Fri 🚫Public hols 🌐schoenberg.at

Vienna's Arnold Schönberg Center, established in 1998, is a unique archive for music scholars and a cultural centre open to the general public. Multitalented Schönberg – a

← The busy thoroughfare of Rennweg in the north of the Belvedere Quarter

↑ The Arnold Schönberg Center, home to a music archive

composer, painter, teacher, music theoretician and innovator – was born in Vienna in 1874 and died in Los Angeles in 1951. Something of a prodigy, he began composing at the age of 9. However, he later dismissed much of his early work as "imitative", gradually developing a more experimental approach to composition, which culminated in the invention of his highly influential twelve-tone technique.

Though Schönberg's work was much admired by fellow musicians, it largely baffled the general public. In 1913 he conducted what became known as the "Skandalkonzert" at Vienna's Musikverein (p177). This featured modern music deemed so provocative that the audience rioted, bringing the concert to a halt.

The centre has numerous fascinating artifacts relating to Schönberg's life and work, a gallery of his paintings, a replica of his Los Angeles study and a library. It stages concerts, lectures, workshops and symposia. Visitors with an academic interest can arrange access to Schönberg's music manuscripts, writings and his correspondence.

A SHORT WALK
KARLSPLATZ

Distance 1.5 km (1 mile) **Nearest U-Bahn**
Karlsplatz **Time** 20 minutes

This part of the city became ripe for development once
the threat of Turkish invasion had receded for good in
1683. The Ressel Park, in front of the Karlskirche, gives an
unobstructed view of this grandiose church, built on the
orders of Karl VI. Take a turn around the park to see a variety
of cultural institutions, notably the Wien Museum Karlsplatz
and, across the road, the Musikverein.

Did You Know?

Joseph Ressel, to whom
the Ressel Park is
dedicated, invented
the first working ship's
propeller in 1826.

*The two **Karlsplatz**
Pavilions were
built as part of the
underground system
of 1899 (p177).*

Karlsplatz U-Bahn

START

*A bronze statue
commemorates the inventor
and engineer Joseph Ressel
(1793–1857).*

FINISH

*The Neo-Classical façade of the
Technical University (1816)
overlooks Ressel Park, which
contains busts and statues of
famous 19th-century Austrian
scientists and engineers.*

KARLSPLATZ

0 metres	50
0 yards	50

N ↑

*Henry Moore's sculpture, **the
Hill Arches** was presented to
the city of Vienna by the artist
himself in 1978.*

←
A bronze statue
of Austrian inventor
Joseph Ressel

Locator Map
For more detail see p166

The Vienna Philharmonic Orchestra performing at the Musikverein

The **Musikverein** *concert hall, home of the Vienna Philharmonic Orchestra, is renowned for its superb acoustics (p177).*

DUMBASTRASSE

KARLSPLATZ

LOTHRINGER STRASSE

The **Wien Museum Karlsplatz** *chronicles Vienna's history from Neolithic times to the present, with weapons, paintings and reconstructed rooms from each period (p176).*

MADERSTRASSE

Built in 1904–12 by the French architect Georges Chédanne, **the French Embassy** *is typical of Parisian Art Nouveau.*

MATTIELLISTRASSE

TECHNIKERSTR

GUSSHAUSSTRASSE

Promised to the people by Emperor Karl VI during the 1713 plague, **Karlskirche** *is Vienna's finest Baroque church (p168).*

→

One of the Karlsplatz Pavilions designed by Otto Wagner

The brightly coloured façade of the Hundertwasserhaus

Must Sees

1. Hundertwasserhaus
2. Prater
3. Schönbrunn
4. Heeresgeschichtliches Museum
5. Zentralfriedhof

Experience More

6. Wagner Villas
7. Kirche am Steinhof
8. Geymüllerschlössel
9. Kahlenberg
10. Grinzing
11. Palais Augarten
12. Donaupark
13. Karl-Marx-Hof
14. Klosterneuburg
15. Wotrubakirche
16. Stadtpark
17. Klimt Villa
18. Kriminalmuseum
19. Wasserturm Favoriten
20. Technisches Museum Wien
21. Otto Wagner Hofpavillon Hietzing
22. Alt-Wiener Schnapsmuseum
23. Amalienbad
24. Lainzer Tiergarten

BEYOND
THE CENTRE

Away from the compact city centre, Vienna unfolds
into densely wooded hillsides, historic vineyard
villages and a scattering of remarkable attractions. This is the preserve of former Habsburg
hunting grounds, with parks and gardens now
open to the public including the vast Prater and
the Lainzer Tiergarten. At Schönbrunn sprawls the
immense 18th-century palace once adored by
Maria Theresa, while to the north, 12th-century
Klosterneuburg monastery houses some of
Austria's great ecclesiastical art treasures.

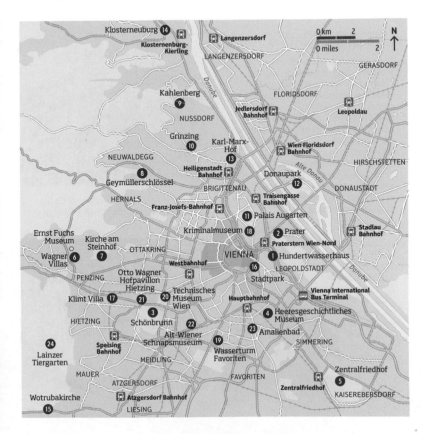

HUNDERTWASSERHAUS

⬛ Löwengasse Kegelgasse ⓤ Landstrasse 🚋 1 Hetzgasse 🚌 4A Löwengasse
🕐 Art Café: 10am–6pm; shopping centre: 9am–6pm daily 🚫 Building: closed to the public
🌐 Building: hundertwasserhaus.at; shopping centre: hundertwasser-village.com

A relatively recent addition to the city's architectural heritage, the 20th-century Hundertwasserhaus is Vienna's most remarkable and striking contemporary structure. This gloriously eclectic block of flats on Löwengasse divides opinion; while some love it, others think it is more like a stage set than a block of flats.

The Hundertwasserhaus is a municipal apartment block created in 1985 by the artist Friedensreich Hundertwasser, who wished to diverge from what he saw as the rather soulless modern architecture appearing in Vienna's suburbs. The result was a structure that has been controversial since its construction, with many critics dismissing it as kitsch. It features undulating floors and large trees growing from inside the rooms. Hundertwasser took no payment for the design, declaring that it was worth it to prevent something ugly from going up in its place. As a private building its interior cannot be visited, but opposite is the Hundertwasser Village shopping centre, a bazaar of shops and cafés open to the public, and a pleasant place to peruse for quirky souvenirs.

> 💬 INSIDER TIP
> ## Art Café
> Grab a coffee at the Art Café on the ground floor of the apartment building (one of the few parts of the structure open to the public). It's bursting with suitably unique decor and has a friendly atmosphere.

FRIEDENSREICH HUNDERTWASSER

Friedensreich Hundertwasser was an artist and designer whose passion for the irregular was largely inspired by Viennese Secessionists. In his use of colour and organic forms, he said, he hoped to realize "a more human and nature orientated architecture". Born to a Jewish mother in 1928, he survived the Holocaust by posing as a Christian: his mother even enrolled him in the Hitler Youth to keep up appearances. After the war, he briefly studied at the Akademie der bildenden Künste Wien *(p159)* before dropping out to travel throughout Europe and Asia. He founded and designed the Kunst Haus Wien, a short walk from the Hundertwasserhaus, where there are also fine exhibits of his work *(www.kunsthaus wien.com)*.

↑ Roof gardens on the multilevel block, a key feature of the building's design

↑ The Hundertwasser-designed shopping centre, inspired by an oriental bazaar

900

Tonnes of earth and grass cover the Hundertwasser-haus roof.

↑ Colour blocks and banding delineating the individual apartments

2 🎿 🍴 🖥

PRATER

🏠 Prater, 1020 Ⓤ Ⓢ Praterstern 🚋 1 (park) 🚌 77A, 80A; 0, 5 (funfair)
🕐 Times vary, check website for details 🌐 prater.at

A vast oasis of green in Vienna's second district, the Prater is enjoyed by locals and visitors alike, with its amusement park and racing track, pleasant tree-lined avenues, verdant meadows and a maze of cycling paths waiting to be explored.

Formerly imperial hunting grounds, these woods and meadows between the Danube and its canal were opened to the public by Joseph II in 1766. Today they make up the Green Prater, a huge park area bisected by a central avenue, the Hauptallee. Once the preserve of the nobility and their footmen, it now attracts joggers and cyclists. At the western end of the Prater is a large amusement park, known sometimes as the Wurstelprater (or Clown's Prater), which dates back to the 19th century and is home to the iconic Wiener Riesenrad Ferris wheel. Access to the Prater itself is free of charge, but each funfair ride is charged individually.

→

Visitors strolling around the Wurstelprater, a huge amusement park filled with rides

↑ The tree-lined Hauptallee, stretching 5 km (3 miles) through Prater's centre

---

WIENER RIESENRAD

One of Vienna's most recognizable landmarks, the giant Wiener Riesenrad Ferris wheel was immortalized in the film of Graham Greene's *The Third Man*. It was built in 1896 by the English engineer Walter Basset, but it has only half the original number of cabins, after a fire destroyed many of them in 1945.

TOP 3 KIDS' ATTRACTIONS

Wurstelprater
There's plenty of fun to be had here, with dodgems, ghost trains and carousels among the many rides.

Planetarium
Kids will be enthralled by the immersive multimedia shows exploring the galaxy.

Miniature Railway
Catch the *Liliputbahn* for a pleasant 4-km (2-mile) trip through the Prater.

The 18th-century Lusthaus pavilion, a former hunting lodge ↑

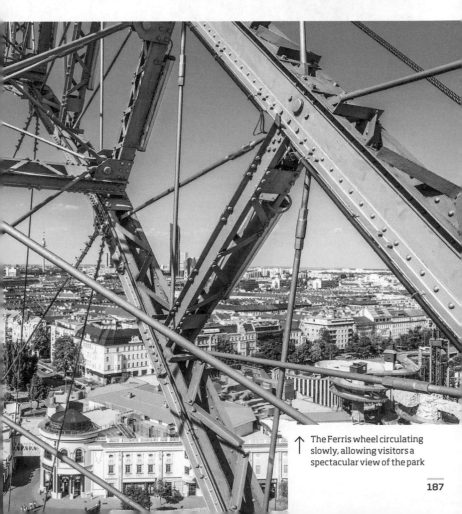

↑ The Ferris wheel circulating slowly, allowing visitors a spectacular view of the park

Did You Know?

The palace was painted its characteristic "Schönbrunn yellow" in 1817-19.

The elegant Ehrenhof fountain in front of the magnificent Schönbrunn Palace ↑

3 ⊕ 🎭 🍽 🖥 🛍

SCHÖNBRUNN

🏠 Schönbrunner Schloss Strasse 47, A-1130 Ⓤ Schönbrunn 🚃 10, 58 🚌 10A 🕐 Times vary, check websites 🌐 Palace: schoenbrunn.at; Imperial Coach Collection: kaiserliche-wagenburg.at; Marionette Theater: marionettentheater.at; Zoo: zoovienna.at

The former summer residence of the Habsburgs, the lavish Schönbrunn Palace is a masterpiece of Baroque architecture set amid exquisite landscaped grounds. Under the rule of Empress Maria Theresa, this was the glittering heart of the imperial court. Today it is one of Vienna's most spectacular and most visited sights.

Schönbrunn is named after a beautiful spring that served the original hunting lodge built here in the late 16th century by Maximilian II. Leopold I initially asked Johann Bernhard Fischer von Erlach (p168) to design a grand Baroque residence here in 1695. However, it was not until Maria Theresa employed Nikolaus Pacassi in the mid-18th century that the project was completed. The sumptuous Rococo decorative schemes devised by Pacassi dominate the State Rooms, where white panelling lavishly adorned with gilded mouldings prevails.

There is a strong Oriental influence in the Blue Chinese Salon and the lustrous Vieux-Lacque Room. Other rooms vary from extravagant – such as the Millionenzimmer, panelled in fig wood inlaid with Persian miniatures – to the rather plain state apartments once occupied by Franz Joseph and Empress Elisabeth. "Imperial" and "Grand" guided tours lead visitors through the palace rooms and the state rooms open to the public are on the first floor.

> 💬 INSIDER TIP
> **Take in a Show**
>
> Puppet shows at the Marionetten Theater in the Little Court Theatre will delight children and adults alike. A version of Mozart's *The Magic Flute* is an undisputed highlight, featuring a feather-clad Tamino and a fantastically vicious snake puppet (*www.marionetten theater.at*).

← The Great Gallery, once used for imperial banquets, hosted state receptions until 1994

→ Allegorical figures by Gregorio Guglielmi riot across the ceilings of the gallery

Timeline

1696
△ Leopold I commissions J B Fischer von Erlach to design a new palace.

1705
Jean Trehet lays out the gardens.

1744–9
Nikolaus Pacassi adapts the building for Maria Theresa.

1805 and 1809
△ Napoleon uses the palace as his headquarters.

1882
△ Palm House is built.

Exploring Schönbrunn

Schönbrunn makes for a wonderful escape from Vienna's city centre, with its lavish state rooms to peruse and manicured gardens perfect for strolling. The strict symmetry of the palace's architecture is complemented by the gardens, with their fountains and statues framed by trees and alleyways. They were first laid out in 1705 by Jean Trehet and completed in 1775 with the addition of the magnificent Gloriette archway. In the Carriage Museum, a building which originally housed the Winter Riding School (p100), ceremonial state coaches and sedan chairs can be seen.

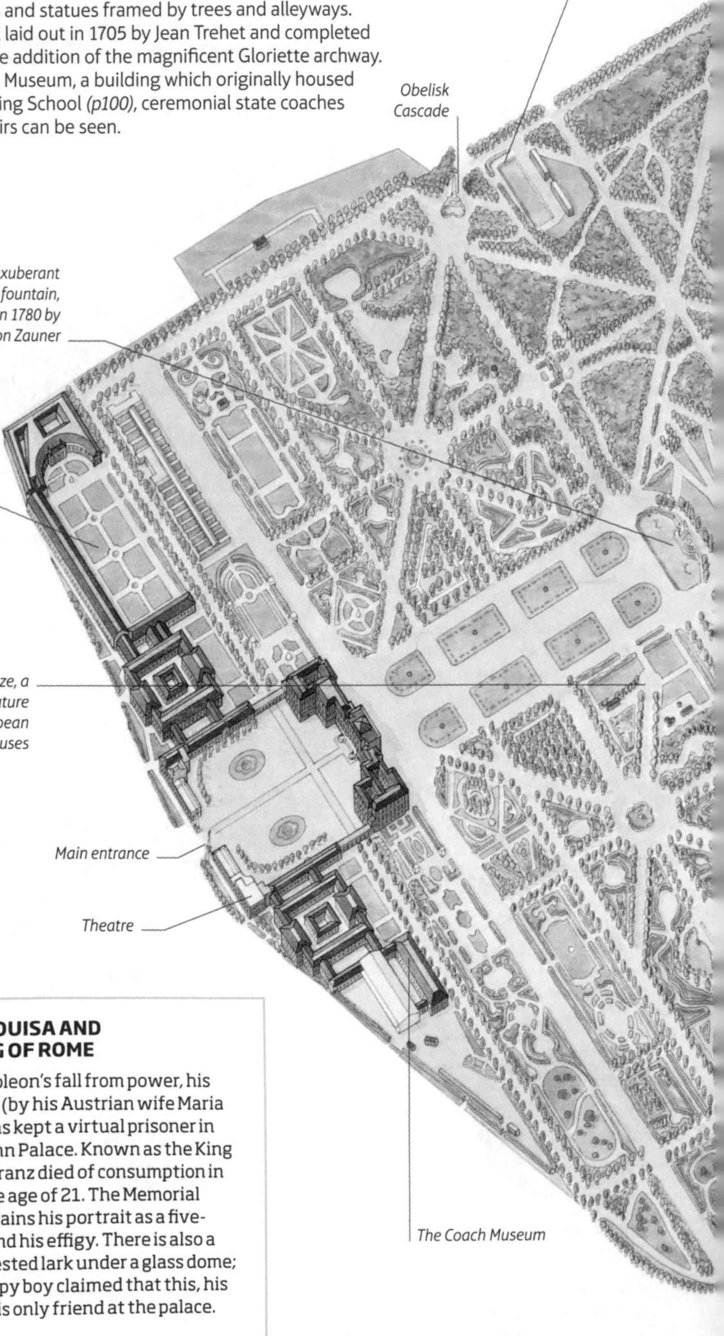

Public swimming pool

Obelisk Cascade

The exuberant Neptune fountain, sculpted in 1780 by Franz Anton Zauner

Orangery

The maze, a favourite feature of European stately houses

Main entrance

Theatre

MARIA LOUISA AND THE KING OF ROME

After Napoleon's fall from power, his young son (by his Austrian wife Maria Louisa) was kept a virtual prisoner in Schönbrunn Palace. Known as the King of Rome, Franz died of consumption in 1832 at the age of 21. The Memorial Room contains his portrait as a five-year-old and his effigy. There is also a stuffed crested lark under a glass dome; the unhappy boy claimed that this, his pet, was his only friend at the palace.

The Coach Museum

The Gloriette

1 A vast collection of tropical plants flourishes in the magnificent Palm House (1882).

2 The Gloriette, elevated on a hill, completes the vista from the palace over the gardens.

3 The Neo-Classical Gloriette arcade was designed by Ferdinand von Hohenberg.

Schönbrunn Zoo

←

The palace and gardens, a UNESCO World Heritage Site since 1996

Japanese Gardens

Palm House

Hietzing Gate

Did You Know?

Schönbrunn's menagerie dates back to 1752; it is the oldest zoo in the world.

The Heeresgeschichtliches Museum's highly ornamented Byzantine-style façade ↑

4 ⓨ ⬚ 🏛

HEERESGESCHICHTLICHES MUSEUM

📍 Arsenal, Ghegastrasse Objekt 18, A-1030 Ⓢ Hauptbahnhof 🚋 18, O, D 🚌 13A to Hauptbahnhof, 69A ⏰ 9am–5pm daily 🚫 1 Jan, Easter Sun, 1 May, 1 Nov, 25 & 31 Dec 🌐 hgm.at

This fine museum is housed in a single block of the Arsenal, a military complex built as a fortress in 1856. With its abundance of fascinating exhibits, it is a must-visit for anyone with an interest in military history.

↑ The bright and airy main gallery of the Heeresgeschichtliches Museum

↑ Albin Egger-Lienz's 1916 painting *Den Namenlosen*, meaning "the nameless"

This impressive museum, designed by Danish architect Theophil Hansen (1813–91), chronicles Austria's complex military history from the 16th to the mid-20th century. Exhibits relate to the Turkish siege of 1683, the French Revolution and the Napoleonic Wars, and include fine paintings, ornate antiques and military artifacts.

The museum is housed across two floors. To view it in chronological order, begin on the first floor on the left, where there are exhibits relating to the Turkish siege. Other rooms chronicle various 18th-century wars and Napoleon's victory over Austria. The 19th- and 20th-century displays, including heavy artillery used in World War I, are on the ground floor. There is also a grand "tank garden" located behind the museum.

Visitors should not miss seeing the car in which Archduke Franz Ferdinand was assassinated, or the modern armaments used in World War I, which the murder of the Habsburg heir precipitated.

> **Exhibits relate to the Turkish siege of 1683, the French Revolution and the Napoleonic Wars.**

THE ASSASSINATION OF FRANZ FERDINAND

On 28 June 1914, Archduke Franz Ferdinand, heir to the Austrian throne, and his wife Sophie von Hohenberg paid a visit to Sarajevo. Gavrilo Princip, a Serbian nationalist, assassinated the couple, provoking an international crisis that led to World War I. The museum houses the car in which the couple were killed.

ARCHDUKE FRANZ FERDINAND'S CAR

5 Ⓜ️ 🖥️

ZENTRALFRIEDHOF

🏠 Simmering Hauptstrasse 234, Tor 2, A-1110 Ⓢ Zentralfriedhof, Kledering
🚃 6, 71 🕐 Times vary, check website 🌐 friedhoefewien.at

Austria's largest cemetery, and its most famous, was opened in 1874 to accomodate the deceased of the rapidly industrializing 19th-century capital. Today it contains 300,000 graves over an area of 2.5 sq km (1 sq mile).

The beautiful old Central Cemetery sits in the verdant outskirts of Vienna's Simmering district – "Central" refers to the site's significant number of graves rather than its location. The cemetery is divided into specific numbered sections: as well as the central garden of honour where VIPs are buried, there are old and new Jewish cemeteries; a Protestant cemetery; a Russian Orthodox section; and various war graves and memorials. Also here is the Bestattungsmuseum, which gives a fascinating insight into the history of Vienna's love affair with lavish burials. A pleasant way to explore the grounds is on the circulating bus.

Luegerkirche

Arcades around the Luegerkirche

The presidential vault contains the remains of Dr Karl Renner.

Sculptor Fritz Wotruba's grave

Modernist composer Arnold Schönberg's grave is marked with this bold cube by Fritz Wotruba.

Beethoven, Brahms Schubert and the Strausses are buried in the musicians' area.

← The Luegerkirche (1907-10) dedicated to patron St Borromeo

① Fritz Wotruba's cuboid sculpture marks the grave of Viennese composer Arnold Schönberg.

② The Russian Orthodox Chapel, completed in 1894, is still used by Vienna's Russian community today.

③ A statue of Johannes Brahms marks his grave in the musicians' section.

Monument to Dr Johann Nepomuk Prix by Viktor Tilgner (1894)

Spectacular monuments are carved in the semicircular arcades facing the main entrance.

←

The expansive Central Cemetery, divided into distinct sections

Bestattungsmuseum

Main entrance from Simmeringer Hauptstrasse

The Russian Orthodox Chapel

THE BESTATTUNGSMUSEUM

Vienna has several rather morbid attractions but none so sombre as this, the Undertakers' Museum *(www.bestattungsmuseum.at)*. Exhibits examine the ways in which death has been dealt with over many centuries by the Viennese, and explore burial rituals and customs; displays include funerary art and a 1784 folding coffin. Though small (allow around 15 minutes to see it all), it will leave a lasting impression.

EXPERIENCE MORE

6 🚲 📍

Wagner Villas

🏠 Hüttelbergstrasse
26, Penzing Ⓤ Hütteldorf
🚌 52A & 52B to Camping
Platz Wien West ⏰ Sun
& Mon by appointment

The Villa Otto Wagner, which
was designed by Wagner
in 1886–8 as his own residence, is stylistically midway
between his earlier grand
Ringstrasse works and the
more decorative elements of
Jugendstil. The house is built
on a grand scale, with Classical
elements like Ionic columns,
and seems more suited to a
north Italian hillside. In 1972,

📷 **PICTURE PERFECT**
**Ernst Fuchs
Museum**

One of Vienna's most
photogenic buildings,
this museum has an
ornate exterior, with
over-the-top portals
and exquisite colour
providing glorious
camera fodder. You can
snap pics inside too.

---

artist Ernst Fuchs (1930–2015)
acquired and transformed the
house, imparting his own
personality on the decor.
Today this forms the fabulous
Ernst Fuchs Museum
  The simpler villa next door
was built more than 20 years
later. Completed in 1913,
Brunnenhaus is lightly decorated in a geometrical style
with deep blue panels and a
glass nailhead ornament by
Kolo Moser.

✦ **Ernst Fuchs Museum**
⏰ 10am–4pm Tue–Sun
🌐 ernstfuchsmuseum.at

---

7 🚲 📍

Kirche am Steinhof

🏠 Baumgartner Höhe 1,
Penzing 📞 9106011007
🚌 48A ⏰ 4–5pm Sat, noon-
4pm Sun by appointment

Completed in 1907, this
astonishing church was Otto
Wagner's last commission.
Within the grounds of the
Psychiatrisches Krankenhaus,
a large psychiatric hospital, it
has a marble-clad exterior
with nailhead ornament and

↑ Kirche am Steinhof's
façade, and stained glass
windows (inset)

spindly screw-shaped pillars,
topped by wreaths which
support the porch. The four
stone columns on the façade
are adorned with angels by
Othmar Schimkowitz (1864–
1947). The statues at each
end of the façade are of
St Leopold and St Severin.
They were designed by
Richard Luksch and are seated
in chairs by Secessionist
craftsman Josef Hoffmann.
  Inside is a single space with
shallow side chapels, decorated with gold-and-white
friezes. Illumination is provided by daylight shining
through lovely blue glass
windows by Kolo Moser.

→

Enjoying good local
wine, food and music in
the village of Grinzing

> The views over the vineyards and the city below are fabulous, with the Danube bridges to the left and the woods to the right.

8
Geymüllerschlössel

🏠 Pötzleinsdorferstrasse 102 🚌 41A 🚋 41 ⏱ May–Nov: 11am–6pm Sun by appointment 🌐 mak.at

In Pötzleinsdorf, northwest of the city, this house is a temple to 19th-century Biedermeier style, with its green-domed roof, geometrically patterned arching windows, and fine parquet floors combining Gothic, Indian and Arabic styles. Dating from 1808, it was built as a summer residence for Johann Heinrich von Geymüller, a rich banker. Now a branch of the Austrian Museum of Applied Arts (p72), it has a collection of intricate Biedermeier and Empire furniture. There are also spittoons, decorative ceramics, and 200 clocks dating from the 18th and 19th centuries, the heyday of Viennese clock manufacture.

9
Kahlenberg

🏠 1190, 10 km (6 miles) N of Vienna 🚌 38A

At 484 m (1,585 ft), this hill is the highest point in the Vienna Woods (p210), with a television mast, a church, an observation terrace and a restaurant. The views over the vineyards and the city below are fabulous, with the Danube bridges to the left and the woods to the right. In 1683, the Polish king, Jan Sobieski, led his troops down from this spot to rescue the Viennese forces fighting for the city (p56).

10
Grinzing

🚇 Heiligenstadt 🚌 38A 🚋 38 to Grinzing

The most famous Heurige village is also the most touristy, with many of the inns here catering to large groups. It is nonetheless very pretty. The village is divided into the Oberer Ort and Unterer Ort (upper and lower towns), the lower town being where you will find more authentic Heurigen and taverns, along lanes such as Sandgasse.

DRINK

Hirt
Set amid its own vineyards on the Kahlenberg slopes, this lovely heurige serves fantastic wines and traditional food.

🏠 Parzelle 165 🌐 heuriger-hirt.at

Weingut Schilling
This traditional heurige offers superb wines and a buffet of local delicacies.

🏠 Lang-Enzersdorfer Strasse 54 🌐 weingut-schilling.at

Buschenschank Stippert
Enjoy local wines, fresh salads and homemade fare at this delightful wine tavern.

🏠 Ottakringerstrasse 225 🌐 stippert.at

Heuriger Leitner
One of the best, run by knowledgeable vintners with great wines and a generous buffet.

🏠 Sprengersteig 68 🌐 weinbau-leitner.at

↑ One of the city's three remaining World War II defense towers in the Augarten Park

🔢 🚫 🍽️

Palais Augarten

📍 Obere Augartenstrasse 1
🚇 Taborstrasse 🚌 5A, 5B
🚋 5, 31 🕐 Park: 6am–9pm daily 🌐 augarten.com

There has been a palace on this site since the days of Leopold I, when it was known as the Alte Favorita, but it was destroyed by the Turks in 1683 and later rebuilt around 1700 to a design attributed to Johann Bernhard Fischer von Erlach. The palace was used for royal receptions and gatherings while the Congress of Vienna was taking place in 1815. Since 1948 it has been the home of the Vienna Boys' Choir and for the most part it is inaccessible to the public. Visitors can explore the **Porcelain Museum** housed in the palace, which examines the history of porcelain and displays pieces from the Rococo and Biedermeier periods, as well as the 20th and 21st centuries.

The Augarten palace has the oldest Baroque garden in Vienna. The park was planted in the second half of the 17th century, renewed in 1712, and opened to the public by Joseph II in 1775. The handsome entrance gates were designed by Isidor Canevale in 1775. Beethoven, Mozart and Johann Strauss I all gave concerts in the park pavilion, behind which is the studio of early-20th-century sculptor Gustinus Ambrosi.

In the distance, you can see two huge *flakturms*, immovable reminders of World War II. Built by German forces in 1942 as defence towers and anti-aircraft batteries, these enormous concrete monoliths could house thousands of troops. So thick are their walls that any explosives powerful enough to destroy them would have a similar effect on the surrounding residential areas. There are two other such flakturms still standing in other parts of the city.

🍽️ **Porcelain Museum**
🕐 10am–6pm Mon–Sat
🚫 Public hols

Did You Know?

At 1.1km (0.75 miles) in length, Karl-Marx-Hof is the world's longest residential building.

VIENNA BOYS' CHOIR

The 26 soprano and alto singers of this ensemble make up one of the finest choral groups in the world. The choir was established in 1498 by the Emperor Maximilian I to accompany church Mass. Through the centuries the choir has worked with illustrious composers including Mozart, Schubert and Bruckner. Today the boys rehearse at the Augarten Palace, where they also attend boarding school.

→

The glorious interior of Klosterneuburg monastery church

12

Donaupark

🚇 Kaisermühlen 🚌 20B
🕐 24 hours

This wonderful park is located on an island in the Danube, northeast of the historical centre. Developed in 1964, the park features a variety of beautiful gardens, cycle lanes and cafés, and is the perfect place for a bit of urban escape. Its most obvious landmark is the great **Donauturm**, which rises 252 m (827 ft) above the park and has two revolving restaurants and an observation platform (last ride up is at 11:30pm).

The park and surrounding area are incorporated into **Donau City**, a vast urban project containing the Vienna International Centre, a complex of United Nations agencies based in the Austrian capital. Guided tours (cash only) of the complex run daily.

Donauturm
🕐 10am–11:30pm daily
🌐 donauturm.at

⊗ Donau City
🕐 Tours are led at 11am, 2pm, and 3:30pm daily 🌐 unis.unvienna.org

13

Karl-Marx-Hof

🏠 Heiligenstädterstrasse 82–92, Döbling 🚇 Heiligenstadt 🚋 D 🕐 Closed to the public

Dating from 1927–30, this is an immense social housing project, containing 1,382 flats. It is the most celebrated of the municipal housing developments built during the period of Red Vienna (p58), when 63,000 new dwellings

←

The front wall of the monumental Karl-Marx-Hof apartment block in Döbling

went up across the city between 1919 and 1934. The Karl-Marx-Hof's architect was Karl Ehn, an apprentice of Otto Wagner.

14

Klosterneuburg

🏠 Stift Klosterneuburg, 13 km (8 miles) N of Vienna 🚈 Klosterneuburg-Kierling 🚇 Heiligenstadt 🚌 238, 239 🕐 9am–5pm daily 🌐 stift-klosterneuburg.at

Above the Danube, to the north of Vienna, stands the vast monastery and fortress of Klosterneuburg.

Dating originally from the 12th century, it houses the astonishing Verduner Altar, whose 51 panels were completed in 1181. In the 18th century it was expanded by Karl VI, who intended to build a complex on the same grand scale as the Escorial palace near Madrid. The work was halted after his death in 1740.

↑ Edmund von Hellmer's gilded monument (1921) to Viennese Waltz King Johann Strauss

15

Wotrubakirche

⌂ Georgsgasse, Mauer
🚌 60A ⏱ 2–8pm Sat,
9am–4:30pm Sun & hols
🌐 georgenberg.at

Built between 1965 and 1976 in an uncompromisingly modern style, this church stands on a hillside very close to the Vienna Woods. The structure consists of uneven rectangular concrete slabs and glass panels, some of the latter rising to the full height of the church. They provide its principal lighting and views for the congregation out onto the woods and hills. The building is raw in style, but powerful and compact.

🗻 GREAT VIEW
Stefaniewarte

This 22-m- (72-ft-) high viewing tower atop the Kahlenberg, towers 300 m (894 ft) above the Danube, and is one of the best vantage points in the city. On a clear day you can see Schneeberg mountain, some 70 km (43 miles) away.

Designed by the sculptor Fritz Wotruba (1907–75), the church looks different from every angle and has a strong sculptural quality. It accommodates a congregation of up to 250.

16

Stadtpark

⌂ Parkring 📞 40008042
Ⓤ Stadtpark, Stubentor
🚌 74A 🚋 2 ⏱ 24 hours

Stadtpark, Vienna's first and largest public park, opened when the old city walls were demolished. Among many monuments – to Schubert and Bruckner among others – is the single most photographed memorial in Vienna: Edmund von Hellmer's golden (gilded bronze) statue of Johann Strauss.

The park was designed in 1861 by Rudolf Siebeck who drew inspiration from English landscaped gardens: there are plenty of ornamental

→

The Wasserturm Favoriten, built in Industrial-Historist style

herbaceous borders for year-round colour. There is also a large playground for children featuring swings, slides, climbing frames, a sand pit and a skate park. The Italian Renaissance-style Kursalon hosts summer open-air concerts and costume balls. The cosy park café **Meierei im Stadtpark** is a popular meeting place.

Meierei im Stadtpark
⌂ Am Heumarkt 2A
🌐 steirereck.at

17

Klimt Villa

⌂ Feldmühlgasse 11
Ⓤ Unter-St-Veit 🚌 53A
⏱ 10am–6pm Wed–Sun
🌐 klimtvilla.at

In a leafy spot in Hietzing, this sumptuous Neo-Baroque villa was built on the site of Klimt's last studio, a simple cottage he rented in 1911 and worked in until his death in 1918. Inside you'll find Klimt's sketches as well as interiors that carefully recreate the style of the period, all based on Moriz Nähr's photographs, and contemporaneous descriptions and letters.

The studio was renovated and opened to the public in

2012, meticulously recreated as the artist would have known it. The exhibition aims to revive the atmosphere and decor of Klimt's living and working space. Tours of the villa run at 2pm on Saturdays.

18

Kriminalmuseum

📍 **Grosse Sperlgasse 24**
🚇 **Taborstrasse** 🚌 **5A**
🚊 **2** 🕐 **10am–5pm Tue–Sun**
🌐 **kriminalmuseum.at**

This medieval house was once known as the *Seifensiederhaus* (the soap boiler's house), and has been the home of Vienna's Museum of Crime since 1991. Its 20 rooms mostly chronicle violent crime, charting the murderous impulses of Vienna's citizens from the Middle Ages through to the present day, as well as the various methods of capital punishment used against some of them. The museum also examines the development of the Viennese police force and its approach to tackling crime. Many

of the exhibits hail from the archives of the Viennese police force and are distinctly gruesome; there is a wide selection of murder weapons, mummified heads of executed criminals, death masks, and case histories illustrated with photographs and prints. Political criminality, from failed coup attempts to the rather more grisly lynching of a government minister during the revolution of 1848 (*p57*), is well covered.Though certainly not for the faint-hearted, this museum provides visitors with a unique take on Vienna's social history.

---

19 Ⓜ

Wasserturm Favoriten

📍 **Windtenstrasse 3, Favoriten** 📞 **5995931070**
🚇 **Reumannplatz** 🚌 **15A, 65A** 🚊 **1** 🕐 **For guided tours (call ahead for an appointment)**

The Favoriten water pumping station was constructed in 1888–9 by Franz Borkowitz as part of a municipal scheme for the transportation of drinking water from the Alpine

foothills to meet the needs of the industrializing capital city's rapidly growing population. By 1910 the construction of other installations around Vienna, including the Vienna High Spring Pipeline, meant that the operations of the complex had to be scaled down. Of the seven original buildings, only the highly decorative yellow-and-red-brick water tower, with its ornate turrets and pinnacles, remains.

The restored interior, in contrast with the attractive exterior, comprises a vast steel structure, ready to store and pump water.

Guided tours are available to members of the public, and visitors who make the climb up the spiral staircase are rewarded with impressive views across the city, including the nearby Prater amusement park, which is pinpointed by its striking Ferris wheel (*p186*).

Exploring large-scale
industrial exhibits at the
Technisches Museum ↑

glass panelling, a peach and
russet asymmetrical carpet,
and a marble and brass
fireplace. The charming
cupola features glass and
gilt flower and leaf motifs.
   Wagner built the pavilion
without a commission from
the emperor in an attempt
to showcase his work. Unfor-
tunately, Franz Joseph used
the station only twice.

20 Technisches Museum

⌂ Mariahilfer Strasse 212,
Penzing ⛟10A ⛟52,58
⊙9am–6pm Mon–Fri,
10am–6pm Sat, Sun &
public hols (free for under-
19s) ⓦtmw.ac.at

Franz Joseph founded the
Technisches Museum Wien in
1908, using the Habsburgs'
personal collections as core
material, but it only opened
its doors to the public ten
years later. It documents all
aspects of technical progress,
from domestic appliances to
large turbines, and includes
fascinating exhibits on heavy
industry, energy, physics and
musical instruments. A major

section features interactive
displays on computer technology, along with exhibits
that explore the extraction of
natural resources such as oil
and gas, and a reconstruction
of a coal mine.
   The railway collection is an
integral part of the museum
with its extensive array of
imperial railway carriages
and engines.

21 Otto Wagner Hofpavillon Hietzing

⌂ Schönbrunner
Schlosstrasse 13, Hietzing
Ⓤ Hietzing ⛟51A, 56B
⛟10, 58, 60 ⊙Mar–Nov:
10am–6pm Sat & Sun
🚫1 Jan, 1 May & 25 Dec
(free 1st Sun of month)
ⓦwienmuseum.at

The pioneering architect Otto
Wagner designed and built
this railway station for the
imperial family and royal
guests in 1899. The lovely
building is in the shape of
a white cube with green
ironwork and a copper
dome. Its waiting room is
decorated with wood and

22 Alt-Wiener Schnapsmuseum

⌂ Wilhelmstrasse 19–21
⊙ By appointment only
ⓦschnapsmuseum.com

Operated by six generations
of the Fischer family, this
distillery runs its own small
museum, which provides
visitors with the lowdown
on both the production of
schnaps and the history of
the company.
   Dating back to 1875, some
of the original furnishings and
fittings are still in use, as are
some of the polished copper
distilling kettles and other
interesting paraphernalia.
   A tour of the facilities
ends with an inevitable
tasting session (teetotallers
are offered fresh raspberry
juice) and there's a gift shop
where you can purchase
some schnaps as a souvenir.
The tour lasts half an hour
and can be booked in English.

→

The richly decorated
Amalienbad main pool, with
its fine stained-glass roof

Amalienbad

⌂ Reumannplatz 23, Favoriten **Ⓤ** Reumannplatz **🚌** 7A, 14A, 66A, 67A, 68A **🚊** 6, 67

Public baths may not seem like an obvious tourist destination, but the *Jugendstil* Amalienbad (1923–6) shows how the municipal administration in the 1920s provided essential public facilities, and did so with stylistic vigour and conviction. Its designers, Otto Nadel and Karl Schmalhofer, were employees of the city's architectural department. The magnificent **swimming pool** is covered by a glass roof that can be opened in minutes and is surrounded by galleries overlooking the pool. Elsewhere in the building are a **sauna** and smaller baths and pools used for therapeutic purposes. The interior is enlivened by imaginative mosaic and tile decoration.

When they first opened, the baths were one of the largest of their kind in Europe, designed to accommodate 1,300 people. The baths were damaged in World War II but impeccably restored in 1986.

Swimming pool
Ⓒ 12:30–3pm Mon, 9am–6pm Tue, 9am–9:30pm Wed–Fri, 7am–8pm Sat, 7am–6pm Sun

Sauna
Ⓒ 1–9:30pm Tue, 9am–9:30pm Wed–Fri, 7am–8pm Sat, 7am–6pm Sun

24

Lainzer Tiergarten

⌂ Lainzer Tiergarten, Hietzing Tiergarten **🚌** 55A **🚊** 60 **Ⓒ** Mid-Feb–mid-Nov: 8am–dusk daily **🌐** lainzertiergarten.at

A former Habsburg hunting ground, now an immense nature reserve in the Vienna

↑ Strolling in the Lainzer Tiergarten nature reserve

Woods (*p212*), the Lainzer Tiergarten opened to the public in 1923. It is encircled by a 24-km (15-mile) stone wall, protecting its herds of deer and wild boar. Scenic viewing posts overlook the favourite feeding areas for wild boar, bighorn sheep, deer and elk. There is also a large bat habitat. From the entrance, a 15-minute walk through woods and meadows brings you to the Hermesvilla, a favourite summer retreat of the imperial family. The interior of the Hermesvilla is currently closed to the public.

Along **Cobenzlgasse**, in the cobbled centre of Grinzing, there are plenty of pleasant and historic Heurigen. At No 30, the Baroque Trummelhof stands on the site of an 1835 brewery.

On the corner of Cobenzlgasse and Feilergasse is the **Altes Presshaus**, whose cellar contains an old wine press.

From Grinzing's Gothic church, continue down the road to the **Grinzing tram terminus**, where this walk ends. The No 38 tram returns Vienna's centre.

PETER-ALEXANDER-PLATZ

RINGWEG

SCHREIBERWEG

Altes Presshaus

FEILERG.

9

30

RINGWEG

SCHREIBERWEG

HIMMELSTRASSE

41-3

COBENZLGASSE

GRINZINGER STEIG

LANGACKERGASSE

RUDOLF-KASSNER-

Pfarrkirche Hl. Kreuz (Gothic Church)

FINISH 🚇 **Grinzing**

STRASSERGASSE

7

SANDGASSE

GRINZINGER STRASSE

Grinzinger Friedhof

SCHEIBELREITER-GASSE

AN DEN LANGEN LÜSSEN

GRINZINGER ALLEE

LEOPOLD-STEINER-GASSE

KRONESGASSE

HUSCHKAGASSE

🚇 An den langen Lüssen

On **Himmelstrasse**, Nos 41–3 share an impressive white Jugendstil façade and at No 25, there is an attractive late-Gothic church with a copper cupola and much-restored interior.

HUNGERBERGSTRASSE

HAUBENBIGLSTRASSE

A LONG WALK
KARL-MARX-HOF TO GRINZING

There are a number of attractive Biedermeier houses on **Grinzinger Strasse**. No 7 was visited by Albert Einstein and No 64 by Beethoven.

Distance 3.5 km (2 miles) **Walking time** 50 minutes **Nearest train** Heiligenstadt **Terrain** Lanes and footpaths, with a gentle incline throughout and cobblestones in places

This walk through part of Vienna's 19th district begins at the site of one of the most important monuments of 20th-century Vienna, the public housing development of the Karl-Marx-Hof. It then takes you through a pretty 19th-century park to the old wine village of Grinzing. Although the village suffered destruction at the hands of the Turks in 1529 and 1683 and from Napoleon's army in 1809, and is now facing changes as a result of modern tourism, its main street preserves its charm.

Locator Map
For more detail see p183

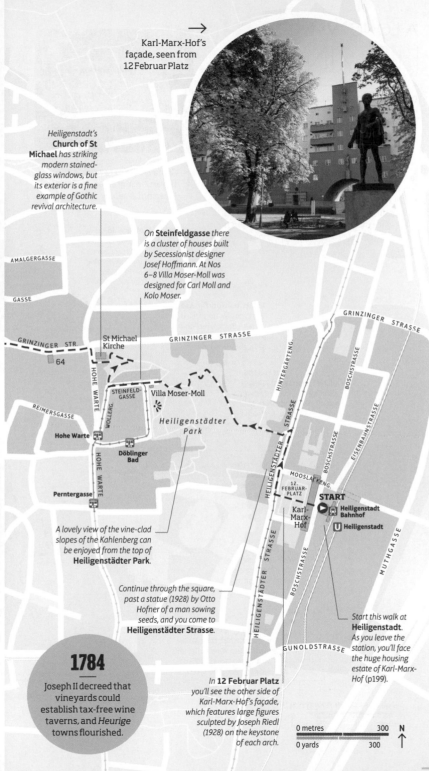

Karl-Marx-Hof's façade, seen from 12 Februar Platz

Heiligenstadt's **Church of St Michael** has striking modern stained-glass windows, but its exterior is a fine example of Gothic revival architecture.

On **Steinfeldgasse** there is a cluster of houses built by Secessionist designer Josef Hoffmann. At Nos 6–8 Villa Moser-Moll was designed for Carl Moll and Kolo Moser.

AMALGERGASSE

GASSE

GRINZINGER STR.

St Michael Kirche

64

HOHE WARTE

STEINFELD-GASSE

Villa Moser-Moll

GRINZINGER STRASSE

GRINZINGER STRASSE

REIMERSGASSE

Hohe Warte

Heiligenstädter Park

HOHE WARTE

Döblinger Bad

HINTERGARTENG.

BOSCHSTRASSE

STRASSE

Perntergasse

A lovely view of the vine-clad slopes of the Kahlenberg can be enjoyed from the top of **Heiligenstädter Park**.

HEILIGENSTÄDTER

MOOSLACKENG.

12. FEBRUAR-PLATZ

START

Karl-Marx-Hof

Heiligenstadt Bahnhof

Heiligenstadt

BOSCHSTRASSE

EISENBAHNSTRASSE

MUTHGASSE

Continue through the square, past a statue (1928) by Otto Hofner of a man sowing seeds, and you come to **Heiligenstädter Strasse**.

HEILIGENSTÄDTER STRASSE

BOSCHSTRASSE

Start this walk at **Heiligenstadt**. As you leave the station, you'll face the huge housing estate of Karl-Marx-Hof (p199).

1784

Joseph II decreed that vineyards could establish tax-free wine taverns, and *Heurige* towns flourished.

GUNOLDSTRASSE

In **12 Februar Platz** you'll see the other side of Karl-Marx-Hof's façade, which features large figures sculpted by Joseph Riedl (1928) on the keystone of each arch.

| 0 metres | | 300 |
| 0 yards | | 300 |

N

A LONG WALK
HIETZING

Distance 5 km (3 miles) **Nearest
U-Bahn** Hietzing **Terrain** Easy walking
with pleasant paths throughout

The former village of Hietzing runs along the
western edge of the grounds of Schönbrunn
Palace (p188). In Maria Theresa's time this was a
fashionable area where the nobility spent their
summers; later it became a suburb for the wealthy
middle classes. The quiet streets contain a
marvellous mix of Biedermeier and Jugendstil
villas, while the square around the parish church
retains an intimate small-town atmosphere.

↑ Gustav Klimt's grave in
the well-maintained
Hietzing Cemetery

*On the corner of **Fasholdgasse**
you'll pass an old Biedermeier
Heurige with ochre walls.
Continue back towards Hietzing
U-Bahn, where this walk ends.*

Trauttmansdorffgasse
*is a pleasant street filled
with Beidermeier and
impressive turn-of-the-
century architecture.*

At Nos 14 and 16
Gloriettegasse *is a villa with
monumental sculpted figures
resting in the pediments, built
in 1913–15 by Josef Hoffmann.*

*At No 29 Wattmanngasse is the
extraordinary* **Lebkuchenhaus**
*(Gingerbread House), so-called
because of its dark brown
majolica decoration.*

Exit the park at
Weidlichgasse *and
continue right
along Maxingstrasse*

*Beyond Maxing Park is **Hietzing
Cemetery**, which contains the
graves of Otto Wagner, Gustav
Klimt, Kolo Moser and Franz
Grillparzer, among others.*

Old Biedermeier
Heuriger

HIETZING

Katharina Schratt
House

Hietzing
Cemetery

0 metres   250
0 yards   250

N ↑

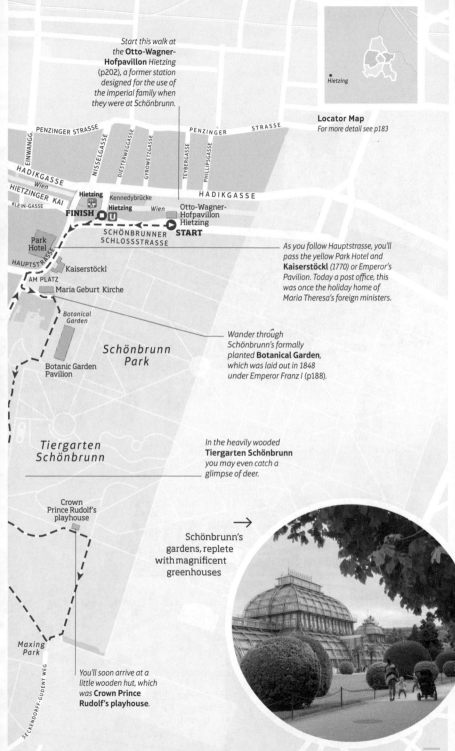

Start this walk at the **Otto-Wagner-Hofpavillon** *Hietzing* (p202), a former station designed for the use of the imperial family when they were at Schönbrunn.

Locator Map
For more detail see p183

Hietzing

PENZINGER STRASSE

PENZINGER STRASSE

EINWANGG.

NISSELGASSE

DIESTERWEGGASSE

GYROWETZGASSE

TEYBERGASSE

PHILLIPSGASSE

HADIKGASSE

Wien

HIETZINGER KAI

KLEIN-GASSE

HADIKGASSE

Hietzing

Kennedybrücke

Hietzing

Wien

Otto-Wagner-Hofpavillon Hietzing

FINISH

START

SCHÖNBRUNNER SCHLOSSSTRASSE

Park Hotel

HAUPTST.

Kaiserstöckl

AM PLATZ

Maria Geburt Kirche

Botanical Garden

Schönbrunn Park

Botanic Garden Pavilion

As you follow Hauptstrasse, you'll pass the yellow Park Hotel and **Kaiserstöckl** *(1770)* or Emperor's Pavilion. Today a post office, this was once the holiday home of Maria Theresa's foreign ministers.

Wander through Schönbrunn's formally planted **Botanical Garden**, which was laid out in 1848 under Emperor Franz I (p188).

Tiergarten Schönbrunn

In the heavily wooded **Tiergarten Schönbrunn** you may even catch a glimpse of deer.

Crown Prince Rudolf's playhouse

Schönbrunn's gardens, replete with magnificent greenhouses

Maxing Park

SECKENDORFF-GUDENT WEG

You'll soon arrive at a little wooden hut, which was **Crown Prince Rudolf's playhouse**.

207

DAYS OUT FROM VIENNA

Within an hour or two's journey from Vienna's centre, astonishing countryside awaits, from Alpine mountains to idyllic lakes. For centuries, the capital has been at the centre of Austria's wine-growing country, and it is surrounded by picturesque towns and villages. Just beyond the city limits, the Vienna Woods await, the scene of the 1889 Mayerling Tragedy. Today this area affords fantastic hiking and lung-fulls of fresh air. It's even possible to hop for the day to neighbouring Slovakia; its capital Bratislava offers a rather different take on central European history. All sights are accessible by bus or train and visits to Baden and Mayerling can easily be combined on one trip.

Must See

❶ Mayerling and the Vienna Woods

Experience More

❷ Baden
❸ Schloss Hof
❹ Eisenstadt
❺ Mariazell
❻ Bratislava

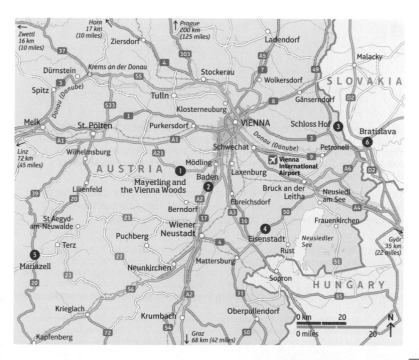

The Mayerling ↑
hunting lodge, now
a Carmelite chapel

THE MAYERLING INCIDENT

In 1889, the Mayerling hunting lodge was the scene of an apparent double suicide of Prince Rudolf and his 17-year-old lover Mary Vetsera. The death of the only Habsburg heir precipitated a dynastic crisis; Karl Ludwig and Franz Ferdinand were each subsequently named heir presumptive.

1 Ⓜ️3

MAYERLING AND THE VIENNA WOODS

🏠Mayerling: 40 km (25 miles) S of Vienna 🄲Mayerling Chapel: 0225 2275 ⑤R2249 from Hauptbahnhof to Baden, then bus 459 to Mayerling 🚌360 from Opera to Baden, then 459 to Mayerling Altes 🕐Mayerling Chapel: 2 Jan–Mar: 9am–5pm Sat, Sun & hols; Apr–1 Jan: 9am–5pm daily; Heiligenkreuz Abbey: daily for tours, check website for details 🌐Heiligenkreuz Abbey: stift-heiligenkreuz.org

The Vienna Woods extend from the western bounds of the city towards the lower slopes of the Alps. They are home to varied wildlife, the notorious Mayerling hunting lodge and the sublime Cistercian abbey at Heiligenkreuz.

The woods make excellent walking country for a half- or full-day outing from Vienna, with densely forested hills home to around 1,000 wild boar, as well as deer, elks and mouflons. In the heart of the woods is a former Habsburg hunting lodge, the site of the 1889 Mayerling Incident, which is now a chapel. After his son's death, the Emperor Franz Joseph gave the hunting lodge to a Carmelite convent and it was completely rebuilt. A few miles north of Mayerling is the medieval Cistercian abbey of Heiligenkreuz. It is the oldest continuously inhabited Cistercian monastery in the world. Inside is a 12th-century nave and a 13th-century chapter house. Its fine features include a Baroque bell tower and Trinity Column, and the tombs of 13 of the Babenbergs who ruled in Austria during the medieval period.

↑ Forested countryside to the west of Vienna, where small farming villages nestle beneath wooded hills

💬 INSIDER TIP
The True Cross

Don't miss seeing what is said to be part of the True Cross, a gift from Baldwin IV of Jerusalem to Duke Leopold V in 1182. You'll find it in the Holy Cross chapel at the Heiligenkreuz abbey.

↑ Tomb of the last Babenberg duke at Heiligenkreuz

→ The Baroque Trinity Column in Heiligenkreuz's inner abbey courtyard

EXPERIENCE MORE

② Baden

🏠 25 km (15 miles) S of Vienna 🚌 360 from Karls-platz 🚆 S2 or 🚆 R2335 & 2337 from Hauptbahnhof 🚋 Badner (WLB) from Karls-platz 🛈 www.tourismus.baden.at

In the southern part of the Vienna Woods are several spas and wine-growing towns. The most famous is Baden (or Baden bei Wien), a spa town with curative hot springs dating from Roman times. As well as bathing in sulphurous water and mud to treat rheumatism, you can enjoy a dip in the soothing hot pools heated to 36°C (97°F). Visitors can also sample local wines in Baden's charming restaurants.

In the early 19th century Baden was popular with the Imperial Court of Vienna. During that period, many elegant Biedermeier villas, baths, town houses and a square were built, and the gardens of the Kurpark laid out. The park extends to the Vienna Woods and has a rose garden and a small memorial to Beethoven and Mozart.

③ 🚴 🏛 🍴 🍽 Schloss Hof

🏠 50 km (30 miles) E of Vienna 🚌 Shuttle Sat, Sun & hols from Marchegg; Hop-on, Hop-off Sat, Sun & hols from Vienna Hilton or Wien Mitte 🕐 Times vary, check website 🌐 schlosshof.at

The restored Schloss Hof is well worth a visit. In 1725, Prince Eugene made it his principal country seat and laid out a formal garden. Extended a generation later under Empress Maria Theresa, the palace contains private and state rooms from each period.

④ 🏛 Eisenstadt

🏠 60 km (37 miles) S of Vienna 🚌 566 from Haupt-bahnhof 🚆 REX 2627 🛈 eisenstadt-tourismus.at

This pleasant town is home to the grand **Schloss Esterházy**, built for Prince Esterházy in 1663–73. It also boasts the

Haydnsaal, a hall of state in which Joseph Haydn conducted the prince's orchestra. Haydn's former home, the **Haydn Haus**, is now a museum. Also nearby is a fascinating **Jewish Museum**.

⊛ Schloss Esterházy

🏠 Esterhazyplatz 5 🌐 esterhazy.at

⊛ ⌂ Haydn Haus

🏠 Joseph Haydn-Gasse 19 & 21 🌐 haydnhaus.at

⊛ Jewish Museum

🏠 Unterbergstraße 6 🌐 ojm.at

⑤ 🏛 Mariazell

🏠 140 km (80 miles) SW of Vienna 🚌 552 or 1130 from Hauptbahnhof 🚆 From Westbahnhof, change at St Pölten to Mariazell alpine railway 🛈 03882 3945

The Mariazell alpine railway takes visitors from St Pölten to Mariazell. The town has

The spire and onion-shaped domes of Mariazell's impressive Baroque basilica

long been a main Catholic pilgrim site of Central Europe, to which the Gothic and Baroque **Mariazell Basilica** bears witness. Inside the basilica, which was enlarged in the 17th century, is a wealth of Baroque stucco, painting and decoration. The treasury also forms part of the church.

A cable car up the mountain leaves every 20 minutes from the town centre. An additional attraction in summer is the world's oldest steam tram, built in 1884, which runs between Mariazell railway station and a nearby lake.

Mariazell Basilica
🅰 Benedictusplatz 1
🆆 basilika-mariazell.at

↑ The imposing façade and formal gardens of the 17th-century Schloss Hof

⑥
Bratislava
🅰 70 km (43 miles) W of Vienna 🆂 From Hauptbahnhof to Bratislava Hl St

A short hop across the border from Vienna, Slovakia's quiet capital makes for a fascinating day trip. Its compact historic centre, located on the north bank of the Danube, is very easily explored on foot.

Much of the rest of the city is the result of 40 years of Communism, which offers an intriguing experience and somewhat of a culture shock for first-time visitors to Eastern Europe.

A good place to start is the impressive **Municipal Museum** with its displays on countless Slovak themes. **St Martin's Cathedral** adds ecclesiastical interest, and the recently renovated **Bratislava Castle**, a highlight of the city, commands fantastic views across the capital.

Municipal Museum
🏛🅰 Radničná 1 🆆 muzeum.bratislava.sk

St Martin's Cathedral
🅰 Rudnayovo námestie 1 🆆 dom.fara.sk

Bratislava Castle
🅰 Zámocká 2 🆆 bratislava-hrad.sk

Sunset over Baden's vineyards

A BOAT TOUR
KREMS TO MELK

Duration 3-4 hours **Stopping-off points** Dürnstein has restaurants and shops **Boat rentals** Take an organized tour from Krems, Dürnst or any river boat pier

Some 80 km (50 miles) west of Vienna is one of the most magnificent expanses of river scenery in Europe, a stretch from Krems to Melk called the Wachau. Castles, churches and wine-producing villages rise up on either side of the Danube valley, which has been settled for over 30,000 years, and breathtaking views unfold. A river trip on an organized tour, run by DDSG (*www.ddsg-blue-danube.at*) or Brandner (*www. brandner.at),* is the best way to take in the landmarks and scenery.

Locator Map
For more detail see p209

Krems to Melk

Spitz, *a Protestant stronghold during the Reformation, is a pretty wine town that lies at the foot of the 1,000-Eimer Berg (1,000-Bucket Mountain).*

High above the river is **Aggstein**'s *medieval castle..*

You'll pass very close to the village of **Willendorf,** *famous for the prehistoric findings made nearby, including the tiny prehistoric statue Venus of Willendorf (p136).*

At the end of this trip, explore the Benedictine abbey of **Melk,** *where Umberto Eco's novel The Name of the Rose is set. It is a treasure trove of decorative art.*

Habruck

Joching

Wösendorf

St Michael

Spitz an der Donau

B217   Spitz   B33

Mitterarnsdo

Schwallenbach

Maria Langegg

Willendorf

Groisbach

Aggstein

Maria Laacham Jauerling

Aggsbach Markt

Aggsbachdorf

Zintring

B3   MELK

Grimsing

Schönbühel

Emmersdorf
Emmersdorf   B33

Pielach

Melk / Altarm
FINISH
Melk   Spielberg

Danube

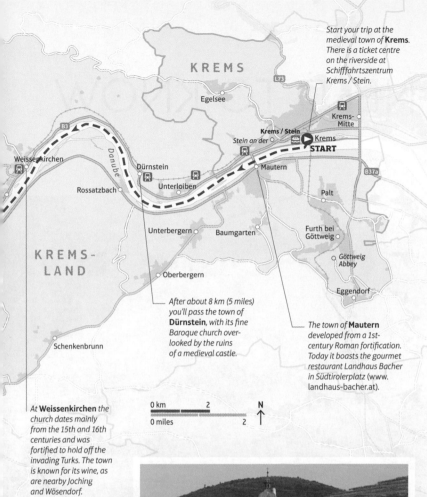

KREMS

Egelsee

Krems-Mitte

Start your trip at the medieval town of **Krems**. There is a ticket centre on the riverside at Schifffahrtszentrum Krems / Stein.

Krems / Stein

Stein an der

Krems
START

Weissenkirchen

Dürnstein

Danube

Rossatzbach

Unterloiben

Mautern

Palt

KREMS-LAND

Unterbergern

Baumgarten

Furth bei Göttweig

Oberbergern

Göttweig Abbey

Eggendorf

*After about 8 km (5 miles) you'll pass the town of **Dürnstein**, with its fine Baroque church overlooked by the ruins of a medieval castle.*

*The town of **Mautern** developed from a 1st-century Roman fortification. Today it boasts the gourmet restaurant Landhaus Bacher in Südtirolerplatz (www.landhaus-bacher.at).*

Schenkenbrunn

0 km   2
0 miles   2

N
↑

*At **Weissenkirchen** the church dates mainly from the 15th and 16th centuries and was fortified to hold off the invading Turks. The town is known for its wine, as are nearby Joching and Wösendorf.*

→

A boat trip departing from the riverside town of Krems

NEED TO KNOW

BEFORE
YOU GO

Forward planning is essential to any successful trip. Be prepared for all eventualities by considering the following points before you travel.

AT A GLANCE

CURRENCY
Euro (EUR)

AVERAGE DAILY SPEND

SAVE	SPEND	SPLURGE
€70	€150	€200+

BOTTLED WATER	COFFEE	BEER	DINNER FOR TWO
€1.30	€2.50	€4	€70

ESSENTIAL PHRASES

Hello	Guten Tag
Goodbye	Auf Wiedersehen
Please	Bitte
Thank you	Danke
Do you speak English?	Sprechen Sie Englisch?
I don't understand	Ich verstehe nicht

ELECTRICITY SUPPLY
Power sockets are type F, fitting type C and type F plugs. Standard voltage is 230 volts.

Passports and Visas

For a stay of up to three months for the purpose of tourism, EU nationals and citizens of the UK, US, Canada, Australia and New Zealand do not need a visa. For visa information specific to your home country, consult your nearest Austrian embassy or check online at **Austria Visa Info**.
Austria Visa Info
🅦 austria.org/visa-application/

Travel Safety Advice

Visitors can get up-to-date travel safety information from the **US Department of State**, the **UK Foreign and Commonwealth Office** and the **Australian Department of Foreign Affairs and Trade**.
Australia
🅦 smartraveller.gov.au
UK
🅦 gov.uk/foreign-travel-advice
US
🅦 travel.state.gov

Customs Information

An individual is permitted to carry the following within the EU for personal use:
Tobacco products 800 cigarettes, 400 cigarillos, 200 cigars or 1 kg of smoking tobacco.
Alcohol 10 litres of alcoholic beverages above 22 per cent strength, 20 litres of alcoholic beverages below 22 per cent strength, 90 litres of wine (60 litres of which can be sparkling wine) and 110 litres of beer.
Cash If you plan to enter or leave the EU with €10,000 or more in cash (or the equivalent in other currencies) you must declare it to the customs authorities.
Limits vary if travelling from outside the EU so check the restrictions before departing.

Insurance

It is always wise to take out an insurance policy covering theft, loss of belongings, medical problems, cancellation and delays. EU citizens

are eligible for free emergency medical care in Austria provided they have a valid **EHIC** (European Health Insurance Card). However it is also advisable to take out some form of supplementary health insurance, as some services, such as repatriation costs, are not covered. If plans include sporting activities, like skiing, make sure the policy covers this.
EHIC
W gov.uk/european-health-insurance-card

Vaccinations

No inoculations are needed for Austria.

Money

Major credit, debit and prepaid currency cards are accepted in most shops and restaurants. Contactless payments are becoming more widely accepted, even on public transport. However, it is always wise to carry some cash, as some smaller businesses won't accept card payments. All vending and ticket machines take notes, usually up to €20.

Booking Accommodation

Vienna has a huge variety of accommodation to suit most budgets, with luxury five-star hotels, family run *pensionen* (B&Bs) out in the Vienna Woods and budget hostels. There's no real low season so it's a good idea to book ahead at any time of year. Prices are inflated during peak times, such as during the summer and Advent. If on a tight budget, consider staying outside the city centre. The **Vienna Tourist Board** and **Camping Wien** websites offer useful booking resources.
Camping Wien
W campingwien.at
Vienna Tourist Board
W wien.info/en/hotels

Travellers with Specific Needs

Vienna is relatively easy to navigate as a disabled traveller. Most major museums are wheelchair accessible and offer audio tours, and the majority of the transport system is equipped for use by disabled travellers. Detailed information is available from the **Vienna Tourist Board** website. Guide dogs are allowed on public transport, and major underground stations have lifts unless otherwise indicated.

Organizations like **Bizeps**, the **Austrian Blind Union** and the **Austrian Association for the Hearing Impaired** offer services to travellers with disabilities.
Austrian Association for the Hearing Impaired
W oeglb.at
Austrian Blind Union
W blindenverband.at
Bizeps
W bizeps.or.at
Vienna Tourist Board
W wien.info/en/travel-info/accessible-vienna

Language

German is Austria's official language but even those with a good grasp may find the Austrian dialect hard to decipher. English is commonly spoken in Vienna, but learning a few niceties in German goes a long way, even if you then continue in English *(p236)*.

Closures

Monday Some museums and tourist attractions are closed for the day.
Sunday Some shops and small businesses close for the day.
Public holidays Schools, post offices and banks and some shops are closed for the day; museums and attractions are usually open.

PUBLIC HOLIDAYS	
1 Jan	New Year's Day
6 Jan	Epiphany
Apr/May	Easter Monday
1 May	May Day
May/Jun	Whit Monday
May/Jun	Corpus Christi
15 Aug	Assumption Day
1 Nov	All Saints' Day
15 Nov	St Leopold's Day
8 Dec	Immaculate Conception
25 Dec	Christmas Day
26 Dec	St Stephen's Day

GETTING
AROUND

Whether you are visiting for a short city break or a rural country retreat, discover how best to reach your destination and travel like a pro.

AT A GLANCE

PUBLIC TRANSPORT COSTS

CITY CENTRE SINGLE

€2.40

Single journey
within one zone

24-HOUR PASS

€8

Unlimited travel
within Vienna

48-HOUR PASS

€14.10

Unlimited travel
within Vienna

These tickets are valid on all means of public transport (U-Bahn, tram, bus and night bus) in Vienna.

SPEED LIMIT

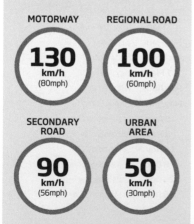

MOTORWAY

130
km/h
(80mph)

REGIONAL ROAD

100
km/h
(60mph)

SECONDARY ROAD

90
km/h
(56mph)

URBAN AREA

50
km/h
(30mph)

Arriving by Air

Vienna's only airport, **Schwechat International**, is well served by most international airlines. Airlines operating services there include easyJet and British Airways, but the main Austrian carrier is Austrian Airlines. Travellers from the United States can fly direct to Vienna from a number of destinations across the US with Austrian Airlines.

Schwechat International Airport is located 19 km (12 miles) southeast of the city centre. With two terminals, the airport is used by over 100 airlines. It is served by the super-efficient **CAT** (City Airport Train), which runs to and from Wien Mitte station in the centre of Vienna. The airport has all of the typical facilities that you would expect, including restaurants, duty free shops, a supermarket, banks and tourist information offices.

A cheaper alternative to Schwechat, Bratislava's **Milan Rastislav Štefánik Airport** in neighbouring Slovakia is less than two hours' drive from central Vienna and is far better served by budget airlines.
CAT
W cityairporttrain.com
Milan Rastislav Štefánik Airport
W bts.aero
Schwechat International
W viennaairport.com

Train Travel

The train is a fast way to get around Austria, which has an efficient high-speed network and reliable local services.

Domestic/Regional Train Travel
The vast majority of Austria's rail services are operated by **Österreichische Bundesbahnen** (ÖBB – Austrian Federal Railways).

The fastest train, the Railjet, can travel at speeds of up to 230 km (143 miles) per hour and links the major Austrian cities, including Salzburg, Graz and Linz, as well as cities across Germany, Italy, Hungary, the Czech Republic and Switzerland. Slower regional trains serve smaller

GETTING TO AND FROM SCHWECHAT AIRPORT

Transport	Journey Time	Fare
City Airport Train (CAT)	16 mins	€12
S-Bahn	25 mins	€4.20
ÖBB Railjet	15 mins	€4.20
Bus	20-40 mins	€8
Taxi	16 mins	€36

towns, but to reach the more off-the-beaten-track locations in the Alps you will need to change to regional local bus services.
Österreichische Bundesbahnen
w oebb.at/en/

Long-Distance Bus Travel

Vienna's main coach station, the **Vienna International Bus Terminal** (VIB), is located close to Erdberg U3 underground station. Services arrive here from most major European cities, including Berlin, Budapest, London and Paris.
Postbus and **Flixbus** run routes throughout Austria and Slovakia. Coaches arrive in Vienna at the Wien Hauptbahnhof bus terminal.
Flixbus
w flixbus.co.uk
Postbus
w postbus.at/en/
Vienna International Bus Terminal
w vib-wien.at/en/

Public Transport

Vienna's transport network is made up of trams (Strassenbahn), buses (Autobus), underground trains (U-Bahn) and overground trains (S-Bahn), all operated by **Wiener Linien**.
The city's transport system works largely on an honesty system – there are no ticket barriers at stations, allowing passengers to hop on and off. However, formal checks by transport authority staff do take place – occasionally you'll be asked for your *Fahrschein* (ticket) by a uniformed guard. Travellers caught without a valid ticket will be fined €103.
Rush hour on weekdays is from about 7am to 9:30am, then again from about 4:30pm to 6:30pm. Smoking is banned in stations and on

public transport. To plan your journey, visit the Wiener Linien website, which has timetables and ticket prices.
Wiener Linien
w wienerlinien.at

Tickets

Vienna's public transport ticketing system is less confusing than it appears at first glance. Buying a ticket in advance is usually the easiest option. Tickets are sold at newsagents *(Tabak Trafiken)*, from ticket machines at stations, or at the counters of U-Bahn and S-Bahn offices.
Vienna city is zone 100 of the Austrian regional fare system; a standard ticket covers all areas of the city and allows passengers to change trains and lines and switch from the underground to a tram or a bus, as long as they take the most direct route and don't break their journey.
Wiener Linien's **EASY CityPass** is a good value option for anyone who is planning on using public transport for more than one day. The pass is available for 24, 48 and 72 hours, or a week, and also entitles the bearer to discounts at some of the city's museums, galleries and shops.
The Wiener Linien 8-Tage-Karte (€40.80) is best for groups of travellers and consists of eight strips which, when stamped, are valid for a day.
Children under 6 may travel for free on the city's transport network, while those aged between 6 and 14 qualify for half-price single tickets. The latter can also travel free during holidays, providing they can show proof of age.
EASY CityPass
w easycitypass.com/en/city/wien-en/

U-Bahn

Vienna's underground system (U-Bahn) is a modern, clean, fast and reliable way of crossing the city. Expansion of the system is ongoing, though this is of more interest to those who live on the fringes of the city.

The U-Bahn operates seven days a week from around 5am to 12:30am. During the day, trains depart every 5 minutes or so, less frequently after about 8pm. A 24-hour service runs on weekends and public holidays. Outside these hours, the U-Bahn service is replaced by Vienna NightLine buses.

The U-Bahn's five colour-coded lines are U1, U2, U3, U4 and U6. Confusingly, there is no U5 line. Check the Wiener Linien website (p223) for information about timetables, tickets and service updates. The U-Bahn is generally safe, but in case of emergencies there are help points on most platforms.

Smoking is prohibited on U-Bahn platforms and on the trains themselves. Displays above the train doors show stations and connections, and a recorded voice announces stops and also connections to trams and buses. Signs indicate where prams can be stored by the doors. Bicycles are allowed on a few carriages, although not before 9am or between 3 and 6:30pm Mon–Fri. Be aware that doors are opened manually and can be stiff and heavy.

Tram

Vienna's tram network is one of the largest in the world, with almost 30 routes. Known locally as "Bim" for its distinctive bell sound, it is a delightful way to get around the city. For the ultimate experience, seek out one of the old, traditional models with their wooden seats and vintage interiors.

Most of the main sights in Vienna's historic centre, such as the Staatsoper, Parliament and Neues Rathaus, are located on the popular Ring Tram route. Passengers will need to purchase a Round-the-Ring ticket (€9) for a complete unbroken journey. On-board services include audio-visual information about highlights along the route, delivered via a multi-lingual multi-media system. Ring trams depart every 30 minutes all year round, from 10am to 5:30pm.

All trams are equipped with seats for travellers with disabilities. However, the modern low-riding trams are a more wheelchair-friendly option. Look for vehicles with the ULF (Ultra Low Floor) sign.

Bus

Bus stops are marked with a green "H" for *Haltestelle,* or stop. All stops display bus numbers, destinations, timetables and route maps. Buses should stop automatically at all bus stops but if you are in any doubt, flag it down.

Tickets purchased from the driver will be valid for one bus journey only. If you have already purchased a ticket from a newsagent or ticket machine, you will need to validate it in the ticket-stamping machine on the bus. If you have already made part of your journey by tram or U-Bahn, there is no need to stamp your ticket again. All buses in Vienna are wheelchair-accessible.

After midnight, Vienna's night bus service takes over. These operate at 30-minute intervals until 4am. There is some variation between the services operating on weekday nights (Sunday to Thursday) and those at weekends and on public holidays. Night buses are marked by the letter "N". All night buses in Vienna start from Schwedenplatz, the Opera and Schottentor, and together serve most suburbs. Tickets can be purchased from the driver and all other pre-bought tickets and passes are valid.

Taxis

Taxis are a comfortable, if more expensive, way of getting around. There is a €3.80 minimum fee during the day, plus €0.20 per kilometre. At night, on Sundays and on public holidays, the minimum charge is €4.30. Round the fare up to the nearest euro or 5 euros.

Taxis in Vienna are instantly recognizable by a "TAXI" sign on the roof, which will be illuminated if the vehicle is available to hail. Phone to book, or hail at a taxi stand – for Vienna-wide locations see the Vienna Taxis section on the **City of Vienna** website or download a free Vienna taxi app. Smartphone taxis now operating in Vienna include Uber, MyDriver and Blacklane.

Vienna's **Faxi Taxi** pedicab service is a quick way to get around the centre of the city: find them at taxi stands, or flag one down in the street. Journeys up to 2 km (1 mile) cost €5. One-way journeys more than 2 km cost €10. Services with cab companies **Taxi 31300, Taxi 40100** and **Taxi 60160** can be booked by telephone or online.

City of Vienna
Ⓦ wien.gv.at/english/transportation/cars/taxistands.html
Faxi Taxi
Ⓦ faxi.at
Taxi 31300
Ⓦ taxi31300.at
Taxi 40100
Ⓦ taxi40100.at
Taxi 60160
Ⓦ taxi60160.at

Driving

Driving licences issued by any of the European Union member states are valid throughout the

EU. If visiting from outside the EU, you may need to apply for an International Driving Permit. Check with your local automobile association before you travel.

Driving to Austria
With the exception of Switzerland, all of Austria's neighbours are EU members, meaning there are no border checks. Driving is a pleasant way to reach Vienna as the roads en route are good. The final part of the journey from Bavaria is particularly scenic as you pass through the Alps.

Driving in Austria
Austria is a fairly straightforward place to drive. Roads are good and Viennese drivers generally sensible. Motorways and regional roads are easy to navigate.

Car Rental
Car-hire firms such as **Hertz** and **Sixt Rent-a-Car** can be found at Schwechat Airport. Drivers need to produce their passport, driving licence and a credit card with capacity to cover the excess. Most rental agencies require drivers to be over the age of 21 and to have an international licence.
Hertz
w hertz.com
Sixt Rent-a-Car
w sixt.com

Parking
Apart from on Sundays, when shops are closed, finding a parking spot in the busy city centre of Vienna can be time consuming.

The City of Vienna operates a park-and-pay scheme in districts 1–9, 12, 14–17 and 20 from 9am to 10pm Mondays to Fridays. Parking disks are sold at newsagents (*Tabak Trafiken*) and petrol stations.

Usually, a maximum stay of two hours is allowed in any space. In other districts, a blue line by the kerb indicates a pay and display scheme. Note that city car parks can cost €8 for one hour or €40 per day.

Rules of the Road
Priority is always given to the right unless a yellow diamond indicates otherwise. Unlike in other EU countries, Austrian stop lights blink rapidly in green before switching to amber. Trams, buses, police cars, fire engines and ambulances all have right of way. Vienna's speed limit is 50 km (30 miles) per hour.

Seat belts are compulsory and children under the age of 12 must sit in the back, with babies and toddlers in child seats. In the event of an accident, or if a traffic jam necessitates an abrupt stop, drivers should turn on their hazard lights to warn drivers behind.

The limit for alcohol is between 0.5 mg per ml of blood (about 330 ml or half a pint of beer or 1–2 glasses of wine) and is strictly enforced. Spot checks are common and anyone over the limit is likely to face a hefty fine and loss of licence.

Always carry your driving licence as well as car ownership and insurance documents. Every car driving on the motorway must display a *vignette* toll sticker, available from all petrol stations.

Cycling
Vienna is a great city for cyclists, as long as the main roads and tramlines are avoided. A 7-km (4-mile) cycle path round the Ringstrasse takes you past many historic sights, and there are also paths to the Prater and the Hundertwasserhaus.

Keen cyclists should look out for **Radlkarte**, a booklet illustrating all of Vienna's cycle routes, which is available from bookshops. Bicycles can be rented at some train stations (discounts are given with a train ticket), or from any of the 100 or so **Citybike** stations.

Cycling enthusiasts can book tours through **Pedal Power** and **Vienna Explorer**, which offers seats for children and e-bikes.
Citybike
w citybikewien.at
Pedal Power
w pedalpower.at
Radlkarte
w radlkarte.at
Vienna Explorer
w viennaexplorer.com

Bicycle Safety
Ride on the right. If you are unsure or unsteady, practise in one of the inner city parks first. If in doubt, dismount: many novices cross busy junctions on foot; if you do so, switch to the pedestrian section of the crossing. Beware of tram tracks; cross them at an angle to avoid getting stuck.

For your own safety, do not walk with your bike in a bike lane or cycle on pavements, on the side of the road, in pedestrian zones or in the dark without lights. Locals may not bother and it isn't compulsory, but wearing a helmet is recommended

Fiaker
Traditional horse-drawn open carriages or *Fiakers*, are a relaxing way to get around, and can be hired at Stephansplatz, Heldenplatz or Albertinaplatz. A 20-minute ride from Stephansplatz to Michaelerplatz with **Carriage Company Wulf** costs around €55 for four people.
Carriage Company Wulf
w vienna-carriage.com

PRACTICAL
INFORMATION

A little local know-how goes a long way in Vienna. Here you will find all the essential advice and information you will need during your stay.

AT A GLANCE

EMERGENCY NUMBERS

GENERAL EMERGENCY	AMBULANCE
112	**144**

FIRE SERVICE	POLICE
122	**133**

TIME ZONE
CET/CEST: Central European Summer Time runs from the last Sunday in March to the last Sunday in October.

TAP WATER
Unless stated otherwise, tap water in Vienna and its surrounds is safe to drink.

TIPPING

Waiter	10 per cent
Taxi driver	Not expected
Hotel porter	€1 per day
Housekeeping	€1 per day
Concierge	€1–2

Personal Security

Vienna is generally a safe place for visitors, but it is always a good idea to take sensible precautions when wandering around the city, especially at night.

Extra precaution should be taken against pickpockets, particularly on public transport and in busy tourist areas – especially in and around the Prater.

Health

Emergency medical care in Austria is free for all EU citizens. If you have an EHIC (European Health Insurance Card), present this as soon as possible when receiving emergency medical treatment. You may have to pay after treatment and reclaim the money later.

For visitors coming from outside the EU, payment of hospital and other medical expenses is the patient's responsibility, so it is important to arrange comprehensive medical insurance before travelling (p220).

Vienna's many pharmacies (Apotheke) are a very helpful source of information on various medicines and treatment for minor ailments. To locate a pharmacy, look out for a bright red "A" sign; there is generally one on every major street.

Pharmacies operate a night and Sunday rota system. Closed pharmacies will display the address of the nearest one open, and the number of the Pharmacy Information Line.

In the event of more serious illnesses and injuries, call the **ViennaMed** doctors' hotline, or make your way to the nearest hospital (Krankenhaus) in the area.

All emergency rooms are part of the public health system, so your EHIC or supplementary insurance will cover you.

Vienna has several private hospitals, clinics and medical centres, but the main facility is Vienna General, the largest hospital in Europe. Most doctors, paramedics and clinic staff speak English.

ViennaMed
☎ 1 513 95 95

Smoking

Austria bucks the European trend in that the law doesn't ban smoking in all enclosed spaces – restaurants and bars are exempt. Smoking is prevalent in Austria and smoky interiors in bars and restaurants are fairly commonplace.

ID

There is no requirement for visitors to carry identification, but in the event of a routine check you may be asked to show your passport. If you don't have it with you, the police may escort you to wherever your passport is being kept so that you can show it to them.

Visiting Churches

When visiting churches and religious sites, visitors should dress respectfully. Cover your torso and upper arms, and ensure shorts and skirts cover your knees.

Mobile Phones and Wi-Fi

There are 400 free Wi-Fi hotspots across Vienna. The most popular are in Rathausplatz, Stephansplatz, the MuseumsQuartier, the Naschmarkt, the Prater and along the Danube Island.

Cafés and restaurants are usually happy to permit the use of their Wi-Fi on the condition that you make a purchase. Wi-Fi is now almost always free in hotels. You can also get online at the tourist information centre on Albertinaplatz.

Visitors travelling to Austria with EU call plans can use their devices abroad without being affected by data roaming charges; instead they are charged the same rates for data, SMS and voice calls as they would pay at home.

Post

Austrian post offices are clearly identifiable by their bold yellow signs. They provide postage stamps (Briefmarken), can send registered letters and arrange the delivery of packages. Foreign currency is handled by the larger post offices.

The Austrian postal system is straightforward and efficient. Postage is charged by weight, and customers can choose between two postal

tariffs: priority and economy. Post offices are generally open between 7am and 7pm Monday to Friday. Stamps are also sold at newsagents.

Taxes and Refunds

VAT is 20 per cent in Austria. Non-EU residents are entitled to a tax refund subject to certain conditions. In order to do this, you must request a tax receipt and export papers (Ausfuhrbescheinigung) when you purchase your goods. When leaving the country, present these papers, along with the receipt and your ID, at Customs to receive your refund.

Discount Cards

A useful discount card is Wiener Linien's **Vienna City Card**. A "Red" adult pass costs €17, €25 or €29 for 1, 2 or 3 days and provides free entry into over 60 of Vienna's attractions and museums. The pass also entitles travellers to the unlimited use of hop-on hop-off buses, a free guidebook and an optional public transport pass. Children's passes cost roughly half of an adult pass.

The **Vienna PASS** is only good value if you intend to visit many sights in quite a short period of time.

Vienna City Card
W viennacitycard.at
Vienna PASS
W viennapass.com

WEBSITES AND APPS

Citybike
An app that helps you to locate your nearest Citybike rental station.

City of Vienna
The City of Vienna website has a useful interactive city map at www.wien.gv.at.

Qando Wien
The official transport app from Vienna's public transport provider, Wiener Linien.

Susi
This app shows you nearby restaurants, free events, ATMs and pharmacies.

Wien Tourismus
Check out www.wien.info, Vienna's official tourist information website.

INDEX

PHRASE BOOK

IN EMERGENCY

Help!	Hilfe!	hilf-er
Stop!	Halt!	hult
Call a doctor	Holen Sie einen Arzt	hole'n zee ine'n artst
Call an ambulance	Holen Sie einen Krankenwagen	hole'n zee ine'n krank'n-varg'n
Call the police	Holen Sie die Polizei	hole'n zee dee pol-its-eye
Call the fire brigade	Holen Sie die Feuerwehr	hole'n zee dee foy-er-vair
Where is the nearest telephone?	Wo finde ich ein Telefon in der Nähe?	voh fin-der ish ine tel-e-fone in dair nay-er?
Where is the nearest hospital?	Wo ist das nächstgelegene Krankenhaus?	voh ist duss next-g'lay-g'ner krunk'n-hows?

COMMUNICATION ESSENTIALS

Yes	Ja	yah
No	Nein	nine
Please	Bitte	bitt-er
Thank you	Danke	dunk-er
Excuse me	Gestatten	g'shtatt'n
Hello	Grüss Gott	groos got
Goodbye	Auf Wiedersehen	owf veed-er-zay-ern
Goodnight	Gute Nacht	goot-er nukht
morning	Vormittag	for-mit-targ
afternoon	Nachmittag	nakh-mit-targ
evening	Abend	ahb'nt
yesterday	Gestern	gest'n
today	Heute	hoyt-er
tomorrow	Morgen	morg'n
here	hier	hear
there	dort	dort
What?	Was?	vuss?
When?	Wann?	vunn?
Why?	Warum?	var-room?
Where?	Wo/Wohin?	voh/vo-hin?

USEFUL PHRASES

How are you?	Wie geht es Ihnen?	vee gayt ess een'n?
Very well, thank you	Sehr gut, danke	zair goot, dunk-er
Pleased to meet you	Es freut mich sehr, Sie kennenzulernen	ess froyt mish zair, zee ken'n-tsoo-lairn'n
See you soon	Bis bald/bis gleich	bis bult/bis gleye sh
That's fine	Sehr gut	zair goot
Where is...?	Wo befindet sich...?	voe b'find't zish...?
Where are...?	Wo befinden sich...?	voe b'find'n zish...?
How far is it to...?	Wie weit ist...?	vee vite ist...?
Which way to...?	Wie komme ich zu...?	vee komma ish tsoo...?
Do you speak English?	Sprechen Sie Englisch?	shpresh'n zee eng-glish?
I don't understand	Ich verstehe nicht	ish fair-shtay-er nisht
Could you please speak slowly?	Bitte sprechen Sie etwas langsamer?	bitt-er shpresh 'nzeeeet-vuss lung-zam-er?
I'm sorry	Es tut mir leid/ Verzeihung	es toot meer lyte/ fair-tseye-oong

USEFUL WORDS

big	gross	grohss
small	klein	kline
hot	heiss	hyce
cold	kalt	kult
good	gut	goot
bad	schlecht	shlesht
enough	genug	g'hook
well	gut	goot
open	auf/offen	owf/off'n
closed	zu/geschlossen	tsoo/g'shloss'n
left	links	links
right	rechts	reshts
straight on	geradeaus	g'rah-der-owss
near	in der Nähe	in dair nay-er
far	weit	vyte
up	auf, oben	owf, obe'n
down	ab, unten	up, oont'n
early	früh	froo
late	spät	shpate
entrance	Eingang/Einfahrt	ine-gung/ine-fart
exit	Ausgang/Ausfahrt	ows-gung/ows-fart
toilet	WC/Toilette	vay-say/toy-lett-er
free/unoccupied	frei	fry
free/no charge	frei/gratis	fry/grah-tis

MAKING A TELEPHONE CALL

I'd like to place a long-distance call	Ich möchte ein Ferngespräch machen	ish mer-shter ine fairn-g'shpresh mukh'n
I'd like to call collect	Ich möchte ein Rückgespräch (Collectgespräch) machen	ish mer-shter ine rook-g'shpresh (coll-ect-g'shpresh) mukh'n
local call	Ortsgespräch	orts-g'shpresh
I'll try again later	Ich versuche es noch einmal etwas später	ish fair-zookh -er ess nokh ine-mull ett-vuss shpay-ter
Can I leave a message?	Kann ich etwas ausrichten?	kunn ish ett-vuss ows-rikht'n?
Hold on	Haben Sie etwas Geduld	harb'n zee ett-vuss g'doolt
Could you speak up a little please?	Bitte sprechen Sie etwas lauter?	bitt-er shpresh'n zee ett-vuss lowt-er?

STAYING IN A HOTEL

Do you have a vacant room?	Haben Sie ein Zimmer frei?	harb'n zee ine tsimm-er fry?
double room with double bed	ein Doppelzimmer mit Doppelbett	ine dopp'l-tsimm-er mitt dopp'l-bet
twin room	ein Doppelzimmer	ine dopp'l -tsimm-er
single room	ein Einzelzimmer	ine ine-ts'l -tsimm-er
room with a bath/shower	Zimmer mit Bad/Dusche	tsimm-er mitt bart doosh-er
porter	Gepäckträger/ Concierge	g'peck-tray-ger/ kon-see-airsh
key	Schlüssel	shlooss'l
I have a reservation	Ich habe ein Zimmer reserviert	ish harb-er ine tsimm-er rezz-er-veert

SIGHTSEEING

bus	der Bus	dair booss
tram	die Strassenbahn	dee stra-sen-barn
train	der Zug	dair tsoog
art gallery	Galerie	gall-er-ee
bus station	Busbahnhof	booss-barn-hofe
bus (tram) stop	die Haltestelle	dee hal-te-shtel-er
castle	Schloss, Burg	shloss, boorg
palace	Schloss, Palais	shloss, pall-ay
post office	das Postamt	dee pohs-taamt
cathedral	Dom	dome
church	Kirche	keersh-er
garden	Garten, Park	gart'n, park
library	Bibliothek	bib-leo-tek
museum	Museum	moo-zay-oom
information (office)	Information (-sbüro)	in-for-mut-see-on (-zboo-roe)
closed for public holiday	Feiertags geschlossen	fire-targz g'shloss'n

SHOPPING

How much does this cost?	Wieviel kostet das?	vee-feel kost't duss?
I would like…	Ich hätte gern…	ish hett-er gairn…
Do you have…?	Haben Sie…?	harb'n zee…?
I'm just looking	Ich schaue nur an	ish shau-er noor un
Do you take credit cards?	Kann ich mit einer Kreditkarte bezahlen?	kunn ish mitt ine-er kred-it-kar-ter b'tsahl'n?
What time do you open?	Wann machen Sie auf?	vunn mukh'n zee owf?
What time do you close?	Wann schliessen Sie?	vunn shlees'n zee?
This one	dieses	deez'z
expensive	teuer	toy-er
cheap	billig	bill-igg
size	Grösse	grers-er
white	weiss	vyce
black	schwarz	shvarts
red	rot	roht
yellow	gelb	gelp
green	grün	groon
blue	blau	blau

TYPES OF SHOP

antique shop	Antiquitäten-geschäft	un-tick-vi-tayt'n-g'sheft
bakery	Bäckerei	beck-er-eye
bank	Bank	bunk
bookshop	Buchladen/ Buchhandlung	bookh-lard'n/ bookh-hant-loong
butcher	Fleischerei	fly-sher-eye
café	Cafe, Kaffeehaus	kaff-ay, kaff-ay-hows
cake shop	Konditorei	kon-ditt-or-eye
chemist (for prescriptions)	Apotheke	App-o-tay-ker
(for cosmetics)	Drogerie	droog-er-ree
department store	Warenhaus, Warengeschäft	vahr'n-hows, vahr'n-g'sheft
delicatessen	Feinkost (geschäft)	fine-kost (g'sheft)
fishmonger	Fischgeschäft	fish-g'sheft
gift shop	Geschenke(laden)	g'shenk-er(lahd'n)
greengrocer	Obst und Gemüse	ohbst oont g'moo-zer
grocery	Lebensmittel-geschäft	layb'nz-mitt'l-g'sheft
hairdresser	Friseur/Frisör	freezz-er/ freezz-er
market	Markt	markt
newsagent/ tobacconist	Tabak Trafik	tab-ack tra-feek
travel agent	Reisebüro	rye-zer-boo-roe

EATING OUT

Have you got a table for… people?	Haben Sie einen Tisch für… Personen?	harb'n zee ine'n tish foor… pair-sohn'n?
I want to reserve a table	Ich möchte einen Tisch bestellen	ish mer-shter ine'n tish b'shtell'n
The bill please	Zahlen, bitte	tsarl'n bitt-er
I am a vegetarian	Ich bin Vegetarier	ish bin vegg-er-tah-ree-er
Waitress/waiter	Fräulein/Herr Ober	froy-line/hair oh-bare
menu	die Speisekarte	dee shpize-er-kart-er
fixed price menu	das Menü	duss men-oo
cover charge	Couvert/Gedeck	koo-vair/g'deck
wine list	Weinkarte	vine-kart-er
glass	Glas	glars
bottle	Flasche	flush-er
knife	Messer	mess-er
fork	Gabel	garb'l
spoon	Löffel	lerff'l
breakfast	Frühstück	froo-shtook
lunch	Mittagessen	mit-targ-ess'n
dinner	Abendessen/ Dinner	arb'nt-ess'n/ dee-nay
main course	Hauptspeise	howpt-shpize-er
starter, first course	Vorspeise	for-shpize-er
dish of the day	Tageskarte	targ-erz-kart-er
wine garden(s)	Heurige (Heurigen)	hoy-rigg-er (-en)
rare	Englisch	eng-glish
medium	medium	may-dee-oom
well done	durch	doorsh

MENU DECODER

Apfel	upf'l	apple
Almdudler	ahlm-dood-ler	herbal lemonade
Banane	bar-nar-ner	banana
Ei	eye	egg
Eis	ice	ice cream
Fisch	fish	fish
Fisolen	fee-soul'n	green beans (haricot)
Fleisch	flysh	meat
Garnelen	gar-nayl'n	prawns
gebacken	g'buck'n	baked/fried
gebraten	g'brart'n	roast
gekocht	g'kokht	boiled
Gemüse	g' mooz-er	vegetables
vom Grill	fom grill	grilled
Gulasch	goo-lush	stew
Hendl/Hahn/Huhn	hend'l/harn/hoon	chicken
Kaffee	kaf-fay	coffee
Kartoffel/Erdäpfel	kar-toff'l/air-dupf'l	potatoes
Käse	kayz-er	cheese
Knoblauch	k'nob-lowkh	garlic
Knödel	k'nerd'l	dumpling
Kotelett	kot-lett	chop
Lamm	lumm	lamb
Marillen	mah-ril'n	apricot
Meeresfrüchte	mair-erz-froosh-ter	seafood
Mehlspeise	mayl-shpize-er	dessert
Milch	milhk	milk
Mineralwasser	minn-er-arl-vuss-er	mineral water
Obst	ohbst	fresh fruit
Öl	erl	oil
Oliven	o-leev'n	olives
Orange	o-ronsh-er	orange

frischgepresster Orangensaft	frish-*g'press*-ter o-*ronsh'n*-zuft	*fresh orange juice*
Paradeissalat	*pa-ra-dice-sa-lahd*	*tomato salad*
Pfeffer	pfeff-*er*	*pepper*
pochiert	posh-eert	*poached*
Pommes frites	pomm-fritt	*chips*
Reis	rice	*rice*
Rind	rint	*beef*
Rostbraten	*rohst-brart'n*	*steak*
Rotwein	roht-*vine*	*red wine*
Salz	zults	*salt*
Sauce/Saft	zohss-*er*/zuft	*sauce*
Schalentiere	sharl'*n-tee-rer*	*shellfish*
Schinken/Speck	shink'*n*/shpeck	*ham*
Schlag	shlahgg	*cream*
Schnecken	shnek'*n*	*snails*
Schokolade	shock-o-**lard**-*er*	*chocolate*
Schwein	shvine	*pork*
Semmel	zem'*l*	*roll*
Senf	zenf	*mustard*
Serviettenknödel	*ser-vee-ert'n-* k'nerd'*l*	*sliced dumpling*
Sulz	zoolts	*brawn*
Suppe	zoop-*er*	*soup*
Tee	tay	*tea*
Topfenkuchen	topf'*n*-**kook**h'*n*	*cheesecake*
Torte	tort-*er*	*cake*
Wasser	vuss-*er*	*water*
Weinessig	vine-*ess-igg*	*vinegar*
Weisswein	vyce-*vine*	*white wine*
Wurst	voorst	*sausage (fresh)*
Zucker	tsook-*er*	*sugar*
Zwetschge	tsvertsh-*ger*	*plum*
Zwiebel	tsvee*b'l*	*onions*

NUMBERS

0	null	nool
1	eins	eye'ns
2	zwei	tsvy
3	drei	dry
4	vier	feer
5	fünf	foonf
6	sechs	zex
7	sieben	zeeb'*n*
8	acht	uhkht
9	neun	noyn
10	zehn	tsayn
11	elf	elf
12	zwölf	tsverlf
13	dreizehn	dry-*tsayn*
14	vierzehn	feer-*tsayn*
15	fünfzehn	foonf-*tsayn*
16	sechszehn	zex-*tsayn*
17	siebzehn	zeep-*tsayn*
18	achtzehn	uhkht-*tsayn*
19	neunzehn	noyn-*tsayn*
20	zwanzig	tsvunn-*tsig*
21	einundzwanzig	ine-*oont-tsvunn-tsig*
22	zweiundzwanzig	tsvy-*oont-tsvunn-tsig*
30	dreissig	dry-*sig*
40	vierzig	feer-*tsig*
50	fünfzig	foonf-*tsig*
60	sechzig	zesh-*tsig*
70	siebzig	zeep-*tsig*
80	achtzig	uhkht-*tsig*
90	neunzig	noyn-*tsig*
100	einhundert	*ine*hoond't
1000	eintausend	*ine*towz'*nt*

TIME

one minute	eine Minute	ine-*er*min-oot-*er*
one hour	eine Stunde	ine-*er*shtoond-*er*
half an hour	eine halbe Stunde	ine-*er*hull-*ber* shtoond-*er*
Monday	Montag	mone-*targ*
Tuesday	Dienstag	deen-*starg*
Wednesday	Mittwoch	mitt-*vokh*
Thursday	Donnerstag	donn-*er-starg*
Friday	Freitag	fry-*targ*
Saturday	Samstag	zum-*starg*
Sunday	Sonntag	zon-*targ*

PICTURE CREDITS

The publisher would like to thank the following for their kind permission to reproduce their photographs:

Key: a-above; b-below/bottom; c-centre; f-far; l-left; r-right; t-top

123RF.com: Marcin Lukaszewicz 198-9b; radub85 144-5t; Richard Semik 199tr; Tupungato 96tl.

4Corners: Franco Cogoli 8cl; Reinhard Schmid 8-9b.

Alamy Stock Photo: age fotostock 44-5b, 69br, 156cl, 170bl, 212-3b; allOver images 52cl, 203b; ALLTRAVEL 31crb; Jonathan Andel 50br; Tomas Anderson 100cl; Frédéric Araujo 89br, 155cl; The Artchives 33bl; Aurora Photos 159t; Azoor Photo 55br, 57tl; Roman Babakin 122cl; Vincenzo De Bernardo 179tr; Bildarchiv Monheim GmbH 196cr; Jon Bilous 177t; blickwinkel 194bl; Boelter 97b; Michael Brooks 42-3t; Luise Berg-Ehlers 31cl; Rostislav Bychkov 33crb; CoverSpot Photography 195cra; Luis Dafos 111cr, 118t; Ian G Dagnall 158tc, 186c, 193cl; De Luan 56br; DPA Picture Alliance Archive 195tl; Bernhard Ernst 186clb; Florilegius 54br; Freeartist 144bl; GL Archive 100clb; Globe Exposure 191cl; Manfred Gottschalk 29br, 82b; Hackenberg-Photo-Cologne 51cl, 87tr, 117cla, 147tl, 158bl, 197b, 203tr; hemis.fr 74tl, 131cl, 133tr, 140bl, 149br, 160bl, / Bertrand Gardel 84-5; Heritage Image Partnership Ltd 56-7t, 189bl; Historical image collection by Bildagentur-online 55bc; Brent Hofacker 22cr; imageBROKER 36br, 38-9b, 53tr, 79b, 87bc, 133cla, 136crb, 211clb, / Bildverlag Bahnmüller 210tl, / Günter Lenz 100bc; imageimage 11br, 160tr; Harvest Images 170cr; Insadco Photography 53tl; INSADCO Photography / Willfried Gredler 206tr; Tiny Ivan 10-1b; Ivy Close Images 56cra; Karl Jena 168cl; John Kellerman 26bl, 76b, 94-5t, 123br, 133cr, 134-5, 136cr; Keystone Pictures USA 170br; Herbert Koeppel 43cr; Art Kowalsky 19c, 150-1; Lautaro 71cra; Chris Lawrence 180bl; Yadid Levy / © The Estate of Sigmar Polke, Cologne / DACS 2018 129tr; LOOK Die Bildagentur der Fotografen GmbH 53br, /© Pipilotti Rist. Courtesy the artist, Hauser & Wirth and Luhring Augustine 51br; Lugris 175bl; Manfredrf 30-1t; Cesar Asensio Marco 12-3b; MARKA 39cb, / jarach 117tr; Stefano Politi Markovina 10clb; Mauritius Images Gmbh 73cl, 130br, / Rainer Mirau 214-5; McPhoto / Bilderbox 69ca; Mikolajn 181br; Hercules Milas 66bl, 88tr, 130-1t, 137, / © Successió Miró / ADAGP, Paris and DACS London 2018 98t; MNTravel 54bc; Robert Murray 119b; North Wind Picture Archives 67bc, 139cla; Painters 139tl; Mo Peerbacus 162cl; Pegaz 69cr; The Picture Art Collection 193clb; Rene Pirolt 37cl; PjrTravel 81b, 110bl; The Print Collector 67br; Prisma Archivo 54t, 57tr, 58t; Khristina Ripak 77tl; Robertharding 211br; Bert de Ruiter 207br; Marcin S. Sadurski 74bc, 177br; Brian Scantlebury 191ca; Markus Schieder 52cla,149br, 210-1t; Jozef Sedmak 80bl; Robbie Shone 68t; Sueddeutsche Zeitung Photo 36-7t; Jack Sullivan 44-5t; Tasfoto 98-9b; Dmitry Travnikov 83tr; Georgios Tsichlis 106-7b; Lucas Vallecillos 22ccrb, 28br, 41cl, 155tr, 170crb; Ivan Vdovin 108tr; Jose Vilchez 40tl; volkerpreusser 26t, 32-3t, 35cr, 59t, 71tl, 134tr, 143tr, 176bl, 187tr, 193br, 195tr, 198tl, 205tr, 213t; Westend61 GmbH 138-9b; Peter M. Wilson 55cr; Scott Wilson 21, 26crb, 66cra; Ernst Wrba 13br, 104t, 120-1b, 169tr; Xinhua 52br; Ekin Yalgin 191tr.

AWL Images: Peter Adams 218-9; Jon Arnold 4, 18, 112-3; Bertrand Gardel 19tl, 124-5; Hemis 20bl, 182l; Jane Sweeney 8clb, 109tr.

Belvedere, Vienna: 171.

Botanischer Garten: 174-5t, 175bc.

Bridgeman Images: De Agostini Picture Library / G. Dagli Orti 55tl.

Burgtheater: Georg Soulek 138cl, 141bl.

Cafe Central: Herbert Lehmann 10c.

Depositphotos Inc: palinchak 52cra; Pressdigital 196t.

Dreamstime.com: Balakate 200-1br; Maciej Bledowski 143-4b; casadaphoto 66br; Castenoid 157tr; Razvan Ionut Dragomirescu 2-3; Eugenesergeev 154-5b; Ginasanders 155cr; Jjfarq 102-3b; Vichaya Kiatying-angsulee 188-9t; Gábor Kovács 200tl; Marcin Łukaszewicz 72; Minnystock 20t, 164-5; Ncristian 189cl; Roman Plesky 107tr, 148cl; Radub85 24t; Rosshelen 6-7, 8cla, 173clb; Brian Scantlebury 121tl; Smallredgirl 184cr; Nikolai Sorokin 79tr; Svetlana195 86tl; TasFoto 24bl, 178b; Lev Tsimbler 135cr; Tupungato 175clb; Vvoevale 105bl; Yup265 16c, 62; Zwawol 186-7b.

DSCHUNGEL WIEN Theaterhaus fu ür junges Publikum: Herr Jemineh hat GlA Åck_4 / Heinz Zwazl 49cr.

Filmarchiv Austria: Rupert Steiner 46bl.

Getty Images: AFP / STR 58bc; Alinari Archives, Florence 58cra; APIC / Retired 38-9t; ASAblanca / Josef Polleross 32bl, 116-7b, 117tl; The Asahi Shimbun 35bl; Bettmann 58tl, 58cr; Amos Chapple 163br; Andy Christiani 11cr, 28-9t, 39cla; Corbis 59bl, / VCGAtlantide Phototravel 101; DEA Picture Library 57cra, 189cr, 189br; Nat Farbman 139tr; George Papapostolou photographer 78tl; Manfred Gottschalk 185; Alexander Hassenstein 24crb; Georg Hochmuth 13cr; Hulton Archive 56bc; imageBROKER / Peter Giovannini 55tr; Imagno 67bl, 170bc, 184bl, 189bc; Hiroyuki Ito 34-5t; Joe Klamar 53bl, 161b; LevTsimbler 76cr; Dieter Nagl 11t, 22t, 53cl; Herbert Neubauer 181tl; Life Ball 2015 / Thomas Niedermueller 139cr, 141tr; Peter Zelei Images 75bl; Josef Polleross 37b, 53cr; James Reeve 22bl; Martin Schalk 52bl, 59br; Manfred Schmid 26cr, 50-1t, 52cr; Gisela Schober 47cl; Silver Screen Collection 46-7t; Sylvain Sonnet 30-1b; Ullstein Bild / Werner Otto 217br; Universal History Archive 55cla, 58br; Flavio Vallenari 43b.

Haus der Musik: 80tr.

Hofburg & Schonbrunn Palace: SKB / A. E. Koller 103crb, 103tl; SKB / Lois Lammerhuber 103tr.

iStockphoto.com: AleksandarNakic 24cr, 48-9t; Amriphoto 48br; AndreyKrav 12t, 191cra; bluejayphoto 41br; RossHelen 41tr; vichie81 40-1b; VvoeVale 17, 90-1; zlisjak 57bl; Vladislav Zolotov 12cl.

Kaffemik: 29cl.

© KHM-Museumsverband: 132-3b, 134cr, 135tl, 135tr, 135bc.

Leopold Museum, Vienna: 129cr, 131br.

MAK-Osterreichisches Museum fur ange wandte Kunst: Georg Mayer 73cr.

MuseumsQuartier E+B GesmbH: 130cr.

Naturhistorisches Museum: 136bl.

ÖNB/Wien: 45cl, 108b.

Reuters: Dominic Ebenbichler 100cla.

Shutterstock: Trabantos 70-1b.

SuperStock: agefotostock / Sagaphoto / Stephane Gautier 45crb, / Lucas Vallecillos 60-1, 184b; AGF / agf photo / Masci Giuseppe 173tl; The Art Archive 56tl; Cultura Limited / Andreas Pollok 42bl; Hemis.fr / Gardel Bertrand 128-9b, / Maisant Ludovic 173tr; Mauritius 192, / Volker Preusser 208tl;, robertharding / Michael Runkel 67t; Westend61 / Werner Dieterich 13t.

Technical Museum: 202tl.

VIENNALE: Robert Newald 47crb.

Wien Museum: Beethoven Pasqualatihaus 146b; Hertha Hurnaus 34bl.

ZOOM Children's Museum: 129cl; J.J.Kucek 49bl, 131tr;

Front flap
Alamy Stock Photo: Stefano Politi Markovina cra;
Mauritius Images Gmbh / Rainer Mirau bl; Jose Vilchez
cla; Scott Wilson 21cb; AWL Images: Jon Arnold br;
Dreamstime.com: Rosshelen tc.

Map cover: AWL Images: Peter Adams.

Cover images
Front and spine: AWL Images: Peter Adams.
Back: Alamy Stock Photo: Bernhard Ernst c,
Georgios Tsichlis tr; AWL Images: Peter Adams bc;
iStockphoto.com: Vladislav Zolotov cla.

Mapping:
Contour Publishing, Cosmographics, original street data:
ERA Maptec Ltd (Dublin).

For further information see: www.dkimages.com

Penguin
Random
House

Main Contributors Stephen Brook,
Marc di Duca, Craig Turp
Senior Editor Ankita Awasthi Tröger
Senior Designer Owen Bennett
Project Editor Lucy Sienkowska
Project Art Editors Tania Gomes,
Bharti Karakoti, Mark Richards, Ankita Sharma,
Priyanka Thakur, Vinita Venugopal
Designer William Robinson
Factchecker Doug Sager
Editors Louise Abbott, Elspeth Beidas,
Penny Phenix, Lucy Sara-Kelly,
Lauren Whybrow
Proofreader Christine Stroyan
Indexer Hilary Bird
Senior Picture Researcher Ellen Root
Picture Research Ashwin Adimari,
Sumita Khatwani, Mark Thomas, Harriet Whitaker
Illustrators Kevin Jones, Gilly Newman,
John Woodcock, Martin Woodward
Cartographic Editor James Macdonald
Cartography Subhashree Bharati
Jacket Designers Bess Daly, Maxine Pedliham,
Simon Thompson
Jacket Picture Research Susie Peachey
Senior DTP Designer Jason Little
DTP Coordinator George Nimmo
Producer Igrain Roberts
Managing Editor Hollie Teague
Art Director Maxine Pedliham
Publishing Director Georgina Dee

MIX
Paper from
responsible sources
FSC
www.fsc.org **FSC™ C018179**

First edition 1994

Published in Great Britain by Dorling Kindersley Limited,
80 Strand, London, WC2R 0RL

Published in the United States by DK Publishing,
1450 Broadway, 8th Floor, New York, NY 10018

Copyright © 1994, 2019 Dorling Kindersley Limited
A Penguin Random House Company
19 20 21 22 10 9 8 7 6 5 4 3 2 1

A CIP catalog record for this book
is available from the British Library.

A catalog record for this book is available
from the Library of Congress.

ISSN: 1542 1554
ISBN: 978-0-2413-6006-4

Printed and bound in China.

www.dk.com